GW01607351

NEED
RESPECT
TRUST

Also by Nemir Kirdar

Saving Iraq

In Pursuit of Fulfilment: My Life Journey

NEED RESPECT TRUST

The core values of one man's extraordinary personal mission – to create a world-class institution built to last

A Memoir

Nemir Kirdar

Founder, Executive Chairman and CEO of the International Investment Bank Investcorp

Weidenfeld & Nicolson
LONDON

First published in Great Britain in 2013
by Weidenfeld & Nicolson

1 3 5 7 9 10 8 6 4 2

A CIP catalogue record for this book
is available from the British Library.

ISBN-13 978 0 297 86858 3

Typeset by Input Data Services Ltd, Bridgwater, Somerset

Printed and bound by CPI Group (UK) Ltd, Croydon CR0 4YY

Weidenfeld & Nicolson

The Orion Publishing Group Ltd
Orion House
5 Upper Saint Martin's Lane
London, WC2H 9EA
An Hachette Livre UK Company
www.orionbooks.co.uk

The Orion Publishing Group's policy is to use papers that are natural, renewable and recyclable products and made from wood grown in sustainable forests. The logging and manufacturing processes are expected to conform to the environmental regulations of the country of origin.

To my dearest Rena and Serra

While I may have missed out on some of your growing up, I was, as these pages describe, working on the realization of a mission. I dedicate this book to both of you with my love and admiration.

CONTENTS

PART III:
Toward a Mission Accomplished

AUTHOR'S NOTE

Some portions of this book – stories about my life that were originally written for *Need, Respect, Trust* – also appear in a personal, limited-edition memoir that I wrote for my family and friends. The author wishes to note and clarify these duplications for any readers who happen to read both.

There are those who look at things the way they are
and ask why ... I dream of things that never were
and ask why not.

Robert F. Kennedy

PROLOGUE

My father used to say that for achieving success in any profession there are three prerequisites: You must be needed. You must be respected. You must be trusted. To be needed, you must have a profession. To be respected, you must excel in what you do and in what you offer. To be trusted, your integrity must be considered beyond question. Guided by that three-pronged principle, Amin Kirdar lived out his days as a dedicated public servant, and I grew up expecting to follow in his footsteps. And I would have, had fate not intervened.

But while circumstances took me on a far different path, I have always carried with me the other-directed philosophy of success that my father preached to each of his five sons. I believe it deeply, I have striven to live it personally, and I have tried always to instill it in my business life. In a very real sense, it is this last effort that is the heart of the story that follows.

From the very beginning, Investcorp – the international investment bank whose founding and subsequent growing pains provide the narrative of this book – was, to me, a bigger idea than that of achieving personal wealth. Believing that a business ought to be an expression of the personal standards of those involved in it, my co-founders and I set out to build not a company but an institution, something whose core values were antithetical to individual self-interest: something that would outlast us all.

While it is common worldwide for entrepreneurs to establish new businesses, it is decidedly uncommon for individuals to dream of establishing new institutions in their own lifetimes. Even more uncommon is the way we went about it. According to prevailing cultural practice in the Arabian Gulf states, business enterprises originate in one of the two following models. The first is the family business. Generally, these enterprises can be traced back to a founding family member who might typically have started with a small amount of capital, perhaps from a rise in the value of real estate. The business would then grow by acquiring prestigious foreign brand agencies seeking newly emerging markets. As wealth increased, the enterprise would expand by adding on further lines of business such as banking, insurance, travel, or local manufacturing. This progression tends to result in family conglomerates and clusters in which younger family members are expected to work and be trained under expatriate managers hired by the founder patriarch to run the various businesses. Normally, such an entrepreneurial enterprise starts out small and, over time – over two, three, or four generations – it may evolve into an institution.

The second model is the government-owned or government-affiliated institution. These entities normally have access to limitless capital and enjoy preferential support by means of access to government business.

Investcorp's creation was an exception in that it followed

neither model. From the start, my co-founders and I intended to establish a world-class organization owned entirely by a widespread private-sector shareholding base in the six Gulf states, with no individual investor in control. As I write this, Investcorp has kept its independence for more than three decades and is unique in the region as a management-driven business enterprise.

It has not been easy. At every stage, we have faced obstacles and challenges. Some were external episodes, but many were internal, people issues. I was well aware of the formidable challenge we would face in the take-off phase of the project. What I could not foresee was the magnitude of the obstacles and the force of the headwind we would then face in maintaining the momentum and building the market penetration of a now-successful brand. Each challenge, once overcome, was potentially a huge gain. If we failed to meet it, however, it might blow us off course or significantly damage the enterprise. When our attempted solutions were not successful, we had to find alternatives. And, whatever we faced, we could never accept the slightest compromise of our core values.

The book you are about to read is the story of how we defined those challenges, and the determination and faith in our mission that we brought to bear in overcoming them. But this book is more than the chronicle of a business entity. It is also – even foremost – the memoir of a vision. It is the story of what happens when an ideal meets real life. It is a story that began many years ago, and continues to this very day. My hope is that it will never end.

PART I

DREAM IN THE MAKING

1
CHANGE OF PLANS

On the morning of July 14, 1958, I was at Yesilkoy Airport in Istanbul waiting for a plane to arrive. I was twenty-two years old, a fourth-year student at Robert College – the American institution of higher education established in Istanbul in 1863 – and the airplane I was expecting was that of the young King of Iraq, Faisal II. King Faisal was a member of the Hashemite family, and the Kirdars and the Hashemites had long been associated. The relationship dates as far back as the Ottoman Empire, when King Faisal's grandfather and my grandfather both served in the parliament in Istanbul – his representing Hijaz and mine representing Kirkuk, our home town.

The Kirdar involvement in Iraqi public service goes back even another generation, to my great-grandfather, Mustafa Kirdar, who became mayor of Kirkuk during the Ottoman rule. It was his son – my maternal grandfather, Haj Mohammad Ali Kirdar – who was elected to be a member of the Ottoman parliament in Istanbul. Following the formation of modern Iraq in 1921 – when the senior King Faisal became its first monarch – he sent my grandfather a message inviting him to come home because 'we're forming a new government.' So Mohammad Ali left Istanbul and returned to Iraq to continue his public service as a member of the new Iraqi parliament in Baghdad.

In all, four Kirdars – on both branches of my family tree, since my parents were first cousins – would serve in parliament from Kirkuk. Upon the death of Mohammad Ali Kirdar, his brother, Mohammad Jamil Kirdar (my paternal grandfather) took his seat. Then when Mohammad Jamil retired, his son, Amin Kirdar – my father – replaced him. When my father decided not to run, my elder brother Nezir, an engineer with an eye for politics, stepped in. It was like passing a torch. We Kirdars considered public service the noblest of callings, and I grew up thinking that that would be my life.

Young King Faisal inherited the throne at the age of four, when his father died in a car accident. During my childhood, my mother would go to visit the Queen Mother several times a year to pay her respects, and I would go along in order to play with the young King. He was eighteen months older than I, and I admired him immensely. I looked up to him. As we grew older, King Faisal would sometimes invite friends to the Rihab Palace to play chess, listen to music, or watch the latest Hollywood movies. He had other, closer friends who would see him more frequently, but a couple of times a year I would receive such an invitation. At the time, I was still a high school student at Baghdad College, the Jesuit school in the capital.

In his preparation for the throne, King Faisal was advised by his uncle, Prince Abdul Ilah, an extraordinarily sophisticated and gentle man who had been appointed Prince Regent until the young King came of age, which occurred in 1953. Even so, Abdul Ilah continued to advise him, staying on as Crown Prince until the King could marry and have a son of his own.

When Faisal II took the throne it was a spectacular time for Iraq, full of promise. The King and his able and wise Prime Minister, Nuri al-Said, were poised to create a highly developed Western-style model state in the Middle East. Among people like me – I was very politically active at university, ferociously defending our government's vision in debates with other Iraqi students who increasingly preached the radical Arab nationalism of Egypt's Gamal Abdel Nasser – King Faisal's ascendance was a source of elation and hope.

In the spring of 1958, when I was home from college on Easter vacation, the King summoned me to visit him – this time at his office rather than at his residence, which was unusual. The atmosphere was much more formal than I was used to – I was received by court officials and ushered to a waiting room – but when I finally saw the King he greeted me with his customary warmth. He was going to be visiting Istanbul in mid-July, he told me, and wanted to make sure we saw each other. 'I'll teach you to water ski!' he said.

And so, on the morning of July 14, I went to Yesilkoy Airport to wait for his plane to arrive. It never did. By the time I reached the airport the young King was already dead, shot down in cold blood in a violent coup by anti-Western military leaders. In addition, the Crown Prince and the entire royal family – women included – were murdered, and Nuri al-Said was mutilated in the street a day later. The perpetrators of these horrendous acts took over the country, bringing in their relatives and cronies and setting Iraq on a perilous political and economic decline destined to last for decades.

For me, July 1958 was an unforgettable, horrifying tragedy. All I believed in had come to an end, and with it all that I might have been. I no longer had the heart for campus politics, which suddenly seemed hollow. I could see no future for myself in Iraq. Right then and there I resolved to leave Robert College and go to the United States, to find a college that would accept all my credits, to finish my degree in a place where it was possible to get a fresh start. The university I found was the University of the Pacific in Stockton, California. By the fall of 1958 I was half a world away from Iraq, finishing up my undergraduate degree in economics.

Six months after the coup, on the last day of December 1958, my father died in Kirkuk of a massive heart attack. It must have been a terrible final few months for him. Nasser's pictures were everywhere, people were shouting revolutionary slogans, new men were in power, members of the old regime were discredited. And yet when Amin Kirdar died, the shops in Kirkuk closed down for three days in deference to a beloved man. 'The father of the city is dead,' the people wailed. His funeral was a civic event, mourners crying openly, following his bier to burial in our family mosque. To the end, my father was clearly trusted and respected, even if no longer needed.

The following year my mother and two brothers were able to escape Iraq and travel to Phoenix, Arizona, where our cousins Fikrat and Nermeen had already lived for some time. Arizona's weather and terrain reminded us of home, and this was where we had decided to make our new base. I moved there in 1960 after getting my degree. While it was comforting to have so many of the family together, I nevertheless recall those days as a very low period. We did not know what our future was, what country we belonged to. How had we – our family *and* Iraq – ended up this way?

I had decided to go to night school to get a postgraduate degree in political science, but first I needed a job. At the university I told the Dean of my credentials, and he said he would call a friend at the local bank. Soon I was interviewed at the head office of First National Bank of Arizona by an impressive gentleman named Ed Carson. He gave me a job as a teller at a branch in the university district, paying $250 a month – my first salary. I thanked him and accepted, but I also asked him where I might go from there. Would I get a chance to develop in the bank?

'Well,' Carson said, 'that's how I started, and today I'm in charge of personnel throughout the organization, all sixty-eight branches. There's no limit to where you can go.'

So that was the beginning of my business career – bank teller by day, graduate student by night. I ended up not pursuing a graduate degree at that moment, though I did attend night classes in political science, history, and philosophy simply for personal improvement.

I have always been good at social networking, and very quickly I began to meet people from the Lions and Rotary clubs. Interested in the story of a Middle Eastern man who had come to the West to reinvent himself, they invited me to speak at their luncheons. News of these talks reached my bank's head office, and I received letters of congratulation from Ed Carson. I thought I was off to a stellar start.

Then I discovered that the bank had a management

training program. Members were rotated through various jobs and accelerated in their move up to assistant manager within eighteen months. I had not even been told about that program, which did not make me happy. Here were other young guys coming into the bank with the same academic qualifications I had, and they were on a fast track while I was stuck as a teller.

But there was not much I could do, so I just resolved to go on with my public speaking while watching for ways to build up my name in the bank. In time an opportunity appeared. In late summer the bank announced a major campaign. All the employees of every branch were gathered around the radio to hear a message from the Chairman of the Board. For the next ten weeks, he said, the entire staff of the bank, from the Chairman to the lowest employee, would be wearing a button that said 'ASK.' The idea was that people on the street would ask what it meant, and that would be our cue to tell them about First National Bank of Arizona and all the excellent services it offered.

The objective was to win new accounts. We were provided with forms to give to customers, and for every dollar of deposits we brought in we would be awarded one point. These we could redeem for prizes. They gave us a catalog with all sorts of incentives listed – everything from a set of cups to a sofa, a tie to a radio, a pair of scissors to a boat.

Here, I saw, was a chance to make my mark, and I attacked the ASK campaign with all the energy I could muster. I took some First National Bank deposit slips and had my name printed on them. Since I was living in a university town, I decided to run a special promotion geared to the start of the school year. The ten-week period ran from August to October, so halfway through it, in September, new students would be coming in. They were bound to open new accounts in the district, so my plan was to go to each dormitory and make a speech. I would ask the students to open an account with First National Bank using the form that I gave them. Whatever branch they made their deposit in, if they used that form I would get the credit, because it had my name printed on it. That was the campaign I organized. All the family helped me, and it worked. I ended up number one, the most successful employee of the bank in the entire state of Arizona.

Immediately head office wanted to know all about this foreigner with the funny name who was working the campus. I was invited to the head office to meet the Chairman of the Board, Sherman Hazeltine, and then I was directed to go see Ed Carson. 'We're putting you on the training program,' Carson told me. 'You've done some of it already, but we'll have to rotate you through the other jobs, then we're going to develop you for a management position.'

So I entered the program and did well. By this time I was a celebrity within the bank. Everybody knew my name because of the ASK campaign. At the end of the year I ran for President of the Men's Club. Had I stayed in Arizona, I would have made my way for sure, because I knew everyone in the system. But instead my life took another abrupt turn. In 1962 I went back to Iraq.

In 1962 we had a full family reunion, and my eldest brother Nezir came to Arizona to see us. Nezir had been a member of the Iraqi parliament for two months leading up to the revolution, and afterwards he had lived in Beirut. Now, back in Iraq, he was convinced that there were opportunities to put things right. Like me, Nezir was deeply committed to the monarchy and unquestioningly loyal to the Hashemites. Of course he was demoralized, but he told me that things were getting relatively better. In the fourth year of the revolution, the leaders of the new military government were seeing their own limitations. Perhaps all was not lost. During that visit I received the full brunt of my brother's deep-rooted political passion. 'What can we do?' he argued. 'It's our country. We have to try and rebuild it.' Passion is contagious, and I quickly became convinced that I should go back too.

I could tell many stories about my six-year return to Iraq, but most of them end in the same sad way: It did not work. Things had not changed enough. And yet, if I had not gone back, who knows what path my life might have taken? As it was, in Baghdad I met and married my wife, Nada, and our first daughter, Rena, was born. I also started a business which precipitated the crisis that pointed me to my job in international banking, and that in turn led to the dream that has become my life's work.

At first I worked with Nezir, helping him in his waterproofing and tourism businesses, but in early 1963 I decided I wanted to do something on my own. I had noticed that there were people in Iraq – people with money – who wanted to establish small industrial projects, but they did not know where to begin. So my notion was to start up businesses ready for sale. My plan was to come up with an idea, study the project, borrow money, import the machinery, hire the staff, and get the thing running – and then sell it as a going concern. It was of course a venture-capital concept, though in those days I had never even heard that term. It was just something I came up with on my own. Between 1963 and 1969 I carried out several projects in the $30,000 to $50,000 range – a bakery, a small plastic molding factory, things of that sort. I also represented some international firms who were looking for contracts in Iraq, and it was a problem with one of those deals that prompted my final departure from the country in which I was born.

One day in April 1969 I was in my office – I remember it was a Thursday at nearly 1 p.m., the beginning of the weekend in Iraq, and I was closing up to go home. Suddenly I heard men's voices out in the reception area, and then the voice of my secretary talking to them. 'But you don't have an appointment,' she was saying. 'No, I'm sorry he's not available right now ...'

I opened the door and saw four men: one military, three civilians. They said they had come to see me. 'Fine,' I said, and invited them into my office. 'What can I do for you?'

'We want you to come with us to Security.'

'Security? Why?'

'There is an investigation.'

'I've done nothing wrong,' I said. 'I'll come with pleasure. But can't we do this on Saturday morning? Right now I'm going home – it's the end of the day.'

'No,' they said. 'You have to come with us.'

I saw they meant it, so I went back to my desk and was picking up the phone when one of them stopped me. 'Put down that phone,' he said.

'I'm calling my home to say I won't be back for lunch. Can't I at least do that?'

'No, you cannot. You're under arrest.'

That was when I started to tremble. 'On what charge?'

One of them became aggressive and accused me of delaying tactics, but another intervened and let me use the phone. So I dialed my number. Nada and I had been married two years, and Rena was ten months old. When I told Nada I was not coming home, she said, 'Why? Lunch is ready.'

'Nada, I'm going to Security,' I said. 'Don't wait for me.' I wanted her to know explicitly where I was going so she could start making inquiries, but I did not have a chance to say more. After that they took me outside and there was some debate about what to do with my car. In the end, two of them sat in the back of my car, and there I was, driving myself to jail.

We drove through the streets of Baghdad, parked the car, and went into a government office in the Saadun district, where they showed me into a room. It was empty except for a metal desk. 'Wait here,' they said, and I did – from one o'clock until six. The room was hot, no fan or air conditioning. The temperature outside was probably 85 degrees. Not a drop of water, no food, no toilet. I had no idea why I was there. No one came to explain. I just sat in that empty room waiting for something to happen.

There were plenty of reasons to imagine the worst. Once the 1958 revolution had succeeded, all the factions involved turned against one another, and the ensuing years had been volatile at best. To start with, the revolutionaries had all been for Egypt's Nasser, who had designs on the wider Arab world. Then the Communists gained the upper hand for a while. There was an ugly period in 1959 – a lot of killing – and that brought a swing to moderation. In 1962, about the time I went back, there were calls to restore the old Iraq, but by this time all the qualified people had left and there was no one to make it work. In 1963 the Ba'athists took control, and then they were thrown out again. All these changes were just revolutionary factions jostling for power. In the mid-1960s a strong Nasserite element returned, and there was a swing towards socialism. That was when they started to nationalize, destroying the economy. The government put my brother Nezir in prison on fabricated charges and sentenced him to seven years, though he was released in three. If 1967 had been a hard year, by 1968 life was extremely unpleasant. That was the year Nada and I started to question whether Baghdad was where we wanted to bring up our children. Nada was particularly horrified when the government hanged a number of people and left their bodies dangling from poles in the town square. The objective was to intimidate and inspire fear. That was bad enough, but then all these supposedly normal Iraqi women with babies on their backs made a show of parading around the swaying bodies, clapping their hands and trilling sounds of joy.

And here I was, one year on, detained by Security with no idea why. At 6 p.m. a policeman came into the room. 'Have you brought your bed with you?' he asked, as though every upstanding Iraqi citizen should always carry a bedroll with him in expectation of the day he is thrown into prison. The man took me to a second building and led me down a flight of stairs and along a corridor where an iron door stood open.

He pushed me into the cell and closed the door behind me. I found myself in a dark room with about sixty people, sitting quietly, all wearing either pajamas or *dishdashas,* the traditional Arab dress. I stood there in my business suit, shaking. They invited me to take a seat.

'Sit?' I said. 'I don't belong here! I want an explanation!'

An old man came up to me. He looked me in the eye and said, very gently, 'My friend, I've been here eighteen months and nobody's even checked my name. Please' – he motioned, ever so kindly, toward the concrete floor – 'sit down. Have you any pajamas?'

'Pajamas? *Pajamas*?'

'Just relax,' the old man said. 'We'll give you something.'

After about twenty minutes I sat down and took off my tie and jacket. It did not take long to become one of them. That night my bed arrived from home, and by the next day the family had started to send me food. When I took a bite of bread, I felt paper. It was a hidden letter from Nada saying people were working to get me out.

I was there ten days. Eventually it emerged that an American company I represented, Continental Electronics of Dallas, Texas, had a contract to sell radio equipment to the Ministry of Information. The procedure was that, while the engineers were installing the machinery, the company would maintain a performance letter of credit (LC) as a guarantee that the job would be finished. When the job was done, this LC would be presented to the government and the company would get paid. But the LC had a time limit, so it had to be renewed if there was any delay in the work. If the LC was allowed to expire, the company could be construed as breaking its contract, at which point the government would retaliate. By putting me in jail as an agent of the company, the new Ba'ath government was seeking to apply pressure on the US firm. Only in this case there had been a mistake: the LC had actually been renewed by the company, appropriately and on time, and Continental Electronics had correctly notified the Central Bank. But no one had thought to notify the Ministry of its safe receipt. Eventually this was sorted out and the letter was shown to the Minister, who was asked to authorize my release.

'Yes,' the Minister said. 'Let him go.'

And go I did. My first act after being released was to apply for a passport, which I eventually got. Nada wanted us to leave straight away, but once I had the passport I felt in less of a hurry. 'I have a lot of obligations,' I said to her. 'Let me clear up my business affairs. In a few months we'll get out.'

'A few *months*?' Nada was incredulous.

And she was right. One week later, Iraq cancelled all passports. People were tossed off the train to Turkey and left in the middle of the desert; cars were turned back on the road to Amman; nobody was allowed through at the border posts. All passports were null and void.

'Didn't I tell you?' Nada said.

I applied again and got another visa, another exit permit – and almost immediately that was cancelled, too. So I applied a third time, and as soon as I had the papers I got myself on a plane for a supposed business trip to Beirut. I had $800 in my pocket: all the foreign currency we could get our hands on. My plan was to check out the job situation in Lebanon and then return for my family, but Nada told me not to come back – I might never get out again. She would find a way to join me later.

That was a difficult trip. I had visited Beirut often; it was a beautiful city in those days – a financial center, a place to see, very popular with the international set. I had a lot of friends there, Americans and others; whenever they came to Baghdad I used to entertain them in my house, along with prominent Iraqis. In Beirut they would reciprocate, taking us to gorgeous restaurants, and so a trip there was always a pleasure for me and Nada – a mixture of business and social life.

This time, however, I was alone, with limited cash. I was looking for a job. I did not want to be entertained because I could not reciprocate. I was even hesitant to call any of my contacts. It was one thing for them to look on me as an equal, a prosperous businessman, but now I was unemployed. People I had once socialized with would be forced to ask me what skills I had, and the answer would have to be none. I was just a man who used to run his own company.

I sent out my résumé, tried this and that, but nothing much happened, and I was not getting far – until one day I met a very bright man named Peter Wodtke. He was in charge of Citibank in the Middle East, a very young man to be holding such a high position. He took a liking to me, we talked, and he gave me a pivotal piece of advice. 'Nemir,' he said, 'you're in the wrong place. There are all sorts of jobs in Beirut – of course there are – but that's not what you want. You should be looking for a managerial post with one of the major organizations. The people who should be hiring you are the people who hired me – and they're not here, they're in New York.'

And so I went again to America, to New York City, where Nada and Rena rejoined me on December 25, 1969. It was one of the best Christmas presents I have ever received in my life.

By that time I had been in the city a couple of months, and after a hard and dispiriting search had managed to land a trainee position at a small start-up bank. Wherever I had been interviewed, the scenario had been pretty much the same: 'You have an impressive personality, Mr Kirdar,' they would say, 'but your age doesn't fit – we take trainees at a younger level. And anyway, you don't have an MBA.'

One day I came across a small international bank that had just started up. The head of it, a man called Jacques Stunzi, had the charisma of a movie star, and this organization he was running was unique. Allied Bank International was a small Edge Act operation in New York owned by eighteen regional banks spread throughout the United States – one in Hawaii, another in Arizona, another in Texas and so on. In their own states they were major regional players, but to conduct international business they needed New York, so instead of going through the giant banks like Citi and Chase, they got together to form their own combined operation, a consortium bank. Allied was a bankers' bank, designed to service their international needs; and the man they chose to run it was Stunzi.

At the time, I was much impressed by Stunzi's operation, especially the style of it. He was a man of vision, and he had plenty of capital at his disposal. Wanting to make a splash, he bought this exquisite town house on East 55th Street off Park Avenue, built as a home in the 1920s by the man who invented baking powder. Inside were spiral staircases, wood paneling, chandeliers, bathrooms with gold taps. It was a spectacular Georgian mansion, right in the middle of Manhattan, and this was where Jacques Stunzi set up the office of Allied. He wanted to give it a European atmosphere, like a merchant bank, so he decorated it with Persian carpets, silk draperies, fine classical furniture. It was more like a luxurious home than an office.

But Stunzi was not merely refined, he was also a good banker. To run Allied he attracted excellent people. He had created four departments – Asia, Latin America, North America, Europe – and to staff them he was hiring experts from other banks. Even though my total banking experience was a couple of years as a teller in Arizona, I immediately sent him my résumé. He responded, and a few days later I was sitting in his sumptuous office.

'Well,' Stunzi said, 'what can you do for us?'

'Immediately, nothing,' I told him. 'But if you train me, I can do a lot for you. First, though, I need to learn.'

'We already have trainees. They're all MBAs, and their average age is twenty-five. You're thirty-two.'

I refused to be thrown. 'If you give me a job, I'll do my MBA at night. I told you, I am eager to be trained.'

Stunzi gave me no answer at that point, but sent me to see some other people in the building. One was a man in the European department. Much later I heard that, after I had left the room, Stunzi called this man and told him I was on the way down. 'I'm sending you a guy I want you to interview. Better take care of him. Someday he might be your boss.'

For whatever reason, I had a good reception from all the people at Allied. I knew it had gone well. I came back the next day and Stunzi hired me. Not everyone agreed with his decision, though. A very bright officer named Robert Sams, who was running Allied's credit department, had initially told Stunzi it made no sense to take on this fellow Kirdar. 'He's too old, and he doesn't understand finance. All right, he's been a businessman in Iraq. But he won't fit here.'

Naturally, Stunzi placed me in the credit department, so the first man I reported to was Robert Sams. I was one of his credit trainees. There was a windowless pit in the bottom of the basement where the trainees sat, and that was where I spent the next two years. Of course I still had to get my MBA, so a couple of months after being hired I registered myself at Fordham University and started going to school at night.

Those were the hardest two years of my life. I used to go to the office in the morning and work like a horse all day long – it was tough work and boring as well. We trainees were the odd-job boys of the office, ordered about by anyone who felt like being bossy. Come the evening, my colleagues in the training pit would all go home to relax, but not me. I had to go to night class at Fordham. Twice a week we had classes and the other evenings I would go to the library, preparing for the classes to come.

We lived out in a suburb called Riverdale in a one-bedroom apartment. The place did have a very small extra room, quarter-sized, but really there was only the one bedroom, and we had a nanny living with us to take care of Rena because Nada was working too. We could not make it on my salary alone. Nada used to pick me up every night after school. By the time we got home, about 11 p.m., I hardly had the energy to change my clothes. Nada would have a meal prepared for me, but often I was too tired to eat. All I wanted to do was go to bed. My daughter was already asleep, so naturally I did not see much of her. And that was how we lived, day after day, night after night – even weekends – for a couple of years. Sometimes I would think about Iraq and how glad I was to be out of there. Then I would look at the life I had made in America and wonder if it was worth it.

I did everything I could to gain recognition at the bank. Every Tuesday morning there was a meeting attended by everybody, including Stunzi, at which we trainees were expected to report on the state of the money markets, and I always prepared hard for those. But I also worked hard at working smart. Somehow I discovered that most nights Jack Stunzi did not go home to sleep. He slept at the office and he liked to start early, so about 6.30 in the morning he could often be found in his office drinking coffee and reading the newspaper. To me this was an opportunity to bond with him, though it required a superhuman effort for me to get up at 4 a.m. to catch the early bus in from Riverdale. I am not by nature an early riser. But two or three times a year I would rouse myself to 'accidentally' run into Stunzi before work hours. 'Nemir, what are you doing here so early?' he would say. 'Come and sit down, tell me how things are going.' One of the things I noticed about Stunzi was that he always wore black cap-toe lace-ups – banker's shoes. Left to my own devices, I preferred loafers, but I decided to invest in a nice pair of cap-toes myself.

I stayed four years at Allied Bank International, progressing through a number of job changes and promotions. The turning point came in 1971, when I finished credit training and received my MBA, both in the same exhilarating month. Suddenly the world opened up, because two of the area heads – North America and Asia – wanted me on their teams. I joined the Asia group and started traveling to Japan, Hong Kong, Singapore, Thailand, Taiwan. That was where I began to build my banking career. I was made an Assistant Treasurer – my first title – and nine months later was promoted again to Assistant Vice President. My foreign trips were a resounding success. I brought new business back from each visit, so my area grew, my position improved. By 1973 I was head of Southeast Asia.

But nothing stays the same forever, and by this time Allied was in trouble. After five years, a few of the parent banks were dissatisfied and there was some jealousy of Stunzi. Each bank wanted to form its own international department, so the parents had started to compete with the child. All the politicking had sapped Stunzi's spirit and there were rumors that he would soon be out. As it happened, my own resignation from Allied coincided – to the day – with Stunzi's, and we left the bank within a few days of each other.

By 1973 I had met a man named James Leary at National Bank of North America. With 130 branches in Manhattan and Long Island, NBNA was ten times the size of Allied. The bank's president, John Vogel, was wondering how to expand internationally, and Jim Leary arranged for me to meet him. After several discussions they asked me to come to work with them.

My mandate at NBNA was to determine what the bank could and should do internationally. What were the opportunities? How could we expand? In 1973 I went to London for a five-week trip and interviewed all the major banks – commercial and investment, both British and American – about what was happening in London. What were the dynamics of the city? What could a bank like NBNA hope to achieve there? What markets might we break into, and what would it take to succeed in them? These were the questions I asked, and I started to accumulate answers, documented in thick reports.

I created all sorts of projections and models, but in the end I concluded that there was no justification for physical international expansion by NBNA. The bank already had a foreign correspondent banking department in New York, and that was working well. Why should they open a branch in London? To do what? It might bring some prestige, but eventually they were certain to close it.

This was a hard decision, because I had been commissioned to start up the business, so there was a conflict between my integrity and my ambition. I was keen to be in charge of such an operation – it was just the chance I needed – and within the bank there was a strong desire to do it. At the same time, I never believed it made sense for NBNA. I presented papers on how it might be done, but I was not convinced, and I told them so.

What I had become convinced of, however, was that my

future did not lie with NBNA. I now realized that international business was beyond the scope of small banks like Allied or NBNA. If I really wanted an international career, I would have to work for Citibank or Chase or Morgan – banks that were already advanced internationally.

2
TURNING POINT

Chase and Citibank had been fierce competitors in the 1950s and 1960s, and then Citi leapt ahead under Walter Wriston, who was a visionary banker and a true internationalist. Under Wriston's leadership, Citi had established a presence everywhere in the world. Now Chase was debating how it could match that. David Rockefeller – a man of outstanding international stature and contacts – had been elevated to the chairmanship of Chase. Chase was my natural next move.

But by 1974 I was a hard man. I was not looking for just any job, and so I went to Chase and told them what I wanted. Becoming a lending officer had no appeal for me, and after my experience having run my own business plus my extended credit training thereafter, I believed I could assume a challenging responsibility. What I wanted from Chase was a branch or subsidiary in a foreign country that I could run on my own authority. I felt ready to do that. By this time I had the business background, the training, and the banking experience to take charge of an operation and be responsible for the end result. Of course I would report to somebody, but I wanted to run my own show. I was pretty brazen.

Chase said I was exactly the kind of man they were looking for. Because of the oil boom, David Rockefeller was pressuring the bank to expand in the Middle East – they were opening in Egypt and Iran at that very moment, and they needed people to run similar entities. But they could not tell me where I might be needed. 'Just join,' they said, 'and then we'll decide where to send you.' So on that basis I joined Chase Manhattan Bank as a Vice President in October 1974.

Two weeks later I found myself in very deep water.

This was the time when oil was on everybody's mind. Since 1973, when rising oil prices had created unheard-of lines at gas pumps throughout the industrialized world, the Middle East had taken on a new importance. The accumulation of wealth in the oil-producing countries was becoming a major issue, and the possibilities for recycling it were being examined by leading financial people around the globe.

Chase, under Rockefeller's leadership, was determined to benefit from these developments. David Rockefeller was a visionary, a world-class statesman; banking was only a part of who he was. His contacts were with kings and queens and presidents, and when he traveled he was treated like a head of state himself. As a thoroughly international business leader, Rockefeller wanted Chase to make up for lost ground and raise its profile in the world.

Chase had asked its Senior Vice President in charge of the Middle East – at that time a man named Derek Richardson – to come up with a business plan for the region, but Richardson was not much for planning. He preferred to get out there and do it – apply for a license, open up shop, see what the market offered. This time senior management was not satisfied with that. What they specifically wanted was The Big Picture – and from that a plan.

Fortunately for Derek Richardson, a cocky young banker had showed up at his office door at exactly the right moment. 'Don't worry,' Richardson, my new boss, told me – 'we'll find a branch for you to run in due course. In the meantime, as you've had some previous planning experience, why don't you handle this project and tell us what Chase should do in the Middle East?'

To me, this sounded like Mission: Impossible. Even though I came from one Arab country, I did not know any other Arab country except Lebanon. I had never been to the Gulf, to Saudi Arabia, to Egypt, to North Africa. But that was a secondary difficulty. The real problem was that I did not know Chase. I did not understand its business or its products and did not know anyone there whom I could call on for help. In the meantime, when you are thrown into deep water, the only thing to do is swim.

I offered Chase a road map for making the plan. 'If you want a plan of this nature,' I said, 'here's how to go about it. This isn't something you can do right away, it's a six-month mission, it needs twenty people, it needs a visit to each of the countries concerned, it needs the following budget. If you agree to all these things, I may be able to do something. But it's a very complex matter.'

I presented this to Richardson, who took it up to senior management, who approved it. Then Richardson came back to me and said, 'There you are, you're in charge. Put your team together and go.'

A team from where, though? People were recommended

to me in this or that branch or department, but I then had to persuade their bosses to release them. I would be ringing the senior officer in Hong Kong late at night asking if I could borrow one of his best men for three months. 'To do what?' he would say. 'Who are you, anyway? When did you join Chase?' It was very hard going because I had no recognition or credibility within the organization. But in the end I got my team, because the Middle East was in the news and I convinced the bigwigs that the project deserved a high priority.

Then a second problem arose. How was I to control this group when they did not really report to me? Without having any authority over them, I had to coordinate twenty-four people, all borrowed on short lease from their jobs and none of them at my disposal for the life of the project. It was two weeks here, three weeks there, so the logistics became very complicated. We established a center in Paris to do North Africa, and then a center in Beirut to do the rest of the Middle East and the Gulf. Moreover, we had to deal with the branch managers in those areas, who were not overly eager to cooperate with a team coming from outside to plan their future.

And while all this was going on, my second daughter was on the way. Nada was in a New York hospital, the birth was due any day. I wanted the doctor to give me the date – the hour – of birth, so that I could fly in and fly right back out again. The only way to make sure of that was to induce labor, which Nada and I jointly agreed was what needed to be done in the circumstances. So I swooped in and sat at the hospital dictating to my secretary while my wife was giving birth. When Serra was born, I went in and kissed Nada and the baby, and then it was back to the airport for the flight to Paris.

This horrendous pressure went on for six months. Volumes and volumes were written about each of the fourteen countries we visited. I went to most of the North African countries myself, and also to Tehran, where I had to sleep in the Hilton Hotel sauna because of a reservations mix-up; there was no other room available. In May 1975, when the final report was being written up, the trouble began in Beirut – the clash with the Palestinians. But I insisted that we could not leave the city until our job was done.

On June 30, 1975, I was to make my presentation to the senior management of Chase in New York. All the top people were present, including David Rockefeller, Willard Butcher, Barry Sullivan, William Ogden, and Thomas Labrecque. Later on these men would become the leaders of the largest banks in America. Rockefeller was succeeded at Chase by Butcher and then Labrecque. Sullivan became Chairman of First Chicago, and Ogden left to run Continental Illinois.

I prepared myself to address these important men. Then, two hours before my presentation, I learned that my boss – Derek Richardson, head of Chase's Middle East department – had left the bank. So I went to the meeting without the protection of a godfather. It did not bode well for the outcome of my presentation.

But the meeting itself was successful. My team's recommendations were that Chase should have three types of operation in the Middle East. One was offshore commercial banking; the second was onshore commercial banking; and the third was investment banking. Offshore banking meant using the existing Chase network worldwide to service the Middle East. Onshore commercial banking meant the establishment by Chase of a direct presence – a branch or subsidiary in a Middle Eastern country; in that instance the aim was to generate new business by exploiting the dynamics of the local market. Investment banking, the third entity, meant setting up as an intermediary between money in the Middle East and opportunities for investment worldwide.

The Management Committee congratulated me warmly. David Rockefeller wanted more meetings with me, country by country, to learn in depth what I had found out. This was arranged. But first, I said, I needed to take some time off. I was a nervous wreck. I had hardly slept for weeks. We had been working round the clock. I wanted to get together with my family and take two or three weeks' vacation.

Now, however, I had a new boss: Richard Higgerson. 'Nemir, I need you,' he said. 'I've just been appointed, I don't know a thing about this plan. I really don't think you should take a vacation right now.'

I told him I was just too tired to be useful. 'Let me have these three weeks, then I'll come back and be at your disposal. I'll do whatever you want.'

I took that vacation. I went to Turkey where I met Nada and the two of us took a cruise around the Mediterranean. Three weeks later I came back and by that time the politics of Chase had changed completely, reversed against me. Higgerson, the new man in charge, had immediately been surrounded by people who discredited our study. All this planning, they said, was expensive and unnecessary – it was all Derek Richardson's expenditure and Nemir Kirdar had no idea what was required, his approach was too theoretical. And they had their way. The plans were buried before they were alive. Corporate politics had won the day.

Now I got the cold shoulder from Higgerson. Though he was complimentary, he told me I was to be reassigned, and asked what I wanted to do next. 'Richard,' I said, 'I came to this bank to go out and run an entity, and that's what I want to do now. If you want to keep me at Chase, send me abroad.'

'No, no, we want you here,' he said. 'There are good jobs going, you could get to know the head office.'

'Not a chance,' I said. 'Even if you send me to a one-man office, I want to get away from all this. Give me a country to manage.'

The choice came down to heading the Gulf business out of Kuwait or Abu Dhabi, but Kuwait at that time would not allow entry to foreign banks. So I went to Abu Dhabi and got a license there, then rented an office and furnished it – just a secretary and myself. Right away I had broken one of Chase's many rules. The bank had a 'premises department' that was supposed to be consulted beforehand about all office-opening arrangements. Someone had to physically come out and look over all plans and give a stamp of approval before anything could be done. I had no patience for that kind of bureaucracy, which would have taken a long time. Naturally I heard about it. 'Oh no, you can't do that,' they said, and immediately dispatched someone to investigate. But the premises inspector realized that what we had chosen was acceptable, and thus he gave us his clearance. We were officially authorized to do business.

★

From the start, my objective was to offer a few products to a few customers, and do it best, and do it big, with an impact on the bottom line. I knew it had to be the kind of business that would make a splash because otherwise time would go by and pretty soon people in New York would be saying 'Who's our representative in Abu Dhabi? Nemir Kirdar? What's he done?' Once they started asking that, I would be done for.

So I set out to build a relationship with the Abu Dhabi Investment Authority (ADIA), the government's arm for investments. Meanwhile, I approached Qatar, where major industrial projects were being planned. I concentrated on a few key contacts, and in eighteen months the Abu Dhabi office of Chase Manhattan Bank – just two people – had achieved amazing tangible results. Among other transactions, in 1977 I put together the largest financing ever done in the Gulf at that time, a facility of $350 million for four industrial establishments in Qatar. Chase got very big coverage in all the banking magazines – *Institutional Investor* called it the deal of the year and awarded Chase a gold medal.

We also took several hundred million dollars in investment from ADIA. With Kuwait, Chase already had relationships, but now these were increased. All our banking ties in the area were strengthened, and this caught the eye of head office. David Rockefeller used to come out once a year. He would take me with him in his plane and we would visit all the states of the Gulf. He introduced me to the rulers of those countries. Rockefeller was well briefed on what I had done there, because by this time Richard

Higgerson had become a champion of mine.

In September 1977, I was promoted to Gulf Division Executive, in which capacity I managed and directed all Chase activities, branches, and offices throughout the Gulf states – except for Saudi Arabia, which became a separate division on its own under another division executive. Working out of Bahrain, I had almost two hundred people reporting to me.

Soon Higgerson moved to Hong Kong and a man named Bill Flanz replaced him as head of the Middle East, based in Athens. The Gulf Division, as we called it, was a big success. Profitability was high, morale was soaring. I handpicked all the key people in that operation. In Bahrain, Nada and I had a beautiful house with a swimming pool where we regularly entertained our growing circle of friends. After years of struggle, life was rich and full. Those were very good years for both us and Chase.

So why did I leave it behind? To explain that, I have to go back to the study I originally prepared for Chase. Even as my team was researching the Gulf region, my boss, Derek Richardson, knew that of the three kinds of banking we were contemplating for the Gulf, investment banking was the one I had set my heart on. There was just more excitement to it – plus, it suited my skills and talents.

But it was not until I became Gulf Division Executive that I realized just how smart an idea investment banking in the Gulf could be. The need for it was palpable – a need I could suddenly see with absolute clarity. This vision came from my observation of two separate emerging trends that I realized were mutually beneficial.

As far back as my time as a young banker in New York, I had often seen old, Western, privately owned family companies facing major challenges. Typically, the story went like this: Fifty or more years earlier, the founder had built up the business. He was proud of it, managed it well, and eventually passed it on to his son, who had been trained all his life to someday take the reins. Now, though, another generation had gone by, and the company had passed to the son's son – or maybe to multiple children. These new owners did not feel the same passion for continuing the family tradition. Basically, they wanted to sell and cash out. Unfortunately for them, the company itself was no longer in any shape to be taken public. While the business had done well under the engaged leadership of the founder, it had since been allowed to languish, to fall behind. In order to sell for good value, the company would require much careful tending and modernizing. Among such improvements would be injections of new capital.

Concurrent with my identifying this phenomenon in the West, another major cultural and economic development was taking shape many thousands of miles away. With the sharp rise of energy prices in the mid-1970s, the energy-exporting countries in the Gulf were suddenly sitting on massive amounts of surplus cash – looking for real places to invest it. Banks at the time were offering only conventional outlets for investment: bank deposits, marketable securities in stocks and bonds, and certain direct investments (buying a hotel or a shopping center, for example). Chase had recognized the growing wealth of the Gulf, which was why they sent me there to grow the Gulf Division in the first place.

And I did see first-hand the potential of just how much surplus wealth there was.

But then I took the thought a step further. At that time, there was no specialized financial institution that operated on both sides of the Atlantic and offered non-traditional investments. Why not build a bridge between the opportunities in the West and the surplus funds in the Gulf?

Back when we were preparing our banking study for Chase, Derek Richardson told me that when we got our operations established in the Gulf, investment banking was 'the one I have in mind for you to run.' Of course I was delighted, and if I had been given that job, Investcorp would not have been started. At that stage I never even thought of leaving Chase. Later, however, I got frustrated, and the first blow was when I came back from vacation in Turkey to find that our plans had been discredited and shelved. All that good work thrown away and ignored, purely for political reasons – I was really upset.

Still, I did not want to resign. I went to the Gulf wholeheartedly, to witness a new world emerging. I wanted to prove what I could generate if I was given the opportunity. With the Gulf Division in Bahrain, I was able to set up a business that was really the embodiment of total modern banking.

What made this possible was the very good relationship I had with Bill Flanz in Athens. I trusted him and he trusted me. With Bill to cover my back, I could run my own business without getting tangled up in the bureaucracy of Chase. And I was dedicated to the job. I was a good soldier for Chase. I served the bank with all my heart, and that was my only wish. David Rockefeller's appreciation meant a lot to me. He respected what I was doing, so the people at head office knew who I was. I could see anyone in the hierarchy and expect a certain degree of support.

The trouble was, I got tired of the games I had to play. I became frustrated by half-measures. My three years in the Gulf Division made it clear to me beyond any doubt that our original study had been right in saying that investment banking was what the region required, more than loan-making, so of course my frustration started to grow again. The plan was a good one, and we were doing some of it, but I kept thinking how much more could be done if I had the proper vehicle for it – and this Chase simply would not create. I talked and lobbied and cajoled until I could do it no longer.

That is really when the seed was sown. It was probably late 1979 or early 1980. I began thinking seriously of getting out and establishing an institution for the region – an organization that would become that bridge I had been dreaming of between the Gulf and the West. For the moment I was not thinking of a full-blown investment bank; my goal was a financial institution focused on investment portfolio management, specializing in non-traditional lines of business.

And I knew exactly how such an organization should be established. What I visualized was no less than a world-class platform adapted to Gulf needs – to be owned by the leading business families in the Gulf.

The six Gulf states – Saudi Arabia, Kuwait, Bahrain, Qatar, the United Arab Emirates (UAE), and Oman – were located in the heart of the world's energy sources. Forty percent of the total world's energy requirements were pumped out on a daily basis from this region. When the prices for this vital product quadrupled in the 1970s, abundant energy under the ground turned to enormous wealth above ground. Part of this wealth was earmarked to change the face of the Gulf states. Highways, housing, airports, hospitals, schools, office space, supermarkets, and so on were all needed to transform the landscape from white sand into modern cities and functioning countries. Nevertheless, the funds needed for all of the above were far less than the inflow of dollars that flooded the region.

These surplus funds had to be invested internationally. There was also another rational reason behind that. The proceeds from the extraction and sale of depleting assets under the ground should not all be spent for the benefit of the existing population. Some of those excess funds should be invested for future generations. Years later, when the income from energy stopped, earnings from investments should continue.

For me, it was clear that governments would create their own official vehicles through which to channel their investments. Moreover, these official entities would prefer to deal with the long-established institutions in New York, London, Frankfurt, or Tokyo. As with all pension funds worldwide, they would demand track records over decades and institutional-quality traditional investments – in other words, global equities, fixed-income instruments, and prime real estate opportunities. World-class financial institutions that had operated a hundred years or more would certainly be able to satisfy the official Gulf government-surplus-fund needs. The Kuwait Investment Authority and the Abu Dhabi Investment Authority, to give two examples, had no need of a new provider of investment opportunities. They knew only too well where to get the most experienced advice with a proven track record.

My vision therefore focused elsewhere – on the potential growth of the private sector, throughout the Gulf.

As governments spent enormous amounts on building the cities and the infrastructure, it would be the private sector that would grow richer and richer by providing the required products and services. Soon the private sector's income would start to exceed its expenses, and then it too would need to invest its accumulating surplus funds.

But this emerging and fast-growing private sector would probably not have the same access to the world's most established organizations as the government money managers did. Nor would these individuals get the same attention from them. Moreover, there were local cultural habits and behaviors that would influence the preference of these private individuals in investing their funds.

As I considered the dynamic opportunities awaiting the right man in the Gulf, it seemed to me there were four prerequisites which, if they could be met, would take me a long way toward my objective.

The first was that the ownership of the new institution should be widely spread among the top ranks of the Gulf business community. This concept went against the grain of the prevailing Gulf practice at the time. The validity of any new institution in the Gulf was measured by the standing of the people associated with it. This being so, the normal way to found a new business enterprise was for a single, wealthy individual to set himself up as a primary owner and chairman and then to invite a group of trusted friends or relatives of equal stature to participate as shareholders and fellow members of the board. Once the institution was established, its technical, day-to-day running would then be delegated to salaried managers hired from outside. But the owners would retain authority over both major decisions and any other matters they felt inclined to question.

For me and the organization I had in mind, there were two problems with that business-as-usual model. My plan depended on the organization's being truly pan Gulf, which meant eliminating the vertical hold of any single or connected families – or, for that matter, any single country. Ownership would have to be widely spread among the elite businessmen of all six Gulf states, and no anchor investor could own too much of it. The presence of such anchor backers from any one country could jeopardize the delicate balance of the entire project as I had conceived it.

But if persuading these high-level owners to accept equal status among themselves was a challenge, even more formidable was the task of convincing them to allow management – myself and my colleagues – to remain in the driver's seat. I wanted these prominent businessmen's names and financial backing, but I could not surrender management control to them. The staff I required would not put up with that. This new organization would have to be managed by the best and brightest talent and skill drawn from around the world. To compete at the level I envisioned, we would have to attract, hire, and retain the top professionals in our field and compensate them competitively, and that would be impossible if they arrived only to find themselves under an unfamiliar ownership's thumb.

My second prerequisite was that this new institution had to be at least as well recognized as the one I had left. However sympathetic these private-sector clients might be to a newcomer, they had worked hard for their money and would never place their investments with an organization they did not perceive as being among the very best. They were comfortable dealing with Chase and the other major names because they trusted their reputation and experience. To persuade them to do business with an untried entity, we would have to demonstrate exceptional quality – and create a brand that reflected that quality – from the start.

It was not my intention, then, to simply replicate any existing institution. To win a hearing from potential clients, I knew I would have to be as good as my competitors; to win their business, I would need to be even better. And while the leading international institutions possessed the name and reputation that I coveted for the new institution, they also had the bureaucracy and baggage that inevitably encumber any large organization. So I had an opportunity, I believed, not only to offer a new kind of investment, but also to be more efficient, more responsive, and more creative. Otherwise, investors would have no reason to switch their loyalties.

The third prerequisite was scrupulous transparency and strict adherence to the banking rules and regulations. I decided we should apply for a banking license and allow ourselves to be scrutinized and regulated by the relevant authorities. Demonstrating our transparency in this way would not only enhance our credibility among our clients but also help to persuade top-flight people to join the firm. To this day, I have insisted that Investcorp's internal auditors have total freedom to talk to anyone in the firm, to examine any documentation they wish, and to tell me if they feel that anyone is trying to block them.

The fourth prerequisite was a thorough understanding of the firm's target market. We had to be rigorously selective in the nature of our business, focusing only on products, services, and markets that would allow us to excel, create value, and offer strong competitive advantage. Above all, we had to understand our target clients – their lack of experience of large, overseas transactions; their aversion to risk, especially when they could not control it themselves; their need for expert, unbiased advice that would sort the good from the bad among the many investment proposals vying for their attention; and, lastly, their demand for superior service. As our public offering memorandum later explained, Gulf investors were largely reactive to opportunities presented to them rather than searching proactively for the best opportunities. We had to offer a product that this type of client would understand and welcome.

The attributes of the new organization were obvious to me. Its cornerstones would be quality, professionalism, transparency, reliability, and integrity. It would be trusted and respected, not just by its clients but by the worldwide financial industry. In all its dealings, it would never be less than world class.

Nothing was more critical to me than ensuring that the new organization considered integrity as its cornerstone. Throughout my life integrity had been vital to me personally, and the same had to apply to any new organization I would launch. No deviation would ever be tolerated. To gain and maintain the all-important trust of our clients, our actions had to be totally transparent. While an occasional error of judgment might be tolerated, any doubts whatsoever as to our integrity would kill the enterprise stone dead.

All this would require a particular – and deliberate – kind of culture. To accomplish this, I had to attract people of superior talent and skill, and motivate them to serve with passion and excitement. I had to empower them with the authority to make decisions, to make mistakes and learn from them. The management style would be open and participatory, with free-flowing communications, constant self-appraisal, and the ability to adapt quickly to changing circumstances. Essential to the culture would be passion, excitement, imagination, and respect for the best ideas, wherever they originated.

These were the imperatives that had influenced my personal conduct throughout my working life; now the challenge was to infuse those same qualities into an institution with an independent life of its own. They had to apply not just to me but to everyone joining the firm, to the service we offered our clients, to our working environment, and to our corporate culture. Fixing it so an entire organization reflected a particular ethos was going to be a lot harder than just applying it to myself – I knew that, even at the beginning.

I just did not know how much harder it was going to be.

Central to any company under my leadership would be the concept of inviolable 'core values.' While our external mission as a business would be to create a value-based and service-oriented firm ensuring client satisfaction and attractive shareholder return, our core values would express our internal mission as individuals and colleagues joined together to create something larger than ourselves. On one of the lined yellow legal pads that I always use for thinking out my ideas, I compiled the following list:

Core values

- Offer attractive investment opportunities
- Convince clients for diversified portfolio
- Earn client respect for our integrity and professionalism
- Earn client respect for the factors that differentiate us
- Commitment to excellence in whatever we choose to do and ensure an outstanding international reputation
- Separate ownership from management. The firm should be majority Gulf owned but managed by top international talent
- Acting as a bridge between the Gulf states and the West should be a key asset
- Transfer competitive edge opportunity to sustainable competitive advantage
- Generate and ensure high performance
- Foster an environment that encourages critical thinking – a working environment that provides freedom and demands that relations between subordinates and their superiors are based on respect and not fear
- Foster vibrant environment ensuring personal growth and enhancement of net worth for our professionals, aligned with increase in shareholder value and client net gains
- Attract and retain talent who are committed to advancing the firm and its core values

- Inspire individuals to innovate and pursue creative value generation to achieve success for the firm and its staff
- Ensure highest ethical standards with no compromise on integrity and transparency

These core values would be our book of laws, and no one who worked for our firm would be above those laws. But the culture that this list defined would only be a means to an end: Building a lasting institution was my true goal.

Even at the time, I think I knew that my motivation went back to my early days in Iraq, when I envisioned a career not in business but in government and public service. For me, the objective had never been to build personal wealth; my goal was to make a difference to other people's lives. Of course, the door to public service closed when I had to leave Iraq. But after my experience at large banking institutions in New York and the Gulf, I believed I could still satisfy my aspirations by fashioning a new institution on my own. I was, at heart, an institutional man, most at home in leading others and in representing a prestigious organization. As I contemplated leaving Chase, I knew I could best function by exchanging one high-powered institution for another. This time, however, the institution would be my own creation.

An institution can be defined as an organization that survives, evolves, and flourishes regardless of changes in ownership and management. It has a life of its own, an indefinite timetable outlasting the organization's founder and the founder's immediate successors. Its values develop over time, becoming part of the personality and culture of the organization. Over the years, it attracts people who share its ethos. For such individuals, a sound institution provides security and a means of advancement for as long as they choose to remain and excel within it.

That said, most institutions are founded not by career men and women but by people who seek fulfillment as entrepreneurs. They may leave their former institutional life after a number of years in order to pursue their dream, or they may decide at a young age to set up on their own and to operate outside the institutional framework. Either way, they create an enterprise and work hard as owners to make it grow. In time, if it succeeds, the small shop becomes a large shop; the pizza parlor becomes a chain; and so on.

In the most successful cases, the original start-up may evolve into an institution. Indeed, most of the institutions we know today began as one person's dream at some point in the past. But such a process requires a long period of constant development. In most cases, several generations will have passed since the founder first launched his idea.

The world of business therefore offers two main routes for ambitious individuals to make their mark: They can climb the ladder within an existing institution; or they can become an entrepreneur and create an enterprise that may or may not evolve into an institution many years in the future. What is not common is for an individual to found a business with the express desire to establish it as an institution, not fifty or a hundred years in the future, but while he is still involved.

Such an ambition requires a different mindset to that of the typical entrepreneur. In this case, the founder will not own the business himself but will attract others to own it from the start. He will join the outcome as an executive. He will drive the enterprise to gain success, fame, and recognition.

He will need to define and establish a corporate culture that distinguishes his organization.

From the start, this model was my choice for establishing an institution.

I knew the challenge was enormous. I knew that achieving my objective required facing constant struggles and setbacks, overcoming obstacles, fighting battles in order to ensure survival. But I knew it was something I was ready and determined to do.

To compound the difficulty, there was no allowance for getting it wrong; no room for trial and error. Had I been setting up a contracting firm, I could have taken my time getting established and building my reputation by degrees. An investment firm, by definition, is different. Unless it is known and trusted as a brand, it cannot even begin to do business. Our clients, their personal fortunes at stake, would demand nothing less than the very best from day one. We would need to be world class – not in five years' time, not even in twelve months, but from the moment we opened for business.

3
LAYING THE GROUNDWORK

My experience at Chase had exposed me to an environment that, at times, seemed over-managed and under-led. Now, as I prepared to move out of a credit-lending function and face an increasingly complex, competitive, and volatile investment world, my new role required true leadership – which I, fortunately, did not find difficult to assume.

There is a distinct difference between management and leadership. Managers do things right. Leaders do the right thing. Leaders produce change and set new directions. Managers establish plans composed of detailed steps for achieving those targets and monitor their progress.

Leaders ensure the realization of a vision by keeping people moving in a common direction. They do that by demonstrating their power for motivation, appealing to untapped human needs, values, and emotions. Setting direction is not planning. Planning is a management process – deductive in nature and designed to generate orderly results, not change. Setting direction is more inductive. Leaders do not produce plans – they create vision. Moreover, leadership requires the ability to identify and attract the right mix of talents and skills to implement that vision.

To translate my concept to reality, I recognized that there

were three prerequisites that must be covered. First, I needed a few trusted and competent professionals to form with me the nucleus of the proposed organization. Second, I needed to relinquish my responsibilities at Chase and have a temporary platform to start contacting possible future founding shareholders. Third, we needed to complete the ownership base (the entire Gulf) and move on to seek the official permits and complete the required formalities.

As I began speaking in confidence with a handful of close associates about forming the executive nucleus of the new company, I was not necessarily looking for specialized technicians – not to start with, anyway. This was partly because I still had nothing to offer by way of reward. I could not yet promise attractive compensation, and I knew that no accomplished professional would ever give up his job with one of the major institutions to come join me on such an uncertain basis.

At that stage what was most important was that the inner circle of the new company should embody the spirit and ethos of the organization. I strongly believed that excitement and emotional commitment had to come first, for without these qualities nothing of permanent value would ever be achieved. I wanted colleagues I could trust and mold into a team. I needed people with a firm belief in the company's future, people who would be able to shape its character with their own integrity and dedication. The prime qualities I sought at this early stage were enthusiasm, loyalty, courage, flexibility, an absence of egotism, deep reserves of energy, and a total commitment to getting the new business off the ground.

Mike Merritt, my second-in-command at Chase, was the first of my colleagues I approached with the idea of the investment firm. His response reminded me of when I had first met him in New York to discuss his joining my Gulf Division team. At that time Mike had been at Chase for several years and was just about to start law school at night, fulfilling a lifelong ambition. But he decided – on the spot – to uproot his family and come work with me in Bahrain.

Now, as I sketched out my vision for the new enterprise, he was immediately on board. For Mike, this was a bold move and potentially an enormous sacrifice. He had played a crucial role in the success of the Chase Gulf Division and was enjoying the rewards and all the trappings of the good life. Greater prospects beckoned. And yet he was willing to give up all that and move to Bahrain in order to become the first associate of a still unformed enterprise.

In the early days it was Mike, more than anyone else, who gave tangible shape to the concept. He and I spent many hours in discussion, often walking the streets after dinner in Kuwait or Bahrain and brainstorming our ideas. As we talked and talked, we generated mountains of handwritten notes and charts, and I gave him the task of turning these into a coherent definition of the concept. With his flair for detail and organization, Mike took a week's vacation over Easter 1980, sat down at his typewriter in Bahrain, and channeled these ideas into a clear, methodical presentation. This concept document, a statement of almost religious significance in the company, was the proposal I would later pass out to prospective backers on my journey around the Gulf. While it was revised twenty-seven times from start to start-up, the first draft was so good and so clear in its vision that when I showed it to another of the founding partners he asked who had prepared it for me. He thought I had hired the giant management consultants McKinsey & Company.

Before joining Chase, Mike Merritt had been a US infantry officer in Vietnam. He had commanded a Pathfinder unit, the elite airborne troops who parachute into battle zones to coordinate helicopter landings, resupply operations, and other air support for the soldiers on the ground. As their name implies, Pathfinders go where others have not yet gone; they impose systems in places where there were none. That is a pretty good description of Mike's role at the company that would become Investcorp. The ultimate implementer, Mike was the man who turned the grand design into hard, practical detail. Without his discipline and drive, Investcorp would not have taken shape so quickly or gained such rapid recognition. Having articulated the concept in that comprehensive business plan, he then would go on to organize the firm's incorporation. It would be Mike who wrote the policy manuals, equipped the business with the necessary computer systems, and put in place its compensation packages, incentive programs, and internal audit machinery.

In contrast to Mike, whose steely core was concealed beneath a placid surface, Elias Hallak – the second colleague I approached to join the new enterprise – was like a firecracker with the fuse burning. A proud, self-contained financial wizard from Beirut, Elie had already served twenty-five years at Chase in the Middle East by the time I took over the Gulf Division. He was very well respected throughout the bank – his work ethic was legendary – and in 1976 he had been sent to Bahrain to set up an offshore banking unit (OBU) for Chase. It was supposed to be a temporary assignment; once he got the unit up and running he would return to Lebanon. But then the Beirut conflict boiled over and Elie stayed in Bahrain. He had had the foresight to insist that he took his wife and two young children with him when he left Beirut.

My first official encounter with Elie says a lot about the type of man he is. Soon after I arrived as head of the Gulf Division, I called all the senior people into my office, one by one. My message was something like, 'Here I am, and I need your help. We've got to make something out of this place.'

Most of my new employees responded with the expected enthusiasm. Elie, however, surprised me. 'We're already doing very well,' he said, 'and whatever changes you introduce are not my concern. I've always done my job. I do it because by nature I'm a deeply committed and honest man, and I like to succeed. I will continue to do my job whether you or somebody else is in charge. So long as the offshore banking unit is safe, that's all I care about. Beyond that, senior management can come and go.'

A different kind of manager might have been irritated. But I recognized in Elie a kindred spirit – a self-starter with high standards and zero interest in the games so many corporate people play. His response to me, and my subsequent response to him, set us on a path to a deeply held mutual respect.

It is no surprise, then, that Elie ultimately felt some of

the same frustration at Chase that I did. Every year we had to submit an annual budget and a five-year plan. Toward the end of our time at the Gulf Division, Mike, Elie, and I worked together to prepare this document. The three of us then flew to Athens to present it to Bill Flanz, who liked it and passed it up the chain of command. It was a great plan, but it went nowhere. Like so many other good ideas, it ended up being shelved.

I did not fully realize how dispirited Elie had become – he is not one for sharing his pain. Not all of his feelings had to do with dashed hopes at Chase. He was also worried about his family. The Gulf is a nice place to live, but to Elie's mind there was not much there in the way of culture – no theaters, not even very good movies – and his children were growing up. He wanted something better for them, and was actually thinking about leaving. As I say, I did not know all of this. But he was projecting something, and I picked up on it. One day in 1980 the two of us were in my office talking about normal business, and out of the blue I said, 'Elie, if you weren't doing this, what would you like to do?'

He proceeded to describe a notion that he had been turning over in his mind. It was still vague – a 'fund management for individuals ... a private banking business, though more advanced' – but I could see that we were on a similar track.

'Well, hang on,' I said. 'We may have something.'

A few weeks later, after Mike had finished polishing the first draft of the concept document, I handed a copy to Elie. He was floored. And from that moment, he began devoting his considerable energies to making this dream a reality. Steeped in the disciplines of currency trading, and a man of formidable intellect, he would become Investcorp's financial architect. He set himself a punishing schedule. Initially concerned with treasury activities and establishing a dealing room, he was soon drawn into wider corporate responsibilities as we increasingly came to rely on his prudence, foresight, and brainpower. He and his workload became legendary. To Elie goes the credit for Investcorp's extraordinary financial record through its first decade and beyond.

The only one of the three co-founders who did not say yes immediately was Cem Cesmig. It bothered me a little, because I value both decisiveness and whole-heartedness. But to give Cem his due, the others had worked alongside me at Chase. They had day-to-day knowledge of the man they were about to link their destinies to, while Cem and I just saw each other socially. How confident could he be about going into business with the prankster pal who had once ambushed him with a spewing hose?

A man of the world from Ankara, Cem (pronounced 'Jem' in Turkish) was the son of a Foreign Service father and a mother who was half French. He was schooled in both Paris – where his father was stationed for a time – and Switzerland, and grew up speaking several languages. Cem was the working definition of the word *polish*.

But there was nothing precious or fragile about him. He was strong-willed and would never take no for an answer. During university in Neuchâtel, he met and married an American girl, Joy, and decided to get his Master's degree in Chicago, where Joy's family lived. When his application to the prestigious University of Chicago was rejected for low SAT scores, Cem refused to accept their rejection.

He promptly flew to the States, secured a meeting with the Dean, and explained to the man that the problem stemmed from his French education – he had only studied English in high school and was not yet comfortable expressing himself in that language. Not only did Cem talk the Dean into accepting him, but when the man told Cem he would have to wait until next semester, Cem convinced him he did not have the money to wait – so the Dean enrolled him immediately in night school. Cem studied English until he was proficient enough to get a job to support his schooling.

Cem and Joy came into my life initially through Nada, who met them in New York while I was doing all that traveling for Allied. I was gone so much that Cem and Joy teased Nada about the man they called her 'Phantom Husband.' Finally, one night when I was home, we ran into them on the street and immediately became close friends. Not only did we have banking in common but all four of us were very gregarious. We liked dinner parties, going out, meeting people, telling stories, engaging in lively debate.

When Chase posted me to Bahrain, Nada and I were thrilled to find that Cem and Joy were there for Bankers Trust. Friday being the first day of the weekend in the Middle East, the four of us soon fell into a Friday pattern: They would come over to our place about midday, and we would have lunch and a long afternoon (and sometimes evening) of lounging by the pool. That is how the hose ambush came about. One Friday when the Cesmigs were coming over – this time for dinner – I hid in the bushes, fully dressed, intending to leap out and spray Cem through the car window when he drove up. But I somehow got tangled in the hose, so when I lunged at him I soaked myself. He never let me forget it.

It was in our swimming pool that I first mentioned the Investcorp idea to Cem. It was late, perhaps 1 a.m., and our wives had long since gone inside and left us bobbing in the water talking about the vicissitudes of life and the frustrations of banking. Because Cem and I were competitors, we never discussed our work in detail, but it was clear that both of us were burned out with commercial-bank myopia. And I knew that Cem understood the Gulf and was a gifted marketer and presenter of concepts – skills that would be valuable to the new company. 'Listen, Cem,' I finally said, 'there's something I want to talk to you about ...' And that was how we started our discussions.

Indeed, Cem's European upbringing gave him detailed knowledge of a part of the world that would prove vital to our success, and he would become a natural trailblazer and spokesman for Investcorp. At critical moments in the firm's history, including the early transactions, he was invariably in the thick of the action. He played a leading role at the Western end of the firm's operations, setting up the London office and leading the thrust into Europe. His charm, sophistication, and personal presence gave him an excellent way with clients and helped to foster many of the firm's best relationships with international banks.

Cem's initial reluctance was not due to any dislike of the project; it was just that, about the same time, Bankers Trust offered him an interesting new opportunity, and it was only prudent for him to consider it fully. In fact, even after he committed, Cem was assigned by Bankers to go back to New

York. By this time I was in Saudi Arabia, calling on potential investors. 'What should I do?' Cem said, and the rest of us advised him to go ahead for the moment. In those very early days, there really was not much for Cem *or* Elie to do, so the two of them stayed put until Mike and Sally – Sally Furniss, my secretary, who would also later resign her job at Chase in order to join us – and I could get the foundation to the next stage.

While there is no such thing as a perfect person, I firmly believe it is possible to build a perfect team. This has become an Investcorp tenet, a day-to-day working philosophy, and it began with the four founding executives. We complemented one another perfectly – Mike the administrator, manager, and conciliator; Elie the trader and financial brain; Cem the diplomat and roving ambassador for the firm; me the leader who kept us all moving in the right direction. But aside from our organizational roles, our personalities added up to more than the sum of our parts. Each man's strengths compensated for the others' weaknesses. Where Cem might shoot from the hip, Mike was the very essence of preparation. Where Elie might lose himself in numbers, Cem had a gift for the human touch. And where those three might lack the skill of strategic thinking, I had an eye for the grand architecture. The assembling of this team was a major step in my own quest to turn the vision into reality.

I will never forget the night we formalized our commitment to the cause, and to one another. Mike, Elie, Cem, and I were in Cem's garden in Bahrain. For months we four had been in clandestine discussions about The Project. I did not like the secrecy, but I had given Chase every opportunity.

If I was ever to launch this company on my own, a certain amount of initial secrecy was inevitable.

Behind the intrigue lay life-changing stakes – and that was what had brought the four of us together at Cem's house, on this night that remains in my memory. We all knew the risks to our families and careers, but the time had come to be in or be out – no more half-measures, ever again.

In Cem's garden I went from one man to the other, looking each square in the eye. 'Are you in?' I said.

'I'm in,' each replied in his turn, and we shook on it in solemn bond to one another and to the adventure we were about to embark on together.

Then, by way of afterthought, I said: 'And let there be no corporate cancer.'

'No corporate cancer,' the others repeated in unison.

It meant no office politics, no individual grandstanding, no hidden agendas, no collusion, no backstabbing – a spontaneous expression of a core value that instantly summed up the others. That pledge of teamwork would become both company legend and company philosophy. And while in years to come I would sometimes be challenged to make it stick, on that balmy Bahraini evening in the spring of 1980 we were four of a kind, a unified team ready to meet and triumph over any obstacle.

With the team in place, my next step was to find a way to research the concept's viability – that is to say, to gauge the support of backers. For that I was fortunate enough to be able to take a leave of absence from Chase on loan to the Arab Monetary Fund (AMF) in Abu Dhabi.

The AMF had started operations in 1977 with capital of $1 billion, a large amount of money in those days. Its headquarters was in Abu Dhabi and its founding president was an Iraqi named Jawad Hashim. I did not know him. But thinking the AMF might be a powerful client of Chase's in the Gulf, I had called on Dr Hashim at his organization's inception. He received me warmly and asked for Chase's help in getting the AMF off to a good start, and I promised to do what I could. Later I told our head office that we should help this man – that we could get in on the ground floor with the AMF, which could be very useful to us in the region. Competing with me were Morgan Guaranty and Citibank, whose management had had the same idea. Chase agreed that we should establish a relationship with Hashim, and that led to several meetings between the two of us over the next couple of years.

The first mention of my joining the AMF occurred in 1979 during a visit by Hashim to Bahrain. After a meeting at my office, I invited him home for lunch, and it was there that he raised the subject – he said it could be a big opportunity for a man of my caliber, a man who was going places. I told him I was perfectly happy at Chase. The only reason I might ever leave, I said, would be to start up an investment firm – an institution that could serve the region and establish bridges with the Western world. There was room for this, I told him, and a need. But I would never leave to work for the AMF or any existing bank, because Chase had been so good to me. 'As you see,' I said, waving my hand at my pool, my garden, my cook, 'I live like a king here. Why would I leave?'

Now, though, Hashim's interest had been piqued. He wanted to know all about my ideas for an investment firm. 'There are certain international investments such as quoted stocks and bonds available to the Gulf,' I explained, 'but there are other non-traditional investment opportunities to which they have no access. A vehicle is needed to bring those investments to them, a firm specializing in the products that aren't available to them now. If that can be created, the region will be better served.'

He asked why I did not just do it. 'It's not that simple,' I said. 'A good idea doesn't always turn out to be good business, and this one needs a lot of study. But at Chase I don't have time for sidelines.' In fact, it was not a study of the concept that I needed – the idea was already crystal clear in my mind. In order to make it a reality, however, I first needed time to explore the appetite of future investors, and I needed my expenses covered during the process. I needed to study the region's receptiveness to, and readiness for, the concept.

Hashim graciously invited me to explore the idea under the auspices of the AMF. One of their objectives was to help the establishment of Arab financial institutions, he said, so I would be making a useful contribution. I could also help them by doing a study of Arab capital markets. He suggested that I come on secondment from Chase, meaning on temporary assignment.

It was an attractive offer, and I told Hashim that it might be possible once I finished my assignment in Bahrain – if Chase agreed – and before I took up my next post. We talked for a long while, and in the end I said I would think about it. We agreed to leave it at that.

A few months later Hashim contacted me again. Had I given the idea more thought? Yes, I had, I said, and indeed I had pondered the matter in great detail. I recognized this as potentially another major turning point in my life, and I wanted to negotiate the move carefully and thoughtfully, if I moved at all. Reputation has always been very important to me; Chase was important to me; and the integrity of any organization I might start was important to me. Certainly this interest from the AMF was convenient to my personal aspirations, but the whole thing had to be done within certain parameters. First, my work had to be useful to the AMF, which Hashim had already confirmed. Now the question was how to deal with Chase. The conclusion I reached was that it was not enough for Chase to simply let me go to the AMF; they had to want me to go there because my work would be so valuable to the region. 'Chase has to *ask* me to go,' I said to Hashim. He then decided to take it up with Chase directly.

His first overture did not work out too well. 'What you want is my right arm!' David Rockefeller replied to Hashim's request. 'We want to be helpful to the AMF, but Nemir Kirdar I will not give.' It was very flattering, I have to say.

When Hashim called back and asked me to push a bit, I flatly refused. 'No, I won't do that,' I said. 'If the bank asks me, I'll come. If they don't, I won't.'

But Chase refused, and that was where the matter lay for a while. Then David Rockefeller retired. Bill Butcher became Chairman, Jawad Hashim wrote another letter asking for me, and Butcher turned to Barry Sullivan, who was then in Butcher's most senior management circle. Sullivan said they should let me go. 'The AMF is an important organization, we need a relationship with it,' he said. 'Let Nemir spend some time there to broaden his scope and he'll come back to us. We can't lose.' Whereupon Bill Butcher wrote back to Hashim giving the go-ahead.

In retrospect, I must say that my secondment to the AMF for ten months proved to be vitally important for launching Investcorp, and I am extremely grateful to Jawad Hashim for having the vision and the courage to support my efforts at that critical time. The AMF provided me with two essential advantages: First, it gave me the time and the platform to test the idea with Gulf investors and solicit their participation. Second, it covered the costs of my travel and accommodation as I visited the various countries of the Gulf. I had no other sponsor to meet those requirements.

From the AMF's point of view, my activities were justified under their charter of promoting the development of Arab capital markets and an effective network of investment firms, either private or government-owned, to meet the ever-increasing demands of the region. The AMF was particularly keen to attract international talent to the region and, more importantly, to use this talent to encourage the development of local skills. To the AMF's credit, they astutely recognized that this could best be achieved over a long period through the emergence of world-class organizations such as the one I had in mind.

For most of the next year, I would be on the road in a strange and enigmatic world, trying to read a region with as many nuances as ripples in its shifting sands. Plus, this appeared to be an especially bad time to be out selling this particular dream: The Iran–Iraq war was blazing, oil prices had plunged, there was recession in the West, and the Gulf was in the throes of a speculative fever that blinded many to the merits of a solid, long-range (and unconventional, for the Gulf) proposal such as I was presenting.

To prepare for it, I had sent my wife and daughters to London to live, to ensure some stability, and I had given up our comfortable house and moved into a Bahrain hotel. The only time I would see it would be on weekends when I came home to confer with my team. They researched the strategic contacts I needed to meet, arranged my travel, and helped me refine the message for the following week's assault. But on a daily basis, there would be only so much they could do from a distance. It was largely up to me.

4
THE GULF CAMPAIGN

The first group I contacted, to test their willingness to invest and play a role in establishing the new firm, comprised individuals I had known well from my Chase days, and these became the nucleus of the founding investors. Some of them were personal friends, such as Khalid Al Zayani and Abdulla Ismail. 'One day we had a conversation in which Nemir put his idea to me, and I jumped at it,' Al Zayani later recalled, 'because I was already trying to do something similar with a partner from Saudi Arabia but it was not going well. Nemir asked if he could send me some papers so I could study his thinking. After that he kept on sending me papers. My father and both my brothers took an interest in the project, then we started to think who else might come in.'

Abdulla Ismail I had met when I went to Abu Dhabi for Chase, in 1976. An Iraqi national, and a highly respected and rising oil and gas expert in pre-Saddam Iraq, Ismail had decided that his future lay not in his native country but in Abu Dhabi, the then-emerging Gulf country to which he had emigrated in the 1960s. There he was given a prominent position in the official oil industry, becoming a deputy oil minister. Nada and I got to know Abdulla Ismail and his wife, Tameema, when we arrived in Abu Dhabi and we soon became close social friends. When I decided to leave Chase to devote myself to creating Investcorp, naturally I approached Ismail, who did not hesitate to offer encouragement and sound advice. His insights into the future growth of the region and the potential for good investment services were invaluable.

Others I approached were people who, while I had dealt with them at Chase, were also widely recognized as distinguished business leaders who enjoyed high stature and influence in their respective communities. In this group were Hussain Alfardan, Mohammed Jalal, and Abdul Aziz Kanoo. Of course Jawad Hashim, at the helm of the Arab Monetary Fund, was very influential. So was Hatim Zu'bi, among the most respected lawyers in the region, operating out of his headquarters in Bahrain.

'The first time I met Nemir was when he came to Qatar with David Rockefeller,' Alfardan recalled. 'We liked each other from the start and felt very close to each other. He had a bright future at Chase, but with his background and culture he felt he could do more for the region. He used to come here a lot, and one day he said, "Why don't we start an investment company for the whole Gulf?" I talked to my friends about it, and the first reactions were good, so I flew to Bahrain and had another meeting with Nemir at his house. We discussed the whole concept and decided to go ahead.'

'Nemir wanted to know if I thought his idea would succeed in Bahrain,' said Mohammed Jalal. '"Yes," I said, "provided you approach the right people and don't restrict it to

Bahrain. You've got to bring in investors from Saudi, for example, and Kuwait." I gave him the names of some Kuwaitis and told him to go and see Aziz Kanoo, who knew more people in Saudi than I did. Those early days weren't easy for Nemir.'

There is a very big difference between calling on people you know and calling on people you do not know. Finding backers and potential founders from the entire six Gulf countries was my next challenge. As it turned out, this phase of Investcorp's birth was the most arduous and frustrating. It took me to the verge of abandoning the whole project.

The closest parallel I can think of to my year criss-crossing the Gulf is the election process in the United States. In the US, if you want to run for president, you have to deal with various factors. First, you must have your idea, your message, absolutely clear in your mind. Second, you must find supporters who believe in the idea as you do. Third, you must organize your supporters so that they form a campaign team, a force that can influence the course of events. Fourth comes the campaign itself, and this breaks down into stages.

The first task is to create a sense in the public mind that you are an unbeatable bandwagon. To do this, you have to win primaries. So you enter the primaries, one after the other, and each time you win you get stronger. Eventually your campaign snowballs, there is nobody left in your way, and suddenly everybody wants to join you because they can smell success. They are scared they will be left out of the game, so now it is their own self-interest that makes them support you. From there the excitement builds nationwide, acquiring a momentum beyond your control and carrying you all the way to the White House.

The hardest part is the beginning. At this stage, no mistakes are allowed. When you are strong you can make a mistake, and it will simply eat away a bit from your support. But if you make a mistake at the beginning, you are out of the race.

To succeed in the status-conscious Gulf, we needed the backing of people of only the highest reputation. In each of the six Gulf states there are always a number of undeniable business leaders, men to whom other men defer – men whose names are golden – and at that beginning stage I was not so much soliciting money as names. If the right names signed on as backers, the investment firm I dreamed of would have credibility and would succeed in attracting clients who would bring us their money to invest.

But in deciding that Investcorp's ownership should be widely spread and inclusive of the top ranks of the entire Gulf business community, I had made the campaign even more difficult. Time and again I was reminded that this was not the way that men of substance in the region operated. Their accepted way of starting a financial institution was for a leading businessman to initiate a joint venture with a few trusted associates, and then hire an expatriate manager to run it as a 'hired hand.' Typically, they would haul in a branch manager from Chase or one of the other banks, double his pay, give him a Mercedes, and put him in charge of operations. While the manager would have day-to-day transactional responsibility, the owners would form the board. Common to all such enterprises was the fact that the members of the board not only owned the business but also ran it.

Had I been showing up with that kind of proposition, I might have been warmly welcomed – even though, as a US-trained Iraqi, I was not the kind of person these powerful, wealthy men were used to receiving. Not only was I not from one of the privileged Gulf families, I had never even set foot in the Gulf until 1976. So I was the wrong messenger with the wrong message. Therefore I had to work twice as hard. Over and over I stressed, in my most charming but insistent way, that in order to rank with the world's best, this proposed new organization would have to be management-driven, and it would have to operate to internationally recognized standards. It could not be subject to the personal whim of any single owner or country.

Some of my contacts proved difficult to meet face-to-face. Of those who did agree to see me, some were puzzled by the proposition. 'You're saying I *might* be offered a place on the board?' was one reaction. 'But I'm chairman of every company I'm in. How can you expect me to participate and not be on the board?' In such cases, I would have to explain that the board would be chosen by the shareholders, not by me, and that I did not have the authority to make advance promises.

One challenge followed another. Most of the people I was calling on could easily have put up a large proportion, if not all, of the capital required to start Investcorp; a trifling proposition was unlikely to interest them. And yet my colleagues and I had also decided that founding shares were to be strictly limited to one-half of one percent per founding investor – no more than $250,000. I had borrowed that amount for my own stake, so that no future backer would be asked to do something that I had not done myself. Yet to these mega-wealthy sheikhs, a $250,000, 0.5 percent share was 'perilously close to an insult,' as an acquaintance of mine once put it. But as I continually pointed out, the concept I was pitching was more than a company; it was a broad-based institution – a professional organization consciously designed to outlast everyone involved in it.

A further breach of normal Gulf practice was my insistence that an allocation of shares should be reserved for management – this to a group of men who regarded management as no more than hired hands. But I knew that I would not be able to attract and motivate world-class professionals without offering them a stake in their own enterprise. As I explained over and over, the company should be a collaboration of inside and outside partners. The inside partners would contribute professional talent, building the firm from within and taking responsibility for all business decisions. The outside partners would contribute their money and trust the management to use it well, ensuring by means of an effective board of directors that the organization remained on track. The interests of both sides would thus be aligned.

The reaction was patchy. A name is everything in the Gulf, and respect is the region's most valued currency. Consequently I soon found that no one wanted to commit unless he knew who else had committed. 'Are the Kuwaitis in this thing?' the Bahrainis would ask – the Kuwaitis are considered the smartest financial people in the Gulf. And of course the Kuwaitis, being so astute, wanted to know if the

Saudis were in. My task was to maintain a delicate balancing act, conducting conversations in six countries with several people at the same time, all of them at the appropriate level, and telling each one about the interest, in principle, of the others. Sometimes I even used the names of men who had indicated a favorable response but had not yet given an unqualified yes – a tactic I had to use with great care. One complaint and my credibility would be gone, and my dream along with it.

Along the way there were setbacks, blind alleys, misunderstandings, and disappointments. In some countries a group of backers began to form; in others, support remained alarmingly thin. Time and again, I returned empty-handed after a fruitless trip to one of the Gulf capitals. It was only with agonizing slowness that a critical mass of backers began to come together in each of the six Gulf states.

To continue the election metaphor, Kuwait and Saudi Arabia were our California and New York – and we had to win both primaries at once. In order to understand Kuwait's importance, it is necessary to understand its origins, which my team and I researched and discussed endlessly before I hit the campaign trail. Prior to the discovery of oil, Kuwait, Bahrain, and Dubai were the three business centers of the Gulf, seaports and trading locations that connected Europe and India to the Arab lands farther north. The English had a mandate over this area, even during Ottoman days, because of its proximity to India, and among the peoples of the region the Kuwaitis were known to be the sharpest traders. They had profited from exposure to the West and were traders by nature. They were also firmly entrenched on their territory, which they had controlled for two hundred years. The al-Sabah family, Kuwait's ruling dynasty, goes back to the eighteenth century.

Then, in 1938, oil was discovered. Oil had already been found in Iraq and Bahrain, but the find in Kuwait was much larger – enormous, in fact. The revenues poured in and the country began to develop very quickly. Kuwait's leaders, who were wise men with foresight, sent their sons to schools abroad and then brought them home to establish the necessary institutions, a task in which they were given unusual freedom of decision. The Kuwaitis are an adventurous people. By nature and tradition they are risk-takers, businessmen rather than bureaucrats. They do not have a nine-to-five mentality. They like to make deals and clinch them on the spot – even when it means involvement around the clock.

So when the oil boom began to heat up, the rulers of Kuwait did what any good businessmen would do. Confronted with the huge amounts of money coming in, they decided to put some aside for the future. When the oil runs out, they reasoned, we should have enough income from diversified investments to keep the nation going. This policy of theirs has been in place for decades now, and it has been so successful that in some good years Kuwait's investment income has been greater than its revenue from oil.

But while the Kuwaiti government has always been sensible, in the boom of the 1970s Kuwait fell victim to a fever of greed. There was a lot of money in private hands and this led to a rush of new companies and an issuing of shares out of all proportion to real economic activity. The share market became hyper-priced. In 1976 there was a collapse, a lot of people got hurt, and the government had to step in. A floor was established and shares were bought in at that mark. But by 1979 the market had overheated again – and this time it was worse. It was the period of the Souk al-Manakh, the market in which shares issued at $1 were changing hands again and again, in a trading whirlpool, until their value reached $20 or $30. Huge fortunes were made in months, sometimes weeks, by people who understood how to manipulate the system.

This went on through 1979 and 1980. By 1981 the bubble was about to burst, but it had not burst yet, and this was exactly the moment when I came on the scene trying to form a solid investment firm. As I went around the Gulf collecting subscriptions, I was asked over and over if the Kuwaitis were in. That was what everyone wanted to know. But when I took the idea to Kuwait, they immediately wanted to grab it. They welcomed me for the wrong reason. To them, this was just another piece of paper to trade. By that time the fever was at its height. If I had wanted to be a rich man, I could have sold those shares and got out and made a fortune for myself. But I had no such intention. With my conventional banking background, I could not understand that crazy market.

On the other hand, I could not ignore it. That was the big game in Kuwait and it was catching on in the rest of the Gulf. Even worse, from my point of view, the investment industry was in a hurry to become part of it. New instantly established companies had been formed which, while claiming similar objectives to mine, were in fact created to engage in trading their shares and contributing to the unreal overheated market.

And now here came Nemir Kirdar, the poor innocent, wanting to establish a *proper* investment firm. At that time my plan was to do it in Luxembourg: a private company, fifty investors, each one putting up $1 million. That was the concept that arose from my studies at the AMF, but I had failed to allow for the complicating influence of Kuwait.

The truth is, I had thought Kuwait would be relatively easy. I had many friends there, and when I went to see them, explaining what I had in mind, they were enthusiastic. 'Names?' said Hamad Al Hamad, speaking on behalf of his group of friends. 'That's easy, don't worry about it. We'll all come in. But, Nemir, you're doing this wrong.'

'Wrong? What do you mean?'

'Luxembourg – no way. None of us will come in. You'll have to make this a quoted company, based in the Gulf. Then it will succeed. Then we'll come in.'

'We can't go that route,' I protested. 'It's a total contradiction of what I'm trying to do. This isn't like the companies you guys are creating, this is a real investment firm, and it has to be private. I want to bring in experts and they'll only join if they can have a say. That's not going to happen if the shares are traded.'

'Then,' said Al Hamad, 'don't talk to us.'

The Kuwaitis refused to hear more. Doors were closed. I was speaking one language and they were speaking another.

Even if I had wanted to take Investcorp public, that would not have been an easy step. It could not be done in Kuwait, because the government was clamping down and the Kuwaitis were having to go to other Gulf states to set up these paper companies. 'Form a public company in Bahrain,' the Kuwaitis had told me, but the trick had been used too often. Other Gulf governments were wising up, and by the time I came on the scene in mid-1981, Bahrain had stopped issuing licenses.

So now I was facing a Catch 22 situation: 'But Bahrain is closed,' I said to the Kuwaitis.

'Sorry, then we're not coming.'

'You mean you're not interested.'

'Nemir, of course we're interested. You have to make it a public company, that's all. If you do, we'll join.'

'How am I going to do that if I can't obtain a license?' At that time Bahrain was the only recognized and respected financial center in the Gulf for a firm of the caliber of the one we targeted.

Faced with an intractable dilemma, I returned to base and talked it over with my team. We all agreed: If we could not convince the Kuwaitis, we would have to budge the Bahrainis. So I went to see the Bahrain Monetary Agency.

'Absolutely not,' they said. 'We're not giving a license to you or to anybody else. We have requests here from some very high-level personalities in the region, but we're turning them down too. We don't want any more banks on the market in Bahrain. If you'd like to do it privately, that's all right.'

'The Kuwaitis won't let me.'

'Well, that's your problem. Don't bring it to us.'

In the meantime, if Kuwait and Bahrain were immovable objects, Saudi Arabia was the irresistible force. As I shuttled around the Gulf, everybody I talked with knew that no investment institution such as the one I was proposing could possibly be established without Saudi Arabia – 80 percent of the market was there. In my days at Chase I had covered Kuwait, Qatar, Bahrain, Oman, and the UAE, and I had good friends throughout the region – except in Saudi Arabia. Saudi Arabia I had not covered. In Saudi Arabia I knew not a soul. In fact, until I touched down in Riyadh in the tense months preceding what would become the long hot siege summer of 1981, I had never even set foot on Saudi soil.

But you have to start somewhere, and so I began by grasping at the only straw in sight. My wife had a friend who was a Saudi, a woman who lived in Abu Dhabi, and her brother was a businessman in the Eastern Province. I had once been introduced to this man on holiday, so now I arranged to meet him in London. He would not sign on, but he offered me his help. 'I will mention one name to you,' said Zaid Ali Al-Quraishi. 'This man is highly respected, a successful businessman in Riyadh who has a lot of followers. Whatever he does, people put money with him. If this man is convinced, you will have no problem. How many names do you need in Saudi Arabia?'

'Ten to fifteen,' I said. 'What I really need there is a coordinator, not just an investor. I want somebody to take care of Saudi Arabia and bring me the best of the names. In the future, if there's a company, he could be the board member representing them all. He can be a power base in the structure and I'm looking for that sort of leader. It's the only way.'

'I have your man,' said Mr Al-Quraishi, and he gave me the name of Omar Al-Aggad. 'If Omar Al-Aggad comes in, a lot of others will follow, because this guy has done several successful industrial projects in Saudi Arabia. As soon as he starts something, everybody else joins in. Originally he was Palestinian, but now he's a Saudi national.'

'That's great,' I said. 'How do I meet him?'

'Call him. Use my name.'

This, I knew, was a poor means of introduction. I would have preferred a letter, but I was in no position to insist. Picking up the phone, I dialed the number in Riyadh and asked for Sheikh Omar Al-Aggad. He was not in, so the operator put me through to Bassam Aburdene, his business manager.

'Mr Aburdene, you don't know me,' I began. 'My name is Nemir Kirdar. I used to work for Chase Manhattan Bank. I was an adviser to the Arab Monetary Fund and now I'm in the process of establishing a new concept, an investment firm which can serve the region. For this to be effective, it has to have shareholders, and they should be prominent people from all the Gulf states. I would like to attract the best available management and make them shareholders as well. So there will be outside partners who are ordinary shareholders and inside partners who are executives. The outside partners bring money and support to the organization, the inside partners bring talent, effort, and skill, and the two will work together ...' Well aware that what I was describing was not the way business was usually done in the Arabian Gulf, I nevertheless bulled forward – they had to hear it before they could accept it.

When I had finished my presentation to Mr Aburdene, there was an uncomfortable silence on his end. Finally, he spoke: 'Do you have anything in writing?'

'Absolutely,' I said. 'I'll send you the papers straightaway.'

A few days later I called him again. 'Very interesting,' he said. 'We see many proposals from all over. Every day there's a new company being formed, but I've never seen a presentation like this. I would like to meet you, but I don't want you to conclude from that that we are interested; please don't come just for that. I don't want to be the cause of your visit to Saudi Arabia, or to create any false expectation.'

'I'll be there anyhow,' I lied. 'Can I see you?'

'Yes.'

'Can I see Sheikh Omar Al-Aggad?'

'If he's here, I'll arrange it.'

About to hang up, I asked Bassam Aburdene when his boss was going to be in Riyadh. He gave me some dates and I said, 'Oh, how convenient, that's when I'm coming too.'

The next problem was to get myself a visa. Saudi Arabia is not the easiest place to get into, and my Iraqi passport caused a few raised eyebrows. I eventually had to ask a friend to convince the Saudi Consul that I was not a mad revolutionary from Baghdad.

The office of Omar Al-Aggad was something to behold.

Time can be a malleable concept in the Middle East, but here was just the opposite: The office was clean, crisp, and very, very efficient, wringing the maximum effectiveness out of the minimum effort. The outer office was staffed by only three people – a telephonist, a coffee server, and Mr Aburdene – all of whom spoke and moved quietly, calling to mind the hum of a well-oiled machine. I had met with Aburdene the day before my appointment and had found him to be an extraordinarily nice man, financially sophisticated but not an egomaniac, unlike a lot of these advisers who are emperors themselves and enjoy making you sweat. 'I respect what I've seen, very professional,' he told me, and proceeded to ask all the appropriate questions.

Now I sat in a row of six people waiting outside Omar Al-Aggad's door, as though at a dentist's office. His appointments fell at precise half-hour intervals. When it was my turn to be ushered in, Omar Al-Aggad jumped up to greet me. He was an impressive man – white-haired, very handsome, self-assured, distinctively elegant. He shook my hand and sat down again. 'I studied your proposal,' he said. 'It looks good.'

Here was a highly intelligent man with zero tolerance for lengthy discussion. In years since, I have learned that he has a short attention span, his mind so quick that he will not sit and listen. He reacts immediately. On that first day I was mightily impressed. His desk was immaculate; any paper that touched it was answered within the same minute.

To open the discussion, I offered to explain the concept. 'I read what you gave me,' he said. 'What else do you want to say?'

'Well,' I said, 'this will only take a few minutes …' But each time I tried to say something, he would interrupt. I could see he was restless, he wanted me out of the room, and so I came straight to the point. 'I want you to coordinate getting widespread Saudi participation in realizing this project.'

'No,' he said, 'I can't do that, I won't take the responsibility. But I will join. I will join as an investor. Where do you want me to sign?'

He was the first investor from Saudi Arabia to sign up, and his money was in the bank within forty-eight hours. When Omar Al-Aggad makes up his mind, his efficiency is admirable – and he is still like that today. 'I found Nemir's concept interesting,' Al-Aggad later recalled, 'because at the time a few Saudi businessmen, including myself, were thinking of starting an investment company of some sort. Unfortunately, everyone in the group was very busy, me most of all. We would meet once or twice a month, achieving nothing really, except to talk about what a good idea it was. Nemir, on the other hand, was a dedicated person with a clear vision of where he wanted to go. All he needed was support and a base.'

'I very much appreciate your coming in,' I said to Omar Al-Aggad the day that he committed to investing – and of course I was thrilled about that: I had cracked Saudi Arabia! But at the same time I could not help being disappointed, which I tried not to show. I still had a very steep climb ahead of me. 'Where do you suggest I go for the rest of the names?'

'I might have a solution for you,' he said, without a second's delay. 'There's a gentleman here who used to be a senior official in government. Well respected, and with excellent contacts. He came to me a year ago with an idea just like yours. Ten people he put together – I'm one of them. We all committed to put money in, but nothing has happened, and frankly I don't think anything will. If I put you in touch with him, maybe his project and yours can be joined together. He'll be your coordinator.'

'Thank you!' I said, relieved beyond measure, as I had no other contact in Saudi Arabia. 'You've solved my problem.' All this took place in exactly thirty minutes. By ten thirty the meeting was over and I got up to go. It was time for Omar Al-Aggad's next appointment.

Within hours I was meeting with the man I will call the Ex-Senior Official. I gave him my presentation and he nodded approvingly throughout, finally saying that he had had the 'very same' idea. 'I wasn't going to do it Gulf-wide,' he said, 'but, sure, we can enlarge it. We can merge our two ideas together.'

So I asked him to explain his concept. He rattled off some scheme to do with the stock market in Saudi Arabia, then another involving an insurance company.

'No,' I said, more firmly than I intended. It was just that my partners and I had worked like dogs to create a blueprint for something with a different focus. To compromise our ideals would not only be wrong, it would be a betrayal. Some good people back in Bahrain had put themselves on the line for what I was doing here.

Quickly adopting a calmer, more reasonable tone, I explained: 'If we attempt too many things, we'll lose our specialization. Our aim must be to do a few things well. Take Morgan Stanley – they have something like eighty-five products. Out of those, I want to do four . . . and in those four I want to be able to compete with Morgan Stanley. That's the most I can achieve in the next ten to twenty years.'

Then I added: 'But I'm under tremendous pressure. By April thirtieth I have to get this whole thing done.' That was four weeks away. 'So when will I know the names?'

'I have them ready,' he said. 'They're all in my company.'

He asked for copies of my proposal so he could send it around with a covering letter, but I thought that was not the best approach. 'Let me make a presentation to each of them,' I said. 'These things don't get done by mail.'

'No, no, you don't need to see them – they're already in. Let me do this my way.'

He suggested that all his people should be introduced to me at a meeting, but again I disagreed. 'I want to meet each one individually,' I said. 'Later on we can have a meeting of those who've said yes, but if we bring together eight people and one says no, the rest could be adversely influenced. I don't like to sell to a group. It never works that way.'

'We'll invite them all and tell them the plan.'

'No, that's not the right way.'

'That's the way it's done here.'

'*Please,*' I said, 'I don't want to take that risk. Let me talk to each one by himself. Let them all sign and then we'll collect them together. I'll come back here in a week and start paying calls.'

'A week is too soon,' he said. 'When's your deadline? April thirtieth? Come back on April thirtieth.'

'But where will I go if it's not done by then?'

'It'll be done,' the Ex-Senior Official said. 'April thirtieth, I'm telling you. These people are *in*, and we'll bring others.'

It was great, for a change, to go back to Bahrain with good news. So often, after a week wandering like a nomad in the desert, I had returned to my colleagues empty-handed. At such times my own sense of business disappointment was nothing compared to the personal pain I felt at having to tell them I had let them down again. At least I was out in the world, calling on prospects, giving it a go; my friends could only hand me the tools, send me off, and wait. They were essentially helpless, and a bad report hit them especially hard. While we believed in our dream, we were still vulnerable to occasional bouts of doubt.

This time, however, I stepped off the plane and said, 'Guys, we've hit a gold mine! Saudi Arabia is done!' Of course everybody was elated. Our struggles weren't over: Kuwait was still a problem, and we had had setbacks in Abu Dhabi too. But Saudi was done. It seemed too good to be true. 'Frankly,' I forced myself to say, 'I'm not a hundred percent sure. But I have a lot of confidence in Omar Al-Aggad. He's a man of action. If he recommended this man, I have to believe it's real.'

On April 29 I went back to Saudi Arabia. When I phoned the Ex-Senior Official, I was told he was in a meeting. I left a message and then sat waiting in my hotel room – two hours, then three. I called again. He had gone home for lunch. In the afternoon he takes a nap, I was told, but he would be back in the office at six in the evening. I asked for an appointment. No, impossible, he did not yet know of my arrival. 'Please,' I said, 'let me come to the office at six. I'll wait in the secretary's room. If His Excellency can see me, I'll see him then.'

First I had to find his office. I had very limited funds, so I could not hire a car – I had to hail a yellow Saudi cab, which are like cubicles, smaller than a Volkswagen. You sit back in them and the dust puffs out of the seat like a nasty cloud, all sorts of hair and wool coming off and sticking to your suit. You tell the driver where you want to go, but the address means nothing to him, so you have to give him localized directions. 'There's a gas station – you turn there and look for the Marlboro sign. After that you'll see a ditch. Keep going until you come to a school . . .'

Finally I made it. I waited in his office – 6 p.m., 7 p.m., 8 p.m. At 8.30 the Ex-Senior Official arrived. He wanted to see me, I was told, and they took me in.

'Sorry I delayed you,' he said. 'Why did you come today? You were going to come next week.'

'No,' I said, 'we agreed to meet tomorrow, April thirtieth. Today is the twenty-ninth, but I came a day early to see if you needed me for a meeting.'

He nodded, beginning to look uncomfortable, which made *me* uncomfortable. 'What should I tell you?' he sighed. 'I mean, you know, these things don't happen easily. How much time do we have?'

'None,' I said. 'Our time has run out. What happened?'

'Some of the people still have a few questions. But it doesn't matter, we'll make another list. There are a lot of people who can come. Let's do this slowly. There's really no problem.'

'Let me ask you a question. As you know, I have one signature from Omar Al-Aggad ...'

'Yes, yes, I encouraged him.'

'No, you didn't. He'd signed already. The question is, do I have yours?'

'Well, no, not really. I don't have the money. When you form the company, I'll join in some capacity, but I'm not an investor. I'm doing this for your sake. I like you – that's why I gave you my ideas. In fact, I've made a decision. I'm not going ahead with my program, I'm supporting yours.'

'Look,' I said, 'I don't want to be rude, but the project is over. I've run out of money. I'm going back to Bahrain. I'm going back to Chase. They've offered me a job in London and I think that's where I'll go.' That was the truth. If my own project did not work out, Chase wanted me to join its investment group in London. And right at that moment, Chase and London were looking pretty good.

'Don't be discouraged,' said the Ex-Senior Official. 'I'll back you.'

'Let's stop right here,' I said. 'Thank you for your help. Incidentally, just for my interest, why did all these guys turn it down without even hearing me? On what basis did they come to that conclusion?'

'I sent them a letter with your study.'

'A letter? You mean they've not been told the details?'

'Well, I recommended you. The letter had my signature on it.'

'You didn't make any presentations to them?'

'No, no, not necessary. They just weren't interested.'

'Thank you,' I said, and went back to my hotel. I could have shot myself.

The next morning, before I left Riyadh, I went to see Omar Al-Aggad. Usually you have to ask for an appointment many days ahead, but I said it was urgent. I told Bassam the whole story, he got me through the door, and I related it to Omar Al-Aggad.

'Oh,' he said, 'I'm very sorry to hear this.'

'Never mind,' I said. 'I'll take over myself.'

'I apologize. Maybe it was the wrong choice.'

'I hope you're still interested.'

He nodded firmly. 'I've signed. My name is in. I have already transferred the funds.'

'Are you sure you won't act as a coordinator?'

'No,' he said, 'I can't tell people where to invest – and I won't. I'll take a risk with my own money, but not with somebody else's.'

And with that I left his office and went back to Bahrain.

Though I felt nothing but the deepest respect for Mr Al-Aggad and his principled manner, my time was almost up. Without the Saudis, we were stuck with a terminal problem.

But then we got another break. At the time, I was talking to the Zayani family in Bahrain, two brothers, and one of them offered to introduce me to Abdul Aziz Kanoo. This became a game changer.

The Kanoos are a prominent Bahraini family whose name we were hoping for anyway, and they have branches throughout the Gulf. Abdul Aziz is a Saudi national who lives in the Eastern Province of Saudi Arabia, but he travels back and forth, and by luck I was able to meet him over dinner in Bahrain. He listened to the whole presentation, said he liked it, and suggested a meeting the next day in his office in Dammam.

Reflecting later on that meeting, Abdul Aziz said, 'Nemir's initiative was welcome, all the more so because of the rather strange atmosphere at the time. This was the period of the Souk al-Manakh, when people were forming new companies every day and selling shares in them before the companies came into being. Nemir and his friends weren't interested in just selling shares, he told me. What he had in mind was a really stable company. That idea I found exciting, because it was something serious.'

So I went back to Saudi Arabia for a second meeting with Abdul Aziz. I told him I was under tremendous time constraints; whatever he thought could be done, we would have to do it immediately – I had to know if we were going ahead or not. So he called some of his friends in the Eastern Province. 'A lot weren't interested because of the bad experience they'd had with overseas investment,' Abdul Aziz later recalled, 'but gradually we made progress. All I had to do was make the introductions. Nemir did the rest.'

Abdul Aziz also arranged for one of his staff, an elderly man, to take me to each appointment. This poor old guy and I, we walked together from one meeting to another, all these dusty places, and every time we came out of what seemed to be a positive meeting the old fellow would smile and say, 'We won.' In reality, we could not be sure, because the prospects had to talk among themselves when we had left the room. But we were getting signs of receptivity.

Returning to Abdul Aziz, I told him about this feedback. 'I think they liked it,' I said.

'You made a good impression,' he said.

'Will they come in?'

'I don't know. We'll see. It looks good. Why don't you leave it for a week or two?'

There was no time to sit around, I said. Could I not go to other places in Saudi – the Western Province, Jeddah? Did he know people in those places too? He said he did, and he would give me letters of introduction. Among the names he gave me, there was one man in particular he wanted me to see – Abdullah Bakhsh. So I went straight to Jeddah while I was already in Saudi, because getting a visa was like pulling teeth.

None of it was easy. While Abdul Aziz had given me the letters I needed, they could not be handed out to just anyone. Until you find a secretary, the offices are totally disorganized. No one knows if the boss is coming, where he is, or what he is doing. With Abdullah Bakhsh, everybody told me he was a prime name, but he did not go to his office until night. 'Don't bother during the day,' they said. 'Go there late.'

So I went to his office, which was in an ancient building with a very old man sleeping on the floor downstairs at the entrance. He must have been the guard, since he shook himself awake and said, 'Where are you going?'

'I'm here to see Mr Abdullah Bakhsh,' I said.

'They're not here,' the old man replied. 'Come back later.'

I wandered around in the dust for a couple of hours, wasting time. By then it was very late, so I went back to the building. 'There's somebody there now,' the old guard said. 'Go on up.'

There was no elevator, so I trudged up the rickety stairs with my letter of introduction in my hand. At the top I knocked on the door to Abdullah Bakhsh's office. I could hear movement inside, and then a man opened the door and ushered me into a room where a man in a white robe was sitting. The man smiled, very pleasant. 'Good evening, sir,' I said. 'I have a letter for you, from Mr Abdul Aziz Kanoo.'

'Let me see it,' he said. I handed it over and he read it, nodding. Then he looked up and motioned me toward a chair. 'Please sit down,' he said. 'Tell me about your project.'

As I began my presentation, he politely interrupted me. 'Coffee?' he asked. 'Tea?' I accepted a coffee and we resumed our business. He listened, occasionally nodding.

After a few minutes he stopped me again: 'More coffee? Tea?' Again I accepted coffee, and again we continued. This went on for about an hour. When I had finished, I switched to tea and he left me sitting there while he went to his desk and worked on some papers. Was he interested? I had no clue. I did not know whether to stay or go. I decided to wait. Occasionally someone would offer me more refreshments. By now it was the wee hours of the morning, but of course I was wide awake because of all the caffeine.

Then, suddenly, I heard a commotion in another part of the office suite. 'The sheikh has arrived,' the man in the white robe said.

'Oh,' I said, realizing I had given my entire pitch to an assistant. 'Will I be able to see him?'

'I don't know,' the man said. 'We'll see.' And he disappeared into another room.

About an hour later, he reappeared. 'Come back tomorrow,' he said. 'Come back late.'

The next night I was there and waiting. At least now I knew the man in the white robe was not the sheikh, so the tone was different from that of the night before. While I waited, he asked me many curious questions about business and the world. I drank a lot of tea and we talked about everything under the sun. I was as engaging with him as possible, since I did not want an enemy in this office. Already I was wondering about this bizarre sheikh who kept me cooling my heels throughout the night. *I'll hate this guy*, I thought, but that is not at all what happened. I loved him from the first minute we met.

Sheikh Abdullah Bakhsh was an older man, very philosophical. We did not talk business at all. We talked philosophy, we talked politics, we talked of personal values. 'The whole thing is,' he said, 'forget about returns. People want to deal with honest people, professionals, people of integrity, long-term builders. That's what I see in you. Projects are thrown at us every day, but I like what you're doing. Let's talk about this some more. What do you do in the evenings?'

'Oh, this and that.'

'Come here every night,' he said. 'Let's talk some more.'

'I'm here to see a lot of people.'

'Oh, you can leave that to me. I'll organize it for you. Who do you want to see?'

I told him about the letters from Abdul Aziz. 'I'll call them,' he said. 'Who are they?' I asked him to recommend some names himself, but that he declined to do. 'I can't tell you who to see. Just tell me who you want and I'll arrange it.'

So the next day I asked someone else about Abdullah Bakhsh. Who were his friends? He knew just about everyone, I learned, including Sheikh Ahmed Zaki Yamani, the Minister of Oil. My informant was very impressed that I was getting help from Abdullah Bakhsh.

'Is it possible to see Sheikh Yamani?' I asked the next evening, when I was back in his office.

'Of course. Who else?' I mentioned another name. 'Sure. No problem. We'll get it organized.'

And he started to make appointments. I'd go to see people, and they began to call others. Nobody was signing, but now at least things were moving in the right direction. 'Right from the start,' Abdullah Bakhsh recalled years later, 'Nemir and I agreed that Investcorp should be built around people, not money. He had many meetings at the time, here in Jeddah and elsewhere. It was amazing how much he did. Even so, it took quite a while to convince the right people to join. After all, Investcorp was the first company to be composed of individuals from all over the Gulf.'

At about this point Abdul Aziz Kanoo called me to say that his people wanted to see me again, so I left Jeddah and went over to the Eastern Province, where I got an encouraging reception. The list of names started to build up. Then I went back to Jeddah and things were still moving. It was all introductory, nobody was signing yet, but at least there was plenty of activity.

All told, I spent sixty days in Saudi Arabia. My visa was extended three times. This was during the months of June, July, and August, when the heat is like a blast furnace, so fierce that nobody moves. That made me a very conspicuous sight in Riyadh and Jeddah, a perspiring man dressed in a Western suit and a cinched tie, carrying a briefcase, pounding the sun-scorched streets knocking on doors. Appearances are important in the Middle East, and to the casual observer I must have appeared to be absolutely mad. There were times that summer when I wondered if it was true.

But it was worse for the three guys waiting in Bahrain. They did not know what was happening. I would call them from time to time, but I was unsure of what to say. I could not tell them everything was fine, because that was not true. And I could not say that everything was bad, because then they would be demoralized. So I just asked for more documents to be sent, more printing to be done, more typing, more back-up. I was giving a mass of instructions, I was short-tempered. They kept asking me about the Kuwaitis. 'Yes,' I said, 'I've talked to the Kuwaitis, but so far nothing.' I did not want to ask for any signatures yet, because if they were not forthcoming it would start a downward spiral. I wanted to create the same interest we had in Bahrain and Qatar, so that I could use this to convince the Kuwaitis.

All that summer I shuttled between Kuwait and Saudi Arabia, Saudi Arabia and Kuwait. Finally we got the names in both places – the Kuwaitis contingent on our going public – and when Abdul Aziz Kanoo saw this progress, he became more active and drew more people in, even some princes of the royal families. The whole thing started to roll. We were winning the primaries now, the bandwagon was on the move.

In the end the operation was a total success. When I saw that the Kuwaitis would not bend, I had to increase my pressure on Bahrain. I took two prominent businessmen with me to see the Minister of Commerce, and he said, 'It's true, we've stopped giving licenses, but all the people who've applied so far have been Kuwaitis. This is the first time we've been approached by prominent Bahrainis.'

'And ours is a very different company,' I added. 'A different concept altogether.' He listened to me while I explained it.

'So why does it have to be public?' the Minister asked. 'Why don't you make it private?'

'Because the Kuwaitis won't let me. And if they don't join, the rest won't join.'

'Yes,' he said, 'I understand the problem. Let me see what I can do.'

So the Minister of Commerce went to the Prime Minister, and eventually a decision was made to give us and four other applicants a license in Bahrain.

The shares were fully subscribed by the founding members. With some left to put on the market, the whole allocation was used up. And then of course we had the opposite problem. Suddenly everybody wanted to be in – every cabinet member, every prince, all the influential people in the Gulf. And this was more than we could handle. The pressure began to build up, big pressure to create further share allocations. The telephone never stopped ringing. Finally, when we put the shares on the market, the issue was 1403 times over-subscribed.

And that, if you will, was the end of the campaign. We had reached the White House.

5
FROM DREAM TO REALITY

The tallest skyscraper is only as solid as its foundation. Every brick, every length of rebar, every slather of mortar is integral to the strength of the whole. During the foundation work, any compromise could prove counter-productive.

This is something to bear in mind when you are building a business out of thin air – which is why, in the thirty months between summer 1981 and December 1983, I was the most ferocious of contractors. My building materials were people, organizational and financial structures, product lines, and, in the end, our physical manifestation itself. At each stage of the construction, it seemed that someone was trying to tell me we needed to slow down, cut back, pace ourselves, grow into our dream. My response was that what we created right now would determine the type of people we attracted, both recruits and clients, and would do so from day one. It was imperative that we begin as we meant to go on. In five years' time it would be too late.

We had to look at it from the customer's point of view. Our client is an investor; each dollar he places is important to him. So from the very beginning I wanted to instill in his mind the idea – the certainty – that if he came to Investcorp he would get the best service his dollar could buy. The customer was not going to give us his money unless he was convinced we were the best. He did not want to hear about temporary offices or the computer system we could not yet afford. He would not subsidize a start-up – why should he? He would go to the organization that had it all. We may have just opened for business, but we were selling the same product as the best in class, and unless it was just as well packaged, well articulated, and well substantiated, the customer would not choose Investcorp.

An impression of solidity can never be created by external means, such as advertising. That impression can only come from the internal message: the way we talk, the way we present, the way we think, the way we deliver, the way we generate results – by every small thing we say and do. That is why every annual report is important, every brochure is important, every corner of the environment we work in is important.

And it all begins with the foundation.

In June 1981, when our second Saudi campaign started rolling and I could see we would go forward, I told Mike I thought it was time to move to the next stage – resigning from Chase. But because I would not submit my resignation until August, when I finished my stint with the AMF, Mike actually resigned before I did.

Soon Mike was living and working in the Grundy Hotel, a cheap establishment right next door to Chase – it is where, because of the convenience, the Gulf Division used to put its out-of-town guests. Now the attraction was a lot of space for relatively little money, which was especially important to

Mike. He and his Vietnamese wife, Rose, had three young sons. The Grundy gave them room to spread out a bit – and also a proper kitchen for Rose to cook her spectacular Vietnamese dishes.

Immediately after resigning from Chase, I got on the phone and began inviting all the people who had signed to join us to come to a meeting in Bahrain. I called it the 'Founders Meeting,' and its purpose was to consolidate the support I had generated and create a formal structure for creating the business.

All along, I had been very careful to deal with potential backers one-on-one. At that early stage, when your support is still 'gelling,' you do not want to risk the vacillating nature of group meetings – this is why I was so adamant with the Ex-Senior Official in Saudi Arabia about the need for individual presentations. In a group, if one person gets cold feet, he can quickly spook the others. If the room turns negative, there is no way to keep the word from spreading. One bad group meeting could sour our prospects throughout the Gulf.

Now, however, we felt we had achieved critical mass and it was safe to bring all these individuals into the same room. That is not to say we would just get together and see what happened; this meeting was vital to our success, and, like everything else we were doing, it had to be tightly choreographed.

There is a term I use for the way I work: *mastermind*. To some, that word will conjure images of Machiavellian movie villains – 'the mastermind behind the evil plot to take over the world,' and so on. Mastermind as a noun suggests pure intellect, but the verb *to mastermind* encompasses something bigger. To me, it describes the combination of vision and action – the process of looking at the total picture, coming up with a plan, and making that plan happen. It is a process that can be applied to anything, large or small, and its value is well illustrated in the history of Investcorp. I use the term both to assess my own performance and to appraise others: 'Can he mastermind?' In the final analysis, none of us – no business, no individual, no family, no country – can survive by sitting and waiting for the world to act upon us. We have to mastermind our progress, continually and consistently, as if we were starting anew each day.

The Founders Meeting was held at the Bahrain Hilton on August 12, 1981. There were forty investors from all over the Gulf at our meeting. I had, of course, invited Jawad Hashim as head of the AMF, and I made a speech explaining how I had researched the project under the auspices of the AMF. That research was the property of the AMF, I said, but now that we had formed a group we were formally asking for the use of it. Dr Hashim responded that he would be delighted – that the AMF was proud to see one of its studies being translated into reality, because that is what the AMF was all about.

There was a lot of goodwill at that meeting, and a number of important decisions were made. We resolved to apply to the government of Bahrain for a license; we thanked the AMF for their valuable contribution; we chose a number of individuals to be on a Founders Committee; and we elected Nemir Kirdar to be the Coordinator of that committee. There was no Chief Executive at that stage, only a

Coordinator, because there was no company yet.

Meanwhile, we drew up a budget and the Founders Committee agreed to meet on a regular basis to approve expenditures and make the necessary early decisions. The forty people who came to the Hilton had each paid $250,000 into the bank – a quarter of their pledged amount – to be held on account for the capital of the company under formation. Additionally, each investor agreed to pay $10,000 to cover the expenses of the formation, which meant that Mike, Sally, and I were put on the payroll from that date. This marked the actual beginning of Investcorp.

A week later we had the first meeting of the Founders Committee. Now the complications began. They questioned our proposed travel expenses and even our judgment in buying Sally's typewriter. This did not shock me – criticism can often be channeled to our advantage. But nitpicking about expenses is something else. I felt that it reflected a lack of understanding of the company we were trying to build, and so began my long process of converting those who had the power to derail us from our chosen path.

As a matter of philosophy, I do not believe in micro-managing. Many companies become lost in the details of expenses and fail to see the value of directing resources for revenue generation. I ask myself a set of questions: What is it that needs to be accomplished? Where is the strategic angle? What am I doing that is different, that is better, than the competition? What resources do I need in order to get that objective accomplished? What is going right, and what is going wrong? Where is my attention required right now?

How about in the future? My focus is all on getting the job done, on achieving the ultimate objective. If it is worth fighting for, let us fight, do it right, and put together whatever is needed to achieve the top line. If we have thought it through properly, it will pay for itself in the long term. 'Expense control is a means to an end,' I told the Founders Committee, 'not an end in itself.'

A fundamental characteristic of Investcorp has been its clarity of direction, and that requires a culture which molds all the talents together so we speak the same language and work to the same agenda. People are bound to have different levels of energy, different intelligence, different skills, but what they must not have is different agendas. To minimize that, there has to be a common belief, a common way of doing things. However distinct an individual might be in talent or in style, in direction he should be identical to the rest of the team.

Of course this might be considered an ideal. It may be hard to erase individual agendas completely, because we are all human beings. We all look at things from our own point of view. So I had to give more attention to this subject – this ongoing obstacle – as the number of people in Investcorp grew. With every new person entering the picture – starting with the Founders Committee members – there was the challenge of converting him to the culture before he began influencing the rest with his own way of doing things. Especially if he was articulate and convincing, he could set off debates and doubts. Then we would have a weakening of commitment, a dilution of the corporate style.

I am a strong believer that individuals are, and should be,

driven by their own aspirations and self-interest. No one should be asked to sacrifice. On the other hand, I firmly advocate – indeed demand – that an individual's self-interest should be entirely aligned to the interests of the corporate entity that he works for. If and when there is any conflict, that individual should no longer work for that company.

A leader's responsibility is therefore to convince his team members that their own personal gain and advancement is directly linked to the growth, success, and prosperity of the firm that employs them. Pursuing any personal gain that is not in sync with the corporate interest is shortsighted, and will end up in an unhappy divorce.

With the Founders Committee and, later, the Board of Directors, the difficulty is that they come to us only four times a year. There is no way they can understand us completely, so I have often had to go back to basics and explain the central concept over and over again. I cannot fire requests at them. I want them to be convinced of what I want. But they have to *choose* it, and that takes time. The important thing is that they understand where the locomotive is heading and why. From the beginning, I was set on achieving a purpose and reaching a certain objective, and I did not want to be derailed. That is the most dangerous thing for an organization. You have got to keep the train on the right track.

The gavel was barely down on the Founders Committee meeting when we locked our files and equipment in the Grundy Hotel and went our separate ways for three weeks of much-needed holiday. My family headed to the South of France, where I lay under the Mediterranean sun and let it bake the tension out of me. What a year it had been.

And what a year lay ahead!

Returning to Bahrain in mid-September, we closed out our space at the Grundy and set up shop in the Holiday Inn of Bahrain – Room 200, a one-bedroom suite. We cleared out the beds and put in desks, and the sitting area became our conference room.

To anyone who did not know us, it might have appeared that we were just another shoestring operation living on borrowed time. But even in those early days, we had two things many companies may never achieve – a well-honed vision and a shared passion. If we sometimes felt daunted by the challenge ahead of us, we faced it with joint humor and private grit.

Mike and his family also took up residence at the Holiday Inn, so while I continued flying around the Gulf calling on potential backers, their lives became confined to a couple of floors in a cookie-cutter hotel. It was probably hardest on Rose, Mike's wife, who suddenly had no proper kitchen for her cooking. We even asked the hotel management if she could have a little two-ring cooker, but they adamantly refused. 'We are a hotel!' they huffed. 'It's against all safety and insurance regulations!' Rose responded to that by smuggling in a toaster and a kettle so they could at least have coffee and toast in their rooms in the morning. Of course she had to hide them whenever the maids came to clean. One day when Mike was making breakfast, the bread got stuck in the toaster and the smoke set off the hotel sprinkler system. The manager came running, flung open the door, and caught a dripping Mike and Rose holding the evidence

– soggy black toast. 'Mrs Merritt!' the apoplectic manager shouted. 'You will *not* cook in your room!'

That fall we completed the founding subscriptions and received authority for the public offering, news that brought in a rush of new people who wanted to be founders. But even though we had sold this investment firm based largely on services in portfolio management, as 1981 drew to a close I felt a nagging need to rethink things. 'Now that we've organized the capital, the ownership, and the decision-making process,' I told the guys, 'let's take a hard look at the actual business. Are we sure we're doing it right? Forget any assumptions we've made up to now – let's go back to a clean sheet of paper. Let's think it through again, re-validate earlier assumptions, and bring in some outside professionals to challenge our thoughts.'

The result was a raucous four days in December that would become a major turning point in the life of this company. With the help of our start-up consultant, Dr Sam Hayes – I had met him when I was at Chase, and had taken the Harvard Senior Management Program under him – we invited a half-dozen financial experts from around the world to come to Bahrain. They included a fixed-income guru from the World Bank, an investment banking specialist from Continental Illinois, an investment adviser to the ruler of Abu Dhabi, and a merchant banker and dealmaker from Chase Manhattan. Elie took time off from Chase to attend, and Cem flew in from New York. Held at the Holiday Inn, the meeting was very unstructured. I told the gathered experts that we wanted them to act as a sounding board, a sort of jury who would listen to our plan, see where the faults lay, and advise us on how to improve it; we wanted to be challenged, item by item, to see if we had gotten it right.

Strong opinions were soon flying around the room and bouncing off the walls. Sometimes the discussion became heated, and not always on the theme at hand. These experts from traditional business became increasingly frustrated with our freewheeling process. 'Where's the agenda?' complained the man from Continental Illinois. 'This is totally unsatisfactory – we're not accomplishing anything.' The World Bank guru echoed that sentiment. He had been expecting to see a business plan, complete with financial details and objectives and resources. To him, the meeting was a disaster.

'No,' I said, at the end of the four days, 'this has been wonderful. This meeting has crystallized in my mind exactly what we should do. I'm really happy with the outcome.' And sure enough, after that meeting our priorities were amended. Instead of our leading line of business being portfolio management, now we saw our top product as corporate investment – the acquisition of private companies in the leading Western economies. Number two was real estate, and portfolio management dropped to third. We had concluded in our session that portfolio management was a commodity line of business – lots of firms offered it. Also, it was labor intensive, requiring heavy operational support, and we wanted to stay small and light and in a high-margin business catering to an exclusive clientele of high-net-worth customers. To those rarefied investors, we wanted to be indispensable. When they thought of high-quality investment, we wanted them to think of us.

The most valuable asset we possessed was our Gulf

customer base – that was our niche and our strength. So, we asked ourselves, what kind of investment would most interest them? If a wealthy individual in Jeddah or Doha wanted to make an investment in his own country, he did not need us; he could do it himself. But what if he wanted to make an investment in the United States? We began to put together a scenario: Here in the Gulf was all this oil money with limited options for investment . . . and there in the West were myriad opportunities for putting that money to work to benefit all involved. Our focus would be on non-quoted companies in the West to which the Gulf investor had no access.

This was essentially the scenario I had recognized back when I was Chase's Gulf Division Executive. Now I began to delve into it deeper, populating it with characters I came to know in my imagination. There was an old, family-owned company with a good name in the industry. Fifty or more years ago, the grandfather built up the business. He was very proud of it, he managed it well and handed it on to his son, who was trained to run it. In due course it passed to his son's son, who owns it today but is probably not in full control because the shares are divided among a swarm of grandchildren. One wants to be an artist, one wants to be a dentist, one wants to be a diplomat, one wants to roam the world. They own the company together but have separate plans for their lives, and they are often in dispute with one another. What they would really like is to sell the company and cash out their shares.

But where does this leave the company's management? 'We've been working for you all our lives,' the managers say to the grandchildren-owners, 'and now you're selling us. Who's going to own the company?' Their fears are real because their jobs are at risk, particularly if the buyer is a competitor. Ideally, management would like to own the company themselves, but they do not have the money. So what they want is a friendly investor who will buy the organization but leave them to run it as they know best.

Enter Investcorp. Drawing upon our wealthy investors in the Middle East, we would access a pool of money with which to buy the Western company from the grandchildren, who could then go off and live the lives they wanted. In the meantime, we have secured management's jobs. Because we want management to be co-owners, we make shares available to them; the rest are sold to a long list of passive investors whom management does not need to know. 'Don't worry,' we tell management, 'you won't be pestered by shareholders again. From now on you'll only have to deal with one – Investcorp. All we want from you is performance. We're getting out in a few years and all you have to do is increase the value of the company between now and then. How you do it is up to you. Our reward comes from taking the financial risk. Your reward is to part-own the company and run it as if you owned it completely.'

In three or four years the cycle is complete. Once the appropriate value has been added, we get together with the management and agree to take the company public. We are cashing out but they can stay in, only now they are running a public company. We are happy because our risk has been rewarded. They are happy because they have kept their jobs and made millions of dollars. And our investors are happy because they have received a huge return on their investment. In fact, the whole Gulf is happy because now there are attractive investment options for all their oil money.

To us, it was an irresistible scenario – and a major piece of the foundation-in-progress.

Nineteen eighty-two opened like the first hand in a high-stakes card game, with all the attendant excitement. 'SHARE FEVER GRIPS BIB INVESTORS' read a mid-January headline of Bahrain's English-language *Gulf Weekly Mirror,* and the article went on to report that 'Investors dressed in the garb of various Gulf states jammed the stairs to accountant Jawad Habib's office this week, their briefcases stuffed with passports. Saudis, Qataris and Bahrainis jostled to register for subscription to the new Bahrain International Bank, the first in a series of public share offers which have raised temperatures on the share market to fever pitch ...' We were mentioned as one of three new investment companies soon to follow with public issues. We could not have asked for a better warm-up.

Not that we needed one. From our earlier focus on persuasion, we now had to go into control mode – too many people wanted a piece of Investcorp. It was a delicate problem. The Gulf is a small, tight region and we did not want to offend scores of important people. To accommodate this late surge of demand, we had to adjust the capital structure. The original number of 100 founding private shareholders was raised, along with the ceiling on formation capital. At the same time, the portion of shares offered both to the public and to management was reduced. Finally, on the last day of March 1982, we closed the list of founding shareholders at 336 names. The complete list appears on page 363 of this book.

It was also in March that Cem resigned from Bankers Trust and started full-time for Investcorp. Elie, who was still moonlighting, had spearheaded the preparation of our prospectus in his off hours from Chase. Now we were about to launch the public offering, which Cem would need to supervise on a day-to-day basis.

When registration for public shares was opened, Bahrain went crazy. Our accountants, Whinney Murray, had rented a big old hall – actually an empty carpet showroom – and for a month crowds of people jockeyed for position in the queue to get inside, where no fewer than one hundred clerks feverishly processed applications. To apply for shares, a person needed to show proof of identity. 'THOUSANDS IN SCUFFLE FOR SHARES' reported the *Weekly Mirror*: 'On the first day, people were lined up before dawn with the usual bundles of passports, and several guards were knocked down in the push to get in when the doors opened at 8 a.m.' The reference to multiple passports described the common practice of brokers showing up with suitcases (I have even heard reports of wheelbarrows) full of borrowed passports, the plan being to get their hands on a couple of hundred times the permitted shares and then dump them on the market. That is how the local game was played. During our registration, one Kuwaiti swooped in on his private jet carrying 160 passports. Cem had to personally supervise the processing of every one, since the Kuwaiti could not fly out without them all.

In the end, we had applications from 640,000 people, and the public offering of shares in Arabian Investment Banking Corporation (Investcorp) EC was a record-setting 1403 times oversubscribed. It was almost embarrassingly successful. And yet, while our reluctant decision to go public turned out to make our name in the Gulf, the sight of all these people fighting for shares gave me no joy – because I knew what they were doing. Most public companies in the Gulf did not even issue a prospectus; all that appeared was an ad in the newspaper, five lines of general explanation. It did not matter. The people who showed up to buy shares did not know or care what the company aimed to do. It was all about making a quick buck. In our prospectus, we clearly stated that Investcorp was a long-term investment and that anyone with other ideas should not apply. Now, as I watched these lines of people who might just as well have been queued up for the circus big top, I wondered if someday we should consider taking Investcorp private.

Only later, when the dust had settled, did we learn that not all those public shareholders were speculators. Among them were good, solid citizens of no great personal wealth – doctors, teachers, engineers and the like – who simply wanted to invest their funds in a serious company. To us at Investcorp, that fact became a matter of profound importance and pride.

At the June 20 Constituent Assembly, the shareholders duly elected a seventeen-person Board of Directors, of which I was one. I cannot over-emphasize the critical importance of the role of Investcorp's Board of Directors in achieving our initial fame and the firm's successful track record thereafter.

The entire Gulf was deeply impressed by the quality of our governing body.

We had two criteria for selecting our board members. First, that they cover the entire Gulf region, geographically; thus we attracted members from Jeddah, Riyadh, the Eastern Province of Saudi Arabia, Bahrain, Kuwait, Qatar, Abu Dhabi, Dubai, and Oman. Second, we stressed that each member must be among the highest profile, most visible, trusted, and respected leaders of his own community.

From Investcorp's beginnings, management has formulated policies and presented them to the board to digest, question, and debate before accepting or rejecting. The board members are expected to satisfy themselves through an interactive process of communication with the management. They must be convinced that the proposed steps to be taken will lead to the advancement and competitive advantage of the firm on a cost-effective basis.

In every Investcorp board meeting, each line of business is invited to make its own presentation. By this, the board members hear the information first-hand. Moreover, it allows them the opportunity to assess the caliber of Investcorp's human skills and talent. Of course, the board also reviews, regularly, the progress of management in achieving the agreed-on plans and targets. But our board's focus is on broader trends and emerging challenges, not on micro-management.

Seven of those first seventeen board members would drop away in time, but the remaining nine – or ten, including me – would serve the company for at least the next twenty years. They were Omar Al-Aggad of Saudi Arabia; Abdullah

Bakhsh of Saudi Arabia; Mustafa Boodai of Kuwait; Hussain Alfardan of Qatar; Mohammed Jalal of Bahrain; Ahmed Ali Kanoo of Bahrain; Abdul Aziz Kanoo of Saudi Arabia; Ahmed Al Mannai of Qatar; and Khalid Al Zayani of Bahrain. These were Investcorp's pioneers, the businessmen who stepped up and supported us when we were still only a dream. They were our fellow visionaries – along with our unparalleled Chairman of the Board, about whom I will tell you shortly.

But first I feel compelled to provide a postscript on the involvement of Dr Jawad Hashim, President and CEO of the AMF. During my ten months at the AMF on secondment from Chase, Hashim was at the peak of his powers – energetic, dynamic, authoritative, decisive, and determined. At the same time he was extremely courteous to me and always supportive of my role and what I was trying to achieve. He was keen to take the idea of Investcorp and help turn it into reality. I also appreciated his vision, courage, resolve, and intellect.

That said, he was, I feel, discredited by certain aspects of his past, and from extensive report in the media, it seems his reputation took a serious dive after he left the AMF. Hashim had previously been an enthusiastic young member of the Ba'ath Party in Iraq and had become close to the power bases in the Party. By his twenties, Hashim had become head of Iraq's Planning Ministry. When the Arab countries decided to establish the AMF in the late seventies, Saddam Hussein insisted that all twenty-two countries should accept Iraq's candidate for running this prestigious organization. Dr Hashim was accordingly appointed.

But following his five-year assignment as President and CEO of the AMF, Hashim suffered huge disgrace as the AMF, it seems, brought lengthy court cases against him for embezzlement. He was convicted in courts in Abu Dhabi and London and disappeared to an unknown address.

I repeat, I personally never saw anything but a bright, courageous visionary and a perfect gentleman. To me he was unfailingly generous and supportive. When I applied for a bank loan to purchase my residence in London, Hashim added his endorsement, knowing very well that I would meet my obligation. His gracious support remains in my memory.

In recognition of his influence and abilities, I asked him to serve on Investcorp's first board in June 1982. Although he was still in position at the AMF, he agreed to join in a personal capacity – which indeed was my request. He attended only two meetings, however, before his troubles began at the AMF.

I should point out that Hashim was not satisfied with simply being a member of the board; he wanted to be chairman. The board, made up of leading Gulf businessmen and nationals, preferred to elect His Excellency Abdul-Rahman Salim Al-Ateeqi, a Kuwaiti who had served his nation as a distinguished government official for more than forty years, including seventeen years as Minister of Finance and Petroleum. Al-Ateeqi's spectacular reputation and status were unmatched by anyone else on the board. His name commanded the utmost respect.

I had met Abdul-Rahman Al-Ateeqi briefly when I worked at Chase, but did not really know him. What I did know, however, I greatly admired. He had dedicated his life to the public sector, working his way up through the police department and the health department to one of the most influential government offices in the world. He owned practically nothing, and retired with only his pension. He lived very simply. After leaving office he served as a senior adviser to the Emir of Kuwait, a post he still holds.

As a private citizen, he could also serve on corporate boards – he was Chairman, in fact, of the Bahrain Middle East Bank at the time we were trying to come up with our board, and one day when they were having a shareholder meeting I asked Elie to go and observe. When he got back, he said, 'We can stop looking. We've found our chairman.' It had apparently been a tough meeting, yet Al-Ateeqi had handled it 'like a general,' Elie said. 'But in a very impressive way.'

Al-Ateeqi demurred at first, concerned about a conflict with his role at the Middle East Bank. 'But that's a commercial bank and we're an investment bank,' I said. 'There is no conflict.' Eventually he agreed to have his name put up for chairman, and in our first board meeting he was elected without dissent. In the years since he took on the chairmanship, I have found him to be a superb choice. He has two qualities of supreme importance to me: One is his superior mind. I can sit down with him and explain the most complex thing, a matter of which he has no prior knowledge, and he will absorb it like a sponge. Two is his absolute integrity. It is beyond question.

Once the board was elected, I was named the new company's President and Chief Executive Officer, for a term of three years. The date was Sunday, June 20, 1982. Our first fiscal year – the duration of which would be eighteen months, to help us get established – was officially under way.

We decided to postpone doing business for six months while we concentrated on building an infrastructure. Elie was aboard now, along with Mike and Cem, and our goal was to hire some fifty people, including eight managers, over our first year and a half. We had compensation and employee policies to work out, equipment to consider, offices to decide upon. The plan was for Elie to invest the capital that had now been released to us, and we would operate on the interest and seek bank lines while we dealt with all these foundation issues. To fulfill the international mandate we had set for ourselves, Investcorp would need a headquarters in Bahrain, a European office in London, and a US base in New York. We had a massive amount of work ahead of us.

In the midst of all this, I had an idea that my co-founders felt bordered on insanity. When I was at Chase, the bank had sent me to Harvard University to attend the Senior Management Program. The experience had been invaluable, in my estimation, and now I insisted that my co-founders attend it as well. They were all embarking on high-level corporate jobs at Investcorp, and the depth and breadth of knowledge that they would gain from the Harvard program would be essential.

None of my colleagues disagreed about the value of the program, but to a man they thought the timing was terribly wrong. When we were only four people, and racing against the clock to be up and running, to send 25 percent of our executive bench on leave was considered unwise.

Although I cannot accept that I am an inflexible man, a stubborn streak has occasionally surfaced, particularly when I believe I see something that others do not see. This was one of those occasions, and I overruled them. 'When else will we have the time?' I said. And so Mike was dispatched first, then Ellie, and finally Cem. Each was away for two and a half months and the firm was established by the other three during the absence of the fourth. At the end, all of them agreed that it had been the right decision – and that, as we got busier and busier, there would never have been a more opportune time.

In the run-up to our incorporation, my co-founders and I had thought long and hard about how the company should be managed – and especially how such a widely dispersed organization could be turned into a tight, effective operating unit. I had three broad answers. The first was to create a culture that insisted on teamwork. The second was to institute a system of annual reviews that would keep the business united in its purpose and heading in the right direction. The third was the formation, in 1982, of what I called the Management Committee – since known as the Mancom. This was the body responsible for shaping and executing all major business decisions. Its original members were Mike, Elie, Cem, and me, but as we began to hire senior professional people, they too joined the group. Each member ran, or helped to run, a business unit or function, taking responsibility for its performance and being rewarded according to results. My idea from the beginning was that the entire

Mancom, from all three offices, would come together twice a year to discuss the firm's past performance and establish future goals. In this way, the culture would regularly be renewed.

In our first round of executive hiring, we generally hewed to the course we had set at the beginning – drawing from people we already knew. Commercial banking was our comfort zone, and my thinking was that it was better – at least at this stage of our development – to go after people we knew and trusted, people we felt could slide easily into our team culture. In early 1983 we brought in both Oliver Richardson and Bob Glaser from Chase. With Bob came Betty Pires, also from Chase. Almost as soon as she arrived, Betty took on the role of managing my office. Although neither of us could know it at the time, Betty would go on to manage my office for the next three decades. She became, and continues to be, a pillar of dependability, on whom I constantly rely.

To head up our Bahrain office, I scrolled back through my contacts to an impressive young man I had met at a social function – Yusef Abu Khadra, who at the time was working for Morgan Stanley in corporate finance.

And although he did not join us until 1984, there was one other early recruit who has played a pivotal role at Investcorp, becoming one of our longest-serving executives. I first employed Savio Tung at Chase Gulf Division, and he impressed me greatly from the start. But while I was away at the AMF, Savio became disillusioned with his job at Chase and jumped ship. Unaware of my plans, he took a job with Arab Asia Bank where his Chinese origins (he was born in

Hong Kong) and his US banking credentials were much in demand.

Once he heard about Investcorp, however, he was quick to renew contact. 'I've made the wrong move,' he told me. 'I didn't know you were going to create a new firm. I'd like to join.'

I was delighted to work with Savio again. Initially in charge of portfolio investment, he would later transfer to corporate investment and become a key partner in New York, much involved in our US transactions. A skilful negotiator, he would eventually become a leading voice in the firm. In 1995, he would take charge of the New York office and within a few months would be coordinating all Investcorp's operations in North America. In 2000 – sixteen years after his hiring – I would ask him to set up the Technology Fund as our fourth line of business after corporate investments, US real estate, and our fund of hedge funds.

Every one of these executives had the qualifications; I had no doubt about that. But what I was looking for was an intangible extra – the ability to subdue personal ego for the good of the team. You never want to hire people without any ego, because they will not be successful. Anyone who accomplishes anything at all in life has to have a personal drive, a need for self-esteem. The challenge is to manage those egos so they do not become a hindrance. They have to be channeled in a way that makes them productive to the firm.

In the meantime, we could foresee our space at the Holiday Inn growing, like a vine, from two rooms ... to three ... to an entire floor. Something had to be done about a Bahrain headquarters – and soon.

For help finding a suitable location in London, we had brought on an English real estate expert named John Thompson, whom I had met when I was based in Abu Dhabi and John was working for the Abu Dhabi Investment Authority. One day in the late summer of 1982 when John was in Bahrain, he, Cem and I left the office in the early evening to walk back to the Sheraton, where we were staying. Along the way, a building caught my eye. 'John,' I said, 'what about this? We should find out who owns it and buy it.'

'Are you kidding?' he said. 'Look at it, Nemir – it's horrible. Badly, *terribly* finished.' Of course, what had attracted me was certainly not the building but the location.

Therefore I persisted, and the next day we learned that it was owned by a Bahraini who had made a bundle in real estate. He also turned out to be the PR man at the Bahrain branch of Chartered Bank. Before we met with him, the three of us checked out the interior of the building, which was highly unattractive. It was all low-class apartments, two to a floor, and every one was full.

'See,' John said, 'not only is it terrible, it's residential. It'll never work. We'll never get vacant possession.'

Tenants aside, I could not believe he was so blind to the potential. To me, here was an existing building of suitable size in a great area of the city. We could save a year and a half by not starting from scratch. 'We can redevelop it,' I said. 'We can give it a facelift. Trust me, it'll work.'

And it did. Cem had to spend three months drinking tea with the owner to persuade him to sell – this ugly building was his pride and joy. And I had to invest untold hours converting the board to the idea of buying straightaway instead of renting. But eventually we bought the building, relocated the tenants, flew in an architect from Boston, and for the next few months I worked with him day and night to achieve the effect we wanted. In addition to being CEO, I became Investcorp's CDO – Chief Design Officer. This was a task I was not going to leave to others, and certainly not to a committee. In my mind's eye, I could see with remarkable clarity the headquarters we wanted: walnut paneling, marble floors, brass fixtures, Oriental rugs, stately furniture, gold-framed oil paintings, deep rich colors – a place that appeared to have been here forever. A place that conveyed the impression it would always be here.

Some of the board members argued with me about cost every step of the way. 'It doesn't matter what we spend on this thing,' I told them. 'I want to do it right. I want the furniture right, I want the color right, I want every bit of it exactly right – not because I want to squander money, but because of the type of service we're selling. The customer isn't going to give us his money unless he's convinced we're the best. So, number one, I have to have the right staff – the best, as good as the best in the industry. And they're not going to come to a shabby place that doesn't have the same standard of research, the same back-up, the same technology. If we want the best people, we have to provide all that from the start. We must be well equipped or we won't make a penny.'

As our building gradually became transformed, it was not just our board that kept an eye on our progress. We made quite a stir throughout Bahrain. At a bankers function at the Hilton, Mike overheard two men talking about us.

'Investcorp? Forget it,' one said. 'Those guys aren't running a bank. They're running a furniture company!'

We all had a big laugh out of that. And I thought: *Just you wait.*

Part II

THE ORGANIZATION IN ACTION

6
TIFFANY AND THE IRISHMAN

We made a 20 percent return on our equity in our first fiscal year, paying our shareholders a 15 percent return on their money. 'GOOD FIRST YEAR FOR INVESTCORP' trumpeted the *Gulf Daily News* in February 1984; '$10.2 MILLION INCOME FOR INVESTCORP IN FIRST YEAR' heralded the *Oman Daily Observer*. The *Financial Times* of London, under the headline 'INVESTCORP STICKS TO ITS LONG-TERM GUNS,' went beyond reporting to provide an incisive analysis of just how revolutionary our approach was in a region accustomed to the speculative fever of Kuwait's unofficial stock market, the Souk al-Manakh, which had so complicated our formation:

> By Western standards, [Investcorp's first-year result] represents a solid achievement on the part of a new company which spent six months setting up its infrastructure. Gulf investors are more impatient, and some criticize its progress as ponderously slow.
>
> But what really hurts is that Bahrain's biggest stagging operation on record failed to come off. Subscribers to the public share issue who had borrowed heavily to finance a large application received a small and therefore costly allocation – and were unable to unload the shares for an immediate profit ... They were disappointed.

> In fact, they have only themselves to blame, since they were warned in advance that Investcorp was geared to long-term returns, and was not a vehicle for speculation. It is hardly the company's fault that the stock market bubble burst so soon after its debut ...

When we had time to reflect on such things, it seemed that the theme of our first couple of years – 1983 and 1984 – was education, both of our investors and ourselves. When John Thompson came to work for us in early 1983, just after we had begun doing business, he immediately gained the distinction of being the only line-of-business expert at Investcorp, since he was already a real estate specialist. The rest of us were learning on the job as we transformed from ex-credit officers to investment managers.

Right away I gave John the mandate of finding us a top-level real estate investment. Gulf investors like real estate. Landmark hotels and sprawling malls are something you can see and touch and point to with pride, and if a hotel is successful the cash flow is attractive. But while many investors had made good money building or buying hotels in their own region, they had just as often lost money when they tried to replicate the process in other countries. For example, some investors had gone to Houston and Dallas because of the oil connection, and John used to joke that 'Texas and Saudi Arabia are essentially identical.' He meant they were similar in geography, in the oil base, in the can-do frontier spirit, and in the tendency to trust individuals over institutions. So now this Gulf investor might look across the table at the new friend he buys pipelines from and think the same man can help him acquire a piece of real estate. There was no scientific approach, no adequate risk analysis.

Investcorp was established to fill in the gap. As it turned out, John heard about a spectacular property opportunity in the US – Manulife Plaza in Los Angeles. The deal was a 50 percent freehold interest in a newly constructed, architectural-prize winning, 75 percent leased, glass-and-granite office tower in the heart of one of the world's top markets. A joint venture with one of North America's leading insurance companies, this would be an impressive first investment – with an acceptable downside risk. Our half interest would cost $52 million.

It was an extremely heady moment, and once we bought Manulife John was all fired up to go out and find others. 'Not so fast,' we responded. 'First you have to place this deal with investors.' It was a shock to his system, but I figured that nobody knew the project better than John. To add marketing savvy to the placement team – Cem was in London heading up preparations for our new office there – I decided it was time to make our next hire, a bright young man who had worked for me in Chase's Gulf Division. This was when we hired Oliver Richardson. Oliver had been anxiously following our progress from his Chase assignment in Denmark. Once we finally landed a product for him to sell, we gave him the call.

Beginning in March 1983, Oliver and John (and I, as time permitted) scoured the Gulf for nine solid months, and there were moments when Investcorp's very first product placement looked as though it might become a disaster. But we learned valuable lessons during that process. One of the most eye-opening was that our shareholders were not automatically going to be our clients, so we would have to widen our net. If we had become somewhat overconfident in thinking we had a ready clientele, we were quickly and forcefully brought back to reality. This first placement so many years ago became a matter of old-fashioned cold-calling, scouting for leads and then looking for people without actual street addresses and knocking on doors at all hours of the day and night. During Ramadan we could not make calls until dark, and during summer we literally could not find anyone under the sun. And after all that, we were told no nine times out of ten.

Oliver knew that selling was long-term missionary work, but John was beside himself, and his revelation accrued to us as a company as well. Knowing real estate as he did, John had thought people would stand in line and bid to get a piece of a deal as magnificent as this. But it turned out to be a hard sell to people whose history was largely merchant trading. They did not understand that kind of syndicated international investment.

For his part, Oliver made a point that was well taken by all of us former commercial bankers now playing in a whole new ballgame. 'Lending money is ten times easier than getting people to give you some of their own for investing.'

We did eventually get Manulife Plaza fully placed, but it was on the market much too long – a fact that was missed by nobody in the Gulf. Besides being costly in terms of return on effort, this was not the image we hoped to project.

Fortunately, while on holiday in Spain that year I met a man named Ziad Idilby, President of the Saudi Investment and Finance Corporation (SIFCO), who introduced me to another deal that was to become Investcorp's first venture in our number-one product line – corporate investment. Joining forces with SIFCO, we acquired a 16.5 percent interest in A&W Brands, a US maker of soft drinks. Few people in the Gulf knew what root beer was, but that did not seem to matter. What mattered was that they could readily relate to the story of a going concern. With A&W, we were in the driver's seat in a way that we had not been when placing Manulife Plaza. In six weeks, we were able to say to the market, 'Sorry, it's gone!' It is always better to leave them wanting more.

While our portion of the $54 million A&W deal was only about $5 million, our involvement was a good example of the power of leveraging – in this case, of our reputation. This small share allowed us to rub elbows with some major players in the US investment market, including Citicorp Venture Capital, one of the largest. With A&W, we made our entrance into a world we would soon come to know much, much better.

From the start, I have envisioned Investcorp as a constantly shifting series of small ad hoc teams working for the good of the larger, wider, permanent team. Let us say that X is doing spadework on a transaction. If he needs Nemir, I am at his disposal, I work for that man. If he needs Y, then Y will be there. If he needs Z, he calls him up, and Z will be there. We are all at the disposal of the project manager for any given task. An important part of my job is to be a subcontractor. Suppose one of our executives is pricing a deal and he needs my involvement – then I get on a plane and join him in pricing the deal. If anyone wants me, they only have to call. 'My time is available to you,' I tell them, 'and if you need four other guys you should call them. All that matters is achieving the task at hand.'

Already, we had been operating in that way to meet our daily demands. For a time, Mike Merritt went to London to oversee our incorporation in the UK and to begin hiring; then Cem took over as general manager there, locating, outfitting, and staffing our permanent London office while Mike returned to Bahrain. John traded his real estate hat for his placement cap to travel all over the Gulf with Oliver. And when Mike left to attend the three-month Advanced Management Program at Harvard, Bob Glaser stepped in as Assistant to the President and Director of Corporate Planning. We were still experimenting with titles in those days, but we eventually abandoned them in deference to the fluidity of our job descriptions.

Our first experience with someone unable to operate in this kind of corporate environment came in 1984, with a man I will call The Irishman. In the wake of the A&W success, we began actively searching for corporate investment opportunities, and in order to do that more effectively we hired an experienced dealmaker. This was The Irishman. Based in London, he soon began traveling back and forth between the UK and the US. The Irishman was the John Thompson equivalent of his line of business: Working for an organization in Chicago, he had negotiated some forty-five corporate acquisitions, and the rest of us were in awe of him. That made it unanimous, since he was in awe of himself.

His academic background was as impressive as his

experience, with an engineering undergraduate degree and an MBA from Columbia University. However, this man proved over time to have some major drawbacks. I dislike a person who blows his own horn, and in hindsight I realize The Irishman's attitude should have been a tip-off. But that was not the only thing I missed about him. He was a very odd man, odd in every way. Even when he began having run-ins with the other guys, I missed the fact that he just did not fit in.

The picture became clearer in the summer of 1984. The Irishman having uncovered a number of exciting prospects – too many to manage without help – I dispatched Cem to the States to lend a hand on a couple of negotiations. One was in New York involving a logging company called Southwest Forests, and another, on the West Coast, was for Bertram-Trojan boats, owned by Whittaker Corporation. Cem later reported that when he arrived in New York, The Irishman greeted him with these words: 'Look, I've got only one thing to say to you. I'm the expert, you don't know anything about this business. So just keep your mouth shut and observe.'

'What are you talking about?' Cem said. 'I'm your partner.'

'You know nothing,' The Irishman said.

We at Investcorp are not afraid of a healthy disagreement, but we do insist on a certain standard of mutual respect. Unfortunately, Cem was in for a rough couple of weeks. Nevertheless, he stood his ground. One day when he and The Irishman were walking down Fifth Avenue, The Irishman said, 'Look, I'm going to be the one negotiating this Southwest thing with Lehman Brothers.' That was his way of telling Cem he could not even attend the meeting.

'Absolutely not!' Cem said. 'No way will I allow you to do that!'

'I'm the boss!' The Irishman said.

That was too much for Cem. He reached up – he was easily a head shorter than The Irishman – and grabbed The Irishman by the lapels. This was right in the middle of Fifth Avenue. Looking The Irishman square in the eye, Cem hissed, 'You ... say ... that ... again ... *and I'll kill you*!'

They had many such moments as they jetted back and forth across the US. Once, in a meeting about Bertram-Trojan with the Chairman of Whittaker and his number two, Cem was making a point when The Irishman kicked him under the table and whispered, 'Shut up! You're putting your foot in your mouth!' Cem said he could have thrown The Irishman out of the window.

The good news from all this is that during his time in New York with The Irishman Cem spotted a newspaper item that would lead to Investcorp's first major corporate investment success. While having breakfast at the Pierre Hotel, he read that the legendary jeweler Tiffany & Co. was for sale. Soon I got a call from The Irishman. 'Nemir, something interesting is going on, and we could be in on it. Tiffany is for sale. Don't you think it would be an exciting deal?'

I was surprised by the question. 'I have no idea whether or not it could be an exciting deal,' I said. 'The Tiffany name is well recognized. But we would have to dig into it to assess the investment merits of the transaction.'

'Well,' said The Irishman, 'I've been talking to Lehman Brothers. They're arranging a management buyout for

Tiffany, and it appears there's room for Investcorp to participate.'

In every corporate deal there are at least two back stories, that of the company and that of the suitors. Tiffany & Co. jewelers was started by Charles Tiffany in 1837, and over time it became one of the most prestigious brands in the world. The little ice-blue Tiffany box was synonymous with luxury and taste. Then in the early 1970s the company was sold by Charles Tiffany's heirs to Avon. To the world it looked like a strange marriage, Avon being a successful purveyor of mass-market cosmetics – so successful, in fact, that it had begun buying up other companies and turned itself into a conglomerate. Indeed, the union was a mismatch: As good as Avon's management may have been at marketing lipstick and make-up, they simply were not attuned to the cultural nuances of the high-end jewelry market. Tiffany's operating income was only about $1 million, and while domestic sales had remained stable, profits had inexplicably dropped for two years running. International sales, which should have been a bonanza, amounted to only about $4 million.

But within Avon there was an executive who appreciated this travesty in the making. William Chaney had been with Avon twenty-eight years, and at one point had been the company's president. In recent years he had been in charge of overseeing some of the conglomerate's subsidiaries, including Tiffany. Though Chaney did not like the way Tiffany was being run, he was apparently powerless to impact its direction. So when Avon's Chairman asked him to sell the company, Chaney saw his opportunity: He convinced the

Chairman to let him run Tiffany as a stand-alone profit center, with Chaney giving up his other Avon duties and reporting directly to the Chairman. Once in charge of Tiffany, Chaney told Avon that he would sell it for them and get back the money they had invested in it.

This, then, is when the investment bankers would have come on the scene, offering to help him organize a management buyout – in other words, to find investors who would support management to buy the company. The early eighties was the sunrise for dealmaking in New York, and this was a perfect opportunity. In those days, an investment banker would approach the management of a struggling company and say: 'We'll help you buy the company.'

'How?' management would say. 'We don't have the funds.'

'Don't worry,' the investment banker would reply. 'We'll organize the whole thing, and bring in investors. You'll own a piece of the action and run the company.'

Lehman Brothers apparently approached Chaney. It was Dennis Levine at Lehman who was working on the transaction when we got involved. Chaney was asked to give Lehman a mandate saying that they represented the company's management on an exclusive basis. Chaney would have also been asked to use his best efforts to get his own bosses to give priority to the management buyout. In other words, if there were two offers, Chaney's and another one, and both were equal financially, Avon would give preference to Chaney's because they knew him and the Tiffany management.

With all those preliminaries checked off the list, the investment bankers would have begun working with Chaney to put a transaction together – the cue for a more powerful group of suitors to make their entrance. This was the Wesray Group, Wesray being former US Secretary of the Treasury William E. Simon and New Jersey businessman Ray Chambers, two partners whose 1982 leveraged buyout of the Gibson greeting card company brought them big fame and big money, and led to the attraction for LBOs. Wesray were known as the smart guys in dealmaking. What made them smart was that with little money down they would buy a company, expecting that its future earnings would be enough to pay off the debt. Then when the company was sold and the new improved pie was divided among Wesray, management, and any other investors, Wesray's piece would inevitably be the largest.

But what grated about a Wesray deal was that while Wesray put in relatively little money and retained the lion's share of the equity, other investors were required to take on the lion's share of the subordinated, or junior, debt. This, we soon discovered, was the role the bigger players had reserved for Investcorp.

Even before the deal structure became a problem, about the only two people in the company who thought we should consider the deal were The Irishman and me. With Tiffany's poor profit picture, it was uncertain that the debt could be paid out of cash flow. And the company's obvious – if still unspecified – management problems would make it tough to convince banks to finance the deal. Most of our executives were intrigued but dubious.

Still, I thought it was a target worth exploring, so I told

The Irishman to go ahead and see what he and Cem could work out. I also asked him to keep me informed on the deal's progress. The discussions went on for a week, then two, with intense meetings every day, lots of bickering and hard bargaining, and endless revisions of figures and forecasts.

By now it was August, and I had rented a house in Marbella for my annual family holiday. It is a rule of mine that I try hard to adhere to: For eleven months of the year I live a crazy life of work and travel, but the remaining month, August, I take off to spend with my family. I still talk on the phone whenever necessary, but I do not travel to do business. I am there just to relax and recharge and have fun with my wife and daughters. It is very important to carve this kind of time out for yourself and your family, and I encourage my executives to do the same. In fact, the Hallaks had also taken a villa in Marbella that year at the same time we had.

But sometimes business will not wait. During August of 1984 I sat in Spain in my Bermudas for several nights in a row, discussing Tiffany by phone with our people in New York. They were outnumbered, so to add firepower to the negotiation team we decided to bring in Savio Tung and Bob Glaser. Bob, the only single member of our executive staff, was the closest at hand: He was enjoying a month-long holiday in Martha's Vineyard with his girlfriend – learning to sail, growing a beard, going to movies. He had just returned from a late-afternoon showing of *Ghostbusters* when he received a call from Cem saying he was needed in Manhattan the next morning for an 8 a.m. meeting. There were no more flights from the Vineyard that night, so Bob had to charter a plane and instruct the pilot to keep flying through an electrical storm. It turned out to be appropriate conditioning for what he was about to experience.

In the prep for that first meeting, The Irishman warned Bob that it was going to be a very, very tough session with the investment banker. 'But I'll handle it,' The Irishman said. 'I know this guy well.'

At the appointed hour, they all gathered in a conference room at the offices of our attorneys, Gibson, Dunn & Crutcher, on 57th street. And sure enough, The Irishman had not exaggerated about the tone of the meeting. As it was later told to me: 'The investment banker, Dennis Levine, turns out to be the rudest, most abrasive, most obnoxious person I've ever been at a meeting with in my life. We're the client, we're paying the bill, yet this guy uses every four-letter word in the book. And all directed at us! What upset him was that Investcorp was unwilling to play the role or pay the price he thought necessary to secure the deal.'

Cem and Bob did not say a word the entire meeting. But when it was over, they took The Irishman aside. 'You told us you know this guy well,' they said. 'The reason we said nothing was to avoid embarrassing you. But do tell Levine that people do not talk to us that way. We have certain standards in the way we do business, and his cursing, yelling, and screaming is quite unacceptable. He doesn't have to agree with us, but, as we are the client, he should at least treat us with respect.'

Bob said The Irishman's reply was, 'I can't tell him that. This guy is too important.'

That confrontation was on a Friday. While it was clear

that there was growing distrust between Tiffany management and Investcorp, one thing both sides wholeheartedly agreed on was that nobody liked Dennis Levine.

Investcorp and Tiffany management tried to make the sale work, but we still had problems with both the deal structure and the financing structure. Donald Trump had also entered the picture with a plan to buy Tiffany and have his then-wife, Ivana, run it. Tiffany management wanted no part of that scenario, but its looming presence undoubtedly added to Bill Chaney's stress and frustration as we continued to struggle without a breakthrough.

Finally, Avon got fed up and gave Chaney an ultimatum: Bring us a deal by five o'clock Tuesday afternoon or else your exclusivity expires and we will consider alternatives. So Chaney put pressure on the investment bankers to wrap it up.

With the deadline just twenty-four hours away, The Irishman called me in Marbella to spell out the final draft of the proposed Tiffany deal. It was very late in Spain, almost midnight on Monday, and he was pulling out all the stops to sell me on the deal's supposed merits.

The conversation went something like this: 'Nemir,' he said, 'we've *got* to accept this. I *strongly* recommend it. It's an *excellent* deal. Yes, I know we're not coming in on level terms. Wesray is taking just equity without putting in any sub-debt. Management isn't putting in anything and is getting equity. But who are we? We're not *known* in the marketplace. It's our *second* year of operation, and this is the price we have to pay to get in. The company is good and these are *very* smart people. Frankly, we should accept this deal.

If we don't, it's going to give us a very bad name in the marketplace for having walked out of a deal at the last minute. We've been negotiating with them all this time.'

'Wait a minute,' I said. 'I hear what you're saying. But this is the first time you've told me about the structure. This is the most ridiculous structure I've ever heard of. We put in forty million dollars of sub-debt just to take two million dollars of equity? That's only twenty percent of the equity, yet we're putting in the entire sub-debt. Why should I agree to that?'

'That's the price of the ticket to get in,' said The Irishman. 'Who are we to get equal terms?'

'No, we do it fifty-fifty with Wesray,' I said. 'Okay, management doesn't put up sub-debt because they're management and are putting in the work. But Wesray should share with us *pari passu*.'

'Then they wouldn't want us in,' he said. 'If they're going to put up the sub-debt, they might as well take the rest of the equity.'

'We can't do it,' I said.

'Nemir, it's going to be very bad for us to walk out of this deal.'

'We win some deals, we lose some deals,' I said. 'We can't accept this one. I won't accept it. It's not approved. You walk out of the deal structured as you have presented it.'

The next night, Tuesday, he rang me again. 'Nemir,' he said, 'this is the worst day of my entire career. The *worst*. You might as well kiss Investcorp goodbye – we'll never be able to do another deal in this town.'

'What are you talking about? What happened?'

'We walked out,' he said. 'We told them we were finished. They took it very badly. Everybody was mad at Investcorp. Our name is mud. Somebody said, "What do you expect from an Arab bank?"'

'Who said that?'

'Everybody.'

'Didn't you explain to the Tiffany management what we were being asked to do?'

'No,' he said. 'Management is mad at us.'

'Okay,' I said. 'You give me Mr Chaney's telephone number, I'll call him.'

'No, Nemir. Please don't call him.'

'I'm asking you for a telephone number – give it to me.'

'I don't think you should.'

'I didn't ask whether you thought I should do it – I'm *going* to call him.'

'He'll just be nasty to you on the phone. It won't help. Just leave it alone. We lost out on a good deal and I think we did the wrong thing.'

'Oh,' I said, 'you're not convinced that what we did was right?'

'No.'

'Well, you give me that telephone number right now. I'll call Chaney. And when you and I next meet, I'll explain to you why we were right.'

Elie Hallak spotted me pacing the terrace of my villa very early the next morning. He later told the story, much appreciated at Investcorp, that he knew something really disturbing was going on for me to be up and dressed at the ungodly hour of 7:30 a.m. Elie was aware the deal had fallen through, and in fact the two of us had stayed up late the previous night discussing it. Now he came over and we sat together on my terrace drinking coffee and reviewing our options.

For me at that point, it was Investcorp's reputation that was uppermost in my mind. At mid-afternoon Wednesday Marbella time I dialed Bill Chaney's number. 'My name is Nemir Kirdar,' I said, when his secretary answered. 'I'm calling from Spain. If Mr Chaney would kindly take my call, I would very much like to talk to him.'

In a few seconds Chaney came on the phone – very cold, of course. 'Mr Chaney,' I said, 'you don't know me, but let me tell you the reason I'm calling.'

'And what is that?' He had a deep voice, very patrician.

'I'm calling about the deal which I understand we've walked away from. I want to explain to you why. Please don't draw any conclusion before you hear my side of the story. After that, you can judge for yourself whether we were right or wrong.'

'Well,' he said, 'I'm very, very disappointed. I'm an honorable man. I don't know investment banking, I don't know the language you guys speak. I was led to believe that we were going to conclude a deal, then at the last minute you walk out and the whole thing falls apart.' He went on to recount how he had gone to his boss and told him Avon could offer to sell Tiffany to anyone it wanted, as he would no longer be a contender.

'Mr Chaney,' I said, 'please just hear me out for thirty seconds. August is the most important month for me because it's the only time I see my family on a regular basis. Even so, will you give me a half-hour of your time? It's not something we can do over the phone. If you'll give me half an hour, I'll be in your office tomorrow morning and explain to you what our position was. Then it'll be up to you to make a judgment.'

'I see no reason for that,' Chaney said. 'Why should you come all the way over here?'

'My reputation is very important to me,' I said. 'And so is Investcorp's. I don't want you to feel that we let anybody down. We were given an option that would've been disastrous for us. Neither you nor anybody else would have accepted it. But let me explain it to you in person. Allow me just thirty minutes of your time.'

'The deal is lost. I really don't see any reason for a meeting.'

'If I'm in New York tomorrow anyhow, and I call your office, would you give me the courtesy of a thirty-minute meeting?'

'If you're in New York anyhow, yes. But please don't come over on my account. There is no longer any deal.'

'Fine,' I said. 'Is eleven a.m. suitable?'

Nada and the girls came in from the beach to find me packing. They were surprised, but I told them I would be back as soon as I could. Just when that might be was anybody's guess, but it did not matter as far as my clothes were concerned: I had only one suit with me anyway; the rest was summer sportswear. I pulled together what I could and closed my bag, and Nada drove me to a travel agent to investigate flights.

The only way I could make it was to go to Malaga and

take an Iberia flight to Boston, then pick up the shuttle to New York. It was very late when I got in. The Irishman was waiting for me at LaGuardia, having told Cem, Bob, and Savio not to come with him to meet me.

In the taxi on the way to the Pierre, he said, 'Nemir, you want to talk about dead or alive?'

'Pardon me?' I said.

'We have a deal on Bertram-Trojan, a very good deal. Let's not screw up that one too like we screwed up Tiffany.'

'I'm here for a meeting with Bill Chaney,' I said.

'Waste of time,' said The Irishman.

'First, I'm going to do what I think is right,' I said. 'After that, I can assure you we *will* have a review meeting with the entire Investcorp team. But right now what's on my mind is our reputation. Once I've addressed that, we'll consider other matters.'

At eleven o'clock Thursday morning I was ushered into Bill Chaney's handsome paneled office overlooking Fifth Avenue, with a view of Central Park. He was a perfect gentleman, offered me a chair, told me he appreciated my visit. I was resolved to stick to my thirty-minute limit, so as soon as it was appropriate I began my explanation.

Taking out my pen and yellow pad, I drew out the deal as it had been presented to us. 'It's the guys with the equity who make money in the long run,' I said, pointing to an E in a box, 'but it's us down here with subordinated debt who take the risk. Now, if you were being asked to take all that risk to get only a fraction of equity while the other parties got all that equity with none of the risk, how would such a deal look to you? How would the market look at you? You'd be a laughing stock. The deal could never be done that way . . .'

He nodded slowly, thoughtfully – he was getting the picture.

'But here's a way it *could* be done.' I flipped to a new piece of paper and began drawing up a different deal. 'We pay forty million in sub-debt,' I began, 'but we take eight million in equity, i.e., eighty percent . . .'

He listened while I went through all the numbers, and I could tell he was impressed. Finally he spoke. 'Where were you twenty-four hours ago? Why didn't you say all this then?'

'It would've been unethical,' I said. 'It wasn't our deal. We were invited to it by Lehman Brothers, who were putting the transaction together. They assigned a role to us, but they kept deteriorating that role, thinking that as the deadline approached we would accept anything, however bad. You had given the mandate to them, so all I could do was to say yes or no to the final deal that they presented. Please don't blame us. We were given a product I simply couldn't accept. If you hadn't gone to Lehman Brothers . . .'

'It was Lehman who came to me,' he said, defensively. 'I don't know about these matters. They proposed the whole thing.'

'I'm just speaking theoretically,' I said. 'I want you to understand that if we had come on the scene first, this is how the deal could've been done.'

'Well, anyway, it's too late now,' Chaney said. 'Avon is being represented by Morgan Stanley, who already have an offer from Donald Trump.'

'Could you tell me how much they're bidding?'

'I heard it's $135 million.'

'Well then,' I said, 'now that the old deal is dead, would you be upset if I went to Morgan Stanley and put before them a fully underwritten offer by Investcorp for the whole amount? We'll deal with the financing later on. I'll take the risk – put up the whole thing at $135.5 million.'

'I'm not going to stop you,' he said.

'That's not enough,' I said. 'I'll only do it if you side with me.'

'I'm not sure I want to go back and tell Avon I have another offer . . .'

'But you have nothing to gain from a Donald Trump takeover of Tiffany. At least I'm talking to you. How about I put together an offer and then we sit down and look at it as a possibility for potential partnership?'

It is a very short distance from the Tiffany building to the offices of our attorneys, Gibson, Dunn & Crutcher, but on that August Thursday in 1984 it felt like the journey of a lifetime. My heart was pounding, the adrenalin pumping. I could feel the prize in my hand, the culmination of all those years of dreaming and hard work. We had not started Investcorp to emulate the sharks and their cynical leveraged buyouts, nothing but greed and numbers. Now we were about to show them how it could be done, with ingenuity and integrity and respect.

The day before in Marbella, after hanging up the phone with Bill Chaney, I had immediately called John Thompson in London. For a week, trying to get a handle on the deal, I had been asking John how much Tiffany's real estate was worth. The answer to that question increasingly appeared to me to be the key to a workable transaction – a structure in which the acquisition of the company and its premises were treated as two separate deals. This was what Elie and I had discussed as a constructive way to go about this deal. Obviously, Tiffany had to remain in its same famous location, so we would take a long lease on the space, sell off the real estate, and get back some of our money – plus a possible profit on the property.

John's best estimate was that the real estate might be worth $65 to $80 million, but I decided to consider it $50 million just to be conservative. The remaining question, then: How much was the business worth?

When we started adding everything up, we found that Tiffany's inventory had a book value of $88 million and a retail value nearly twice that; the fabled Tiffany Diamond was appraised at $10 million; and the company had some $30 million in receivables from corporate clients like Shearson Lehman, American Express, and Chase Manhattan Bank, who regularly bought promotional items. Suddenly, instead of a giant risk, we saw the deal as an opportunity to buy more than $200 million worth of assets for $135 million.

But we would still have to come up with the cash on signing, so before submitting our offer, I put the bottom-line question to Elie: 'Can we raise the money?'

'Yes,' he said. 'I'll take care of it.'

All Thursday afternoon we and our lawyers worked at hammering out the offer, and on Friday morning I took it over and presented it to Morgan Stanley. 'The offer's closed,' they said.

'No,' I told them, 'at least give Avon the chance to refuse it if they wish. They are a public shareholding company, and if they receive a higher offer, are they going to say no? It's a fully underwritten offer. No ifs, ands, or buts. No financing. No way out.'

By Friday afternoon I asked Bill Chaney if I could meet with him over the weekend, and he invited me to his home in Connecticut. I drove up on Saturday morning and was greeted warmly by Chaney and his wife, Caroline. The three of us had a pleasant lunch, chatting amiably about our respective backgrounds and the meandering paths that had led us to this moment. After lunch, Bill and I went and sat on his front porch and I took out my yellow pad and outlined our respective roles once Investcorp bought Tiffany. Neither of us signed it. It was just a few notes so we both understood our positions and the philosophy behind them. He already knew, from the generous 20 percent ownership I had allotted to management, that Investcorp considered him and his team our inside partners, working in tandem with us and our outside investors to create the kind of win-win-win situation that was so desirable in these buyout deals. We did not skirt the fact that there was very hard work ahead of us, most of it falling squarely on Bill Chaney's shoulders. But he was appreciative of our supportive attitude, and this was the spirit of our meeting.

On Monday morning Avon received our offer, and Bill told the Chairman who was behind it. Although he had already shaken hands with Trump, Avon's Chairman was now compelled to compare the offers. There was really no comparison. Besides being slightly higher in price, our bid was also fully underwritten, which Trump's was not. Also, Bill told the Chairman that we were backing the management, so Avon should support us.

Very quickly, I was invited to a meeting at Avon with all the company's top brass and their financial advisors from Morgan Stanley. I took Charlie Marquis from Gibson, Dunn & Crutcher to explain who we were, but, even so, a brash young man from Morgan Stanley piped up and asked me, 'How can *you* raise this money? What financial resources do *you* have?' Perhaps he did not emphasize the word *you* quite so heavily, but that was the implication I heard. And I was not having it.

'If you want references,' I said to the young man, 'please check with your boss about the financial capabilities of Investcorp.'

At that meeting Avon granted us a period in which to mount a second attempt at a management buyout, so now we had to assign an investment bank to work with us on the negotiations – and especially to help guide us through the arduous process called due diligence. This was the detailed investigation any investor performs on the company he is about to buy. No stone – be it of the management, operational, or financial variety – would be left unturned. The question was, which investment bank to assign? Some of our team argued for Lehman Brothers, but others said no, Lehman had lost out on the former deal and we should go with someone new.

In the end, we chose Lehman. Frankly, I felt we had some moral obligation to them since they had invited us to the deal in the first place, and there was also the benefit of their having done considerable work on Tiffany already. But I told Lehman they had to assign a brand-new team to us – we would not work with Dennis Levine. Months later The Irishman, with misguided regret, would inform us that Levine had been passed over for promotion because we had had him removed from the Tiffany deal. To which both Cem and Bob, wiping away crocodile tears, said, 'It couldn't have happened to a nicer guy.'

Our new Lehman team was headed by a man named William Shutzer, who would go on to win the confidence of both Tiffany and Investcorp, but about whom I initially had reservations. He identified himself as being a 'managing director and also number two on the M&A side with eight managing directors reporting to me.'

But it was only when he said, 'Anyway, we've agreed on our fees,' that I felt compelled to redress the balance of power that New York investment bankers seem so hell-bent on claiming for themselves.

'We've agreed on nothing,' I said. 'The deal you brought in the past is dead. You lost, we lost. Now this is Investcorp's deal. We're free to appoint anybody, but we're appointing you. Do you want the job, or not? And it is I who will tell you what your fees are *and* what your role is.'

No doubt that smarted. Lehman was big in New York and we were new – that had been the recurring theme through all our negotiations. But it was a theme whose time was up.

'Can I make a phone call?' Shutzer asked, and I said fine. He stepped out and was gone a few minutes. When he returned, there was hardly a vestige of the swagger that apparently came with the big investment-bank résumé.

'I guess we'll take the job,' he said.

On Wednesday, one week after leaving Marbella, I boarded a plane back to Spain and the resumption of my summer vacation. It had been an exhilarating seven days, and though I did not fully appreciate it at the time, it was a week that contained the seeds of all of Investcorp's greatest future triumphs and hardest challenges. In a sense, this had been a trial run for the next twenty-five years.

By the time I left Manhattan I was already embroiled in a risky standoff with a couple of powerful members of my Board of Directors. After sending a memo to the board explaining the transaction and the offer we were making, I received a quick call from my secretary in Bahrain telling me to phone Vice Chairman Ahmed Kanoo immediately. 'I want to talk to Nemir,' he had said to her. 'I don't want this deal. It's a major risk and we should be out of it.'

When I reached the Vice Chairman he insisted on an extraordinary meeting of the board to decide the Tiffany matter. 'I want a meeting *right now*,' he told me.

'There's no time for a meeting,' I said. 'The deal will be presented, in full, at the next board meeting. We will follow the majority vote.' He was not pleased, and wrote me a firm letter instructing me to abandon the deal. Mohammed Jalal sent one saying the same thing. But I heard nothing from the other fourteen board members. Later, in our regular November board meeting, I would have these two letters read out for all to hear before I argued my case to the entire board. That would be followed by one of the fieriest discussions we would ever have in an Investcorp Board of Directors meeting – and then, thankfully, a resolution in favor of the Tiffany purchase.

But by then Cem and Bob would have reached an agreement with Avon and I would be facing vastly greater danger than the wrath of a couple of unhappy board members. In time, Tiffany would become a resounding success for us, a model deal, but not right away. No bank would touch it at first, and I would burn with humiliation at that fact. Cem would remain in New York for eight months, calling on no fewer than thirteen banks, before he finally found a taker in the General Electric Credit Corporation (GECC) – which, given their leverage over us, would drive a tremendously hard bargain. As for the real estate, it would take John Thompson nine long months to land a buyer for the Tiffany building. We would sell it for $66 million (against our cost of $50 million) – only to watch our buyers flip it later on to a group of Japanese investors for $90 million.

But all of that was still in the future on that August day when I flew back to Spain and my interrupted holiday. What had just become part of the present was Investcorp's, and my own, portentous clash between big deals and big-deal dealmakers. I left New York knowing I had an instinct for deals, but I was less certain of my knack for hiring the people who could make them happen. The Irishman had thoroughly baffled me. In our review session at the Pierre the night of my first meeting with Bill Chaney, we had all stayed up in my suite until 4 a.m. wrangling over what had gone wrong with the first Tiffany deal. At one point, The

Irishman addressed Cem, Bob, Savio, and me: 'The trouble is that you're all commercial bankers. You don't know *how* to make deals. This is how deals are done.'

'I was making deals before you were born,' I responded, but secretly I was flabbergasted: Such an ego, absolutely impossible to work with. And if he was that difficult with me, what must he have been like with the rest of the guys?

A few days later, I told him I was taking him off Tiffany. 'But it's my deal,' he said.

'No, your deal is gone. I'm assigning you to Bertram-Trojan. Cem and Bob will take over Tiffany.'

And they did, while climbing a very steep learning curve. I took Cem aside and told him the Investcorp team was behind him, and that he also had the expertise of Lehman Brothers, Gibson, Dunn & Crutcher, and Coopers & Lybrand. With them he had to conclude the financing part.

As for The Irishman, I gave him one more chance. I dispatched Mike Merritt to accompany him on the Bertram-Trojan deal, my thought being that if The Irishman ruffled the feathers of the world's most easygoing man, there was no hope for him at Investcorp.

The Irishman failed the test. He was ushered out of the firm.

7
THE TRAIN

Conventional wisdom holds that you should not attempt to open two offices at the same time – you open one, get it up and running, then move to the next one. We did not follow conventional wisdom. And so, in 1984, we celebrated the grand openings of offices in both London and Bahrain.

During 1982 and 1983 Mike, and later Cem, had done the hard work of establishing our London outpost from temporary offices with rented desks, and plastic canopies to protect them from falling plaster. Now the newly revealed Investcorp House, London, was a handsome, strategically placed, elegant building at 65 Brook Street, in Mayfair, where – as with our plans for Bahrain – visitors were welcomed into a haven of old-world taste and stability with Middle Eastern accents. When searching for art for the walls, Cem had run across a Sotheby's sale of tinted prints by the famous Scotsman David Roberts, whose evocations of his journeys to Egypt and the Holy Land had so impressed Londoners in the mid-nineteenth century. By the time Cem had bought the books of prints at auction – bidding against an enthusiastic Kuwaiti collector – they were too valuable to dismantle, so we purchased copies for our walls and the original books went into a bank vault.

It was just this kind of attention to detail that had made our Bahrain office such a cause célèbre. Investcorp House, Bahrain, opened with much fanfare in May 1984, the highlight being the ribbon-cutting by the Prime Minister, His Excellency Sheikh Khalifa bin Salman Al Khalifa. After the ceremony, I escorted the Prime Minister, our board members, and other important officials on a tour of the building that had been the subject of so much local gossip and rumor over the preceding year. Now there was only praise. This, people said, was the kind of office more likely to be found among old merchant banks in London or New York, and suddenly the marble floors, Oriental carpets, and wood-paneled walls made perfect sense. On the outside, dark glass deflected the searing Gulf sun while encasing Investcorp in a cool blue cube that stood out boldly from the white buildings around us. The board was proud, and the local press was beside itself – not least for the fact that we moved in only fourteen months after buying the building, nearly a year ahead of schedule.

The Prime Minister's agreement to come to Investcorp to celebrate the opening of our building was an unprecedented event of extraordinary impact. The entire cabinet of ministers attended the celebration, which lasted two and a half hours. That evening it was the lead story on Bahraini television and radio news, and the next morning all the newspapers contained front-page articles complete with pictures. I do not think any bank in Bahrain has ever had a similar experience. The recognition for Investcorp was unmatched.

But while the external compliments were rewarding, it was the quiet, transformative pride of our staff that touched me most. At the time of our move, we were up to eighteen rooms at the Holiday Inn, and I well remembered what Betty Pires had said when she joined the company in early 1983: 'I told my husband I was going to work in Room 200 at the Holiday Inn, and he said, "What kind of job is *that*?"' Those days were finally over.

Or were they?

Tiffany was a whole new beginning for Investcorp. Suddenly, starting in the fall of 1984, we found ourselves invited to every deal in New York, and that meant more and more of our team were in Manhattan for long stretches at a time. With no office of our own, our people – Cem, Oliver, Savio, and Bob, occasionally buttressed by the judicious addition of new London hires Paul Dimitruk and Linda Cates – were graciously granted full-time use of a small conference room at the law offices of Gibson, Dunn & Crutcher. As the Holiday Inn had been our early toehold in Bahrain, this windowless room high over 57th Street – anchored by a single round table – would be our New York working center until 1988, when we would finally open our headquarters on Park Avenue.

From these disparate points on three continents we coordinated our first major phase of dealmaking. It was the mid- to late-eighties, an exhilarating period, intense and brimming with adrenalin. We were like a shiny new locomotive picking up steam. It was only later that I realized we had become addicted to the steam.

There are two ways to pursue an acquisition, passively and actively. In the passive method, we simply wait for an investment bank to send a deal to us. We received many of those in our post-Tiffany period, when the word on the street was that there was this Gulf institution called Investcorp with a lot of money to spend. In those days we might see as many as three hundred possible deals a year, which is too many even for big firms full of people who know what they are doing. But besides having Gibson, Dunn & Crutcher and Coopers & Lybrand as guides, our tight little team was inherently smart and resourceful. Most had been through Chase's credit training program, and they applied that experience to corporate acquisitions. Now, instead of figuring out if a potential borrower could pay back a loan, the task was to determine if a potential acquisition company could pay off its liabilities and generate incremental net worth.

Although our acquisition criteria have evolved over the years, some aspects of it have remained stable. We look for an established company with a good name, a good market niche, a good earnings potential, good cash flow, and a good growth forecast. Following the Tiffany purchase there was a certain amount of euphoric interest in fame and glamour, but – as I have repeatedly told our people – we are not in show business. Our investors simply want an attractive return on their investment.

Whenever an investment bank sent any of our group a deal, the person who received it would read it over and determine if it was suitable for Investcorp or not; those that were not acceptable were courteously rejected, but potential deals were passed around to other team members and a consensus was reached. If a deal looked viable, the next step was to put our heads together and come up with a number we thought it might be worth – $100 million, say. Then we contacted the bank that sent us the deal, saying we would be interested in looking at the company and this is what we think we might be willing to pay for it.

That is called the preliminary offer, and it concludes the first round in a corporate acquisition transaction. If the bank likes our general level of interest, they include us in the second round – and at that point we have to start spending money, because we have to hire lawyers, accountants, and maybe even an investment bank to conduct due diligence, and based on that we would determine whether or not we really want to buy the company. Out of the three hundred or so deals we received annually in those years, we might have sent thirty letters expressing interest. Later we realized we had to become more selective, and by the end of the 1980s we were looking at perhaps ten deals seriously and succeeding in acquiring only three. You can spend a very large amount of money going after deals that turn out to be of no interest, or impossible to finance, or that are also pursued by people who can outbid you.

Between 1983 and 1989, we completed sixteen corporate acquisitions. At each stop we slowed the locomotive just long enough to take on our newest passenger, then steamed off down the track seemingly faster than before. Each deal fed the fire, and the energy that emanated from it could become extremely intoxicating if you let it. It would be easy, for example, for the corporate acquisitions team to think they were driving the train, and in fact some members of that unit began to view the North American team as 'the factory' – the manufacturing center where the business and profit were produced. London they saw as the promotional, marketing, and advertising arm. Placement was merely 'the sales people.' These identifications were, of course, not accurate.

For the most part, I was not personally involved in deals during that period. Operating now out of London (with an identical office in Bahrain), I had plenty to keep me busy – the board, a steadily increasing staff, the placement team, the real estate side, internal and external financial issues. All of it was important. But of everything I had to contend with, nothing loomed as more pivotal to the fortunes of the firm than keeping tabs on the performance of the corporations we acquired. And that very much included the attitudes of our own people. Walking into a corporate board room to sign a deal committing millions of dollars promotes a great feeling of power. Once we buy a company, whoever is heading up the acquisition becomes to a great degree the company's overseer. There is a seat on its board, golf outings with its CEO, periodic calls on head office during which the Investcorp representative is received as a visiting dignitary. It can turn a person's head, and that can affect morale inside my own firm. Early on, I recognized this as yet another ego danger I had to watch out for.

In the 1980s, our corporate investment portfolio reflected an extraordinary sampling of the everyday – jewelry, boats, golf carts, department stores, fire plugs, photo processors, auto service centers, women's clothing, dairies – and each acquisition added a ring of names and faces to our ever-widening constellation of relationships. Robert Smith, CEO of America's top producer of recreational power boats, Bertram-Trojan, and its Italian subsidiary,

Riva, became a member of the extended family; over time, every one of Investcorp's New York executives made the trip to his Miami headquarters. At Club Car, a manufacturer of golf carts based outside Augusta, Georgia, genial CEO George Inman welcomed our team to an office that was no less than a miniature golf museum filled with mementoes of the game. In Virginia, William Peebles, scion of a century-old family department-store chain that had run out of family, graciously greeted Cem and Bob as allies in his goal of preparing his beloved Peebles Department Stores for its next chapter of life. And then there was Ed Powers, the only CEO of an acquisition company from that period that I met before we closed the deal.

Ed ran the Mueller Company, a very successful manufacturer of valves, hydrants, pumps, and fittings used in the distribution of water or natural gas. Founded as a family business in 1857, Mueller remained firmly in family hands through several generations, until, in the 1980s, there was nobody left to steer it day-to-day. Fortunately for the family stockholders, this was when Ed Powers took over. A blunt, straightforward man as unflashy as Mueller's products, Ed increased profits nearly tenfold in an eight-year run. Now he was talking about retirement, and, with his blessing, the Mueller family had decided to sell the company with Ed becoming a shareholder and then staying on to run it.

I met Ed in the offices of Morgan Stanley one morning in 1986, on yet another dramatic New York day. In the weeks leading up to this moment our team – headed by Paul Dimitruk and Oliver Richardson, later joined by Savio Tung – had won Ed over, forging an agreement for a management buyout and bidding more than we had ever offered for any company – $320 million. Then, at the last minute, a rival offer – a higher rival offer – came in from the Kuwaiti Investment Authority, represented by the ex-Chairman of the US Federal Reserve, Bill Miller. This put Ed Powers in a very tough position. He had committed to us, but he had a duty to his stockholders to seriously weigh both offers. So on that day at Morgan Stanley the Investcorp team was in one room, Bill Miller and his people were in another, and Ed was shuttling back and forth. Apparently, even though the Kuwaitis had put in a better bid, their offer was subject to obtaining senior approvals in Kuwait which were not yet in hand. They were waiting for a telex from Kuwait to confirm the final go-ahead. Miller kept asking for another twenty-four hours, while we insisted that today was the day.

Naturally, Ed was trying to get us to sweeten the offer to the point where his decision would be easy, and we were saying, 'Ed, don't increase the price. You're going to be our partner and have to *pay* for it. Let's get it at this price, right now.' But he said he could not pull it off.

I was contacted by my colleagues and asked to intervene. So I met with Ed Powers. We sat in a room together and I looked him straight in the eye and assured him of the trust and respect he would receive as a working partner of Investcorp. When he asked if I could improve our bid, I agreed to a nominal increase only.

'But,' I told him, 'it will all expire at noon. At twelve o'clock today we either have a deal, or we pull out. Tomorrow you'll be left with only one offer, and if that fails to come through, you'll have to tell your board you lost them both. Okay, so

Investcorp's offer is lower, but it's right here, signed and sealed. Theirs is a bird in the bush, while ours is a bird in the hand. Remember, it will be your company, Ed. Do what you think is best.'

He never revealed to me what swayed him, the carrot or the stick, but a few years later he told an interviewer, 'I have a fond place in my heart for that man. Nemir is a closer.'

I do not remember when I began seeing the train metaphor. I tend to think in images anyway – sometimes Investcorp is a watch whose smooth running is dependent on every single part, no matter how tiny, doing its assigned job; other times we are a building whose foundation is of the utmost importance, stone by stone. A metaphor can help explain your complex ideas to others. It can even help you see them clearer yourself.

For Investcorp, the train metaphor encompasses something the others do not: It extends to the companies we acquire. Investcorp is a train running through time and the acquired companies are our passengers. We stop for them, take them and all their baggage on board, and carry them as comfortably as possible to the next stop on their journey. They get where they want to go and we achieve our mission to create wealth for our investors. That is our role and that is their role. Thus, during the ride there is a value-adding process, which at Investcorp we call post-acquisition management.

The train concept refers to corporate investments and not to real estate, because over the train ride we are partnering with the managements of those companies to achieve a certain destination within a certain time. When we get to the target destination, the managers of those companies leave us and our partnership as well. While the Tiffany management appreciated the process and happily moved on to the next stage in their journey, other corporate managers did not feel the same. They thought their experience with Investcorp was so successful that they regretted our parting of ways.

In real estate, from 1985–1992, instead of focusing on asset deals such as Manulife Plaza and the Tiffany building, an expanded Investcorp real estate team aggressively pursued development deals on both sides of the Atlantic. The very first one, a joint partnership in a London apartment complex called Beverly House, later came to look like an object lesson. Our process was to find an experienced, reputable development partner and help him get the project under way – line up financing, get construction contracts signed, and all that. To protect our clients from any losses related to development glitches, we waited until construction was set to go before placing a portion of the deal with investors. Their return, we felt, should be governed by the sale price of the finished building, and how long it took to sell. Their risk would then be a financial one, much like any other, and not a technical one.

But a construction site is rife with technical risk. Though work on Beverly House proceeded smoothly and some £35 million in pre-sold contracts came in, just before completion a fire tore through the building and destroyed the elevators. The project was set back by six whole months. Miraculously, this turned out not to be the disaster we first thought it was. Completion had been set for October 1987, the month of the stock market crash, but the six-month delay pushed us past the fear caused by the unsettled market. By the time we were ready to close the sale contracts, confidence had returned. Investcorp's first real estate development ultimately produced an annual return of 8.1 percent to our investors – not great, but it could have been so much worse.

Going forward, while we were no longer blind to the unpredictability of both construction and markets, we still had innumerable lessons to learn about the vagaries of project development. Our first US development, a business park called Dominion Point near Dulles International Airport in Virginia, offered us a primer on the dangers of over-building. 'In America, it's almost too easy to build,' our real estate people later said. 'When conditions are good, the banks throw money at developers, so you get a huge over-supply, and then the inevitable downturn. A local market can collapse overnight.' And that is what happened with Dominion Point.

On and on it went – through luxury residential complexes in San Francisco, office developments in Boston, urban renewal projects in Washington, DC, and high-rise apartments in Manhattan. Almost all suffered costly construction delays for one reason or another. 'Whatever your calculations are at the start,' John Thompson said in the early 1990s, by which time the truth of the matter was finally clear to all, 'you can never predict what the market will be when you reach the other end. That is the major problem of property developments.'

★

In June of 1987, four months before the stock market crash, we invited the chief executives of all the companies Investcorp had acquired to come to London for a conference, and to bring their wives. The night before our meetings, Nada and I hosted a dinner at our house. The food, the wine, the table setting, the service – there was a glow over the evening when I stood up to make my welcoming toast. And that was when I talked to them about the train.

Our relationship, I said, was like a shared train ride. Each company in the portfolio was traveling toward its own chosen destination, and Investcorp would take them part of their journey. Then we would stop the train and let them off, to continue their progress by other means.

The shift in mood was nearly imperceptible, but not completely. Perhaps I felt the sudden cooling effect of frozen smiles, or detected a degree of sparkle fading from certain eyes. Robert Smith, CEO of Bertram-Trojan, later told an interviewer that he was surprised and disappointed by my words. 'Though I knew Investcorp wasn't in the business of owning boat companies for an eternity, I was really enjoying the relationship. I felt I was learning and growing, and I didn't want it to end.' My comments were not aimed at anyone in particular, nor were they intended to shock. But it was a message I wanted to convey to recipients both outside and inside the company. We can know something intellectually without confronting it emotionally. For quite some time I had been feeling that changes were on the way, and I thought it was my job as a leader to start edging people toward emotional acceptance.

In any human organization there has to be someone who

acts as a focal point. There are several styles of leadership, of course, including those executives who insist on making centralized decisions. That is not me. My style is more a matter of vision, setting the direction and controlling the outcome. In my view, effective leadership requires an ability to see and choose the road, a willingness to assume the risk entailed in that choice, and the power to motivate a team of people, inspiring them to contribute their best. Team members need to be persuaded that achieving the chosen target ensures that the firm, its shareholders, and indeed the team members themselves will be the winners. I have to keep all the separate parts of the organization in view and make sure all are evolving in the right direction. If they are, then well and good, I can stand back. But if something is drifting out of line, I have to step in and correct it before it becomes a larger problem.

By the time our portfolio CEOs and their wives visited London that summer, I had had many intense conversations about the overheating stock market with Elie and Mike, as influenced by our able economist Professor Geoffrey Maynard. He forced us to believe that the market bubble was dangerously close to bursting, and it was time to liquidate our managed funds. So when the Dow plummeted on October 19, we had less than $3 million still invested out of a total value of $172 million. It was that kind of foresight that I wanted to apply elsewhere throughout the firm.

There was not much to do on the real estate side – once we had embarked on project developments, we could not change direction without suffering major losses. But corporate investment was another matter. Soon my opportunity appeared – wrapped, as opportunity so often is, in a disguise of bad luck. One would have thought the market crash would dampen the buyout trend, but the opposite seemed to be the case. With the advent of junk bonds, corporate buyouts became more feverish than ever. Now, suddenly, whenever we got serious about an acquisition, we found ourselves outbid by 20 to 30 percent. After a few such instances, it was clear to me: If we cannot buy, then it must be a good time to sell.

We had taken Tiffany public in May 1987 – always the plan – and that same year had sold Jiffy Lube and Mallison-Denny, a UK timber company. But our intention had been to hold our recent corporate purchases – Bertram-Trojan, Riva, Club Car, Peebles, and Mueller – until their values reached target levels, which we thought might take three to five years. The market, however, had accelerated everything. Prices were remarkably high. Rather than stay in, hoping for even larger gains, I believed now was the prudent time for a major sell-off.

That was the message I conveyed to the executive staff at our annual first-of-the-year Management Committee (Mancom) meeting in January 1988. And what happened was ... nothing. It was as though no one had heard a word I said.

In April we had another group get-together – all the Mancom members from all three offices – and this time I gave the order more forcefully. 'No more buying,' I said. 'The tap is turned off. I want you to sell everything.' They looked me straight in the eye and nodded, and I thought they had got it. Once we all returned to our respective offices, I kept expecting a flurry of phone calls announcing divestitures. Instead, it was the same as before: not a word.

By now I was furious. At our mid-year Mancom meeting, I laid it out in terms they could not ignore. 'I have told you and told you I want you to *sell* these companies,' I said. 'This year, your bonuses will not be based on buying. They'll be based only on what you sell.' Soon I started receiving that flurry of calls I had expected before.

It is instructive to explore what was happening here. From my perspective, when external conditions presented us with an inability to buy, I was forced back to basics – to examining not only what we could do, but what we *should* do. Again, the train idea came into play. As I had told our portfolio CEOs, they would be passengers for a time and then we would let them off the train to continue their journey by other means. But letting them off the train implied something further – something related to our investors, who, it suddenly dawned on me, were not riding on the train at all. They were waiting at the station. And waiting ... and waiting ... Up to now, we had only bought companies, we had never sold one. So our investors had not received a single dime from us. Our track record consisted solely of reports saying how well these companies were doing. It was time to change that, time to complete the cycle that was our mission as a firm: buy, manage, sell.

While I had noted to myself how possessive members of our corporate investment team had become with their acquisitions – necessarily so, up to a point – I was still surprised at how difficult this sell order had been for them.

Even though they knew – intellectually – that we were not

a holding company in the business of owning companies forever, for various reasons they had blocked out that fact emotionally.

'Until you send your clients a check, they've got no proof that they've invested in a successful deal,' Linda Cates told an internal interviewer in 1991, as she explored the difficulty she and others had in following my order. 'Nemir wanted everybody to know that the job consisted of buying, managing, and then selling. We had bought and managed, but we didn't know how to sell. And it was a tremendous shock to our system to have to do so. The worst aspect was losing control. When you're buying a company you're in total control ... But when you become a seller you're at the mercy of the buyers. That loss of control just goes against the nature of Investcorp, and it caused great personal stress.'

Now they understood what the placement team had been dealing with every single day.

But even as the corporate investment group began beating the bushes for buyers, they remained generally unconvinced that this was the right time to sell. Partly this was a technical difference of opinion. Companies are bought and sold at a price determined by two factors – 'profitability' and 'multiple.' You can buy a company whose profitability – i.e. its EBITDA (earnings before interest, taxes, depreciation, amortization) – is, let us say for ease of example, $80. The multiple is determined by the external market demand for that type of company or industry. Assuming the multiple is 10x at that point in time, our $80 company would be sold at $80 x 10 or $800.

When Investcorp buys a company with EBITDA $80, our

aim is to work with management to increase its EBITDA to $100 over three to five years. And when the EBITDA is at $100, we *hope* to sell at the same multiple or better – in other words, $100 x 10 or $1000. If the multiple goes down – say, to 5x – the company we had bought at $800 would be worth only $500, even though its profitability had improved from $80 to $100.

So when I sensed that the market was high, it meant that the multiples were high and so a good time to sell. My associates who did not favor selling were still focusing only on profitability. They claimed the potential for growth in profitability was still high, so why sell before the company had reached its target profit potential? And if we could have been certain that the multiples would not drop, my associates would have been right – in that case, higher profitability would mean higher enterprise value and therefore greater return to investors. But I felt in my bones that the multiples were too high and might not stay at that level for very long.

In addition to this technical difference of opinion, there was another cause of our disagreement: emotion. '[Nemir's] fear,' Savio Tung once told an interviewer, 'is that one of us will fall in love with a company, something which is very easy to do. When you live with a company every day, you get to know its strengths and weaknesses. You think you can address the weaknesses while maintaining the strengths, and so turn it into a successful company. The temptation to do that can be overwhelming ... It can creep up on you, and I think it did in '88. Some of us had got too close to the portfolio companies under management.'

Generally, when I am putting over a new idea I do not

believe in transmitting it through group meetings. If someone needs convincing, I prefer to spend time with that person separately, talking it over one-on-one. As a leader I believe in that method, and frankly that is my strength, so I want to use it. I also dislike deadlines. If something is worth doing, I would prefer not to put an artificial time frame on it. It is more important to get it right – to keep working with the individual executives until everyone is aboard and we are all heading in the same direction. I find the quality of the outcome is better through persuasion.

But in the case of selling our portfolio companies, there were a couple of major obstacles to my usual method of convincing. The first was distance: Since we were now so spread out, I was finding it harder to have a series of face-to-face conversations. And second, I felt there really was a time pressure, though I did not know how long we had. I just knew the economy was on a euphoric high that could not last. Professor Maynard had convinced me it was only a matter of time before the bottom dropped out.

So our people had to go out and sell even if they did not fully agree. 'One of my jobs at the time,' Linda Cates later recalled, 'was to take prospective buyers around Peebles and Club Car so they could spend a whole day looking at them. Management would give a presentation and I would show them the store and the warehouse, and so on. Every morning I had to stand up and explain why we were selling these companies. I found it very difficult, because I really didn't believe it was the right time to sell.

'But it was. Nemir was absolutely right. We sold them

at precisely the right moment and got the highest price we could ever have gotten for them.'

Now we know that that was the moment Investcorp grew up. It took six years, but finally we had confronted the cycle that was our reason for being. Investcorp is an intermediary. It acts as a link between the risk-taking investors and a particular investment opportunity. The fiduciary responsibility of any such institution is to realize the best possible return for its clients, and that is why we devote such enormous effort to supporting and guiding the growth of each portfolio company. The idea is to maximize its value at exit. But the by-products of that effort, when successful, are twofold: Yes, we generate an attractive return for our investors; but we also leave behind a stronger and more prosperous business.

On a warm June morning in 1988, when Club Car's George Inman arrived in New York to attend the festivities surrounding Investcorp's new Park Avenue offices, Savio Tung pulled him into a quiet anteroom and handed him a proposal, prepared by Shearson Lehman, for the sale of Club Car. Inman was shocked. Prepared for just such a reaction, Savio suggested Inman look at the sale price before responding. 'When I saw those numbers,' George later recalled, 'any objection that I might have had was considerably muted.' Club Car sold for $83 million, which meant the company's management multiplied their money nearly eightfold. For Investcorp's clients, Club Car produced an annual return on equity of 98.7 percent.

Similar scenes were acted out with Bertram-Trojan, Riva, Peebles, and Mueller. Bertram-Trojan sold for almost double the cost of acquisition, yielding our clients an annual return of 41 percent, and every one of the company's 1300 employees received a bonus. Mueller was sold to Tyco Laboratories for $366 million, generating an annual return to our Gulf investors of 40 percent. And in January 1989, a financial buyer acquired Peebles for $160 million, nearly twice its cost to us some three years before. The annual return to our investors was 63.4 percent. Like Club Car's George Inman, the CEOs of these other companies had only praise for their time with Investcorp.

'We were treated so well, there was no way we could get off the train without smiling,' said Robert Smith. 'For the rest of our lives we will have a feeling of gratitude and respect for our former owner.'

'It was a happy relationship,' recalled William Peebles in 1992, '... and we're still good friends today. I guess that tells you something.'

Ed Powers, predictably the least effusive of the bunch, simply said, 'I never regretted my association with Investcorp. They never failed to do what they said they would do.'

And sometimes the train comes back along the same track: Just three months after Mueller was sold and Ed had retired to his home on the Chesapeake Bay, I found myself picking up the phone and asking him if he would mind taking a look at a troubled company we owned in Columbus, Georgia. Soon Ed had bought a house in Columbus and become CEO of the company, and it was six more years before he was able to get back to retirement.

Of the seven corporate investment deals that had gone full cycle by 1989, the average annual return was 74.8 percent.

It was a golden age of sorts. Within months, the recession of the early nineties was upon us. Life was about to become much more complicated. ‘If we’d tried to sell Peebles in 1990 or 1991,’ said Bob Glaser later, ‘it would have been difficult to find a buyer at any price, let alone an attractive price. Here, once again, as with Bertram-Trojan, we learned that it’s prudent to sell when the multiples are high.’

Our new maturity was not lost on the financial community. Now, instead of being just the hot up-and-coming firm with money to spend, we were seen as something infinitely more solid. Investors greeted our placement team with new warmth. Banks contacted *us* about financing our deals. Buying may be more fun, but selling is the real test.

It took a while for the rest of the firm to grasp that, but in 1988 they began to get it. Today when I think back to the unsung heroes who built the foundation of our placing power in the Gulf, three individuals stand out. Oliver Richardson, a gifted and charming man with an iron will, was the first to establish a network of client relationships for us. He displayed great ability to achieve his goal irrespective of the time needed or the magnitude of the obstacles to overcome. Later, Yusef Abu Khadra joined the team from Morgan Stanley, and his intellectual capacity and high discipline added great strength to the firm’s placing ability. Yusef’s honesty, dedication, and commitment cannot be overstated. Finally, as younger professionals joined the placement team in increased numbers, the group needed a strong leader at the top. Salman Abbasi, who succeeded me as Chase’s Gulf Division Executive when I left in 1981, was the person I contacted to assume that responsibility. An outstanding banker with great leadership and management skills, Sal worked harder than anyone else on his team and always set an example to be followed. His decisiveness, intellect, and strong personality were respected by his clients, colleagues, and competitors alike.

As a way of commemorating the lessons of 1988, Savio Tung commissioned a memento for all the CEOs involved in the four pivotal sales we made that year: a brass diesel locomotive. I have three of them myself, one for each of my offices – Bahrain, London, and New York. I display them prominently, a reminder of a defining moment in the life of Investcorp – not just the year the train ran exactly on time, but the year placement took its rightful place as the engine driving this firm.

8
STATES OF WAR

On August 2, 1990, three divisions of Iraq's elite Republican Guard invaded neighboring Kuwait and quickly took over the country. The resulting standoff between Saddam Hussein and the rest of the world would last six months, involve trade embargoes enforced by NATO troops, throw global financial markets into turmoil, and culminate in the US-led bombing and invasion of Iraq. As an Iraqi national, I watched the unfolding crisis with feelings of anger toward the dictatorship in Baghdad. But as the CEO of a Bahrain-based international financial firm, I could not afford personal emotion. At best, Iraq's invasion of Kuwait promised major disruptions for Investcorp; at worst, it threatened something much more dire.

Today when I think casually of that year, the catastrophic Gulf War stands out as the prime benchmark. Going deeper, however, I have to say it was the first volley of an internal culture war that proved most propitious for Investcorp. The Gulf War hovered over us and made our lives harder, but we would have encountered significant stress without it.

By 1990, we were a company that had grown larger and more successful, but also somewhat unwieldy. The Mancom members, all fifteen of them, still reported to me. While this structure sometimes taxed my day-to-day focus, we remained a tight unit linked by a larger long-range vision and clarity of future direction. At the January 1990 Mancom meeting, for instance, we jointly decided to go after the biggest quarry we had ever pursued – the retail giant Saks Fifth Avenue. Having heard about the sale the previous fall, we had tried to join with Saks management on a buyout; they graciously declined, saying they were already too far along with a Japanese buyer. But Saks was perfect for us – leading brand name, loyal customer base, strong market position, nationwide coverage, impressive performance, good cash flow, capable management – and at the Mancom meeting we vowed, as a team, not to let this one get away.

Saks would not be formally offered for sale until February 15, but, acting as though it were already ours, we spent more than a million dollars in due diligence between early January and the March 15 deadline for preliminary bids. In what has been called 'the greatest collective effort of Investcorp's first twenty years,' we rearranged ourselves into small guerrilla teams – comprising our own people and advisers from Coopers & Lybrand – and dispatched them across America to walk the floors of every one of Saks' forty-six stores. We found growth opportunities and potential cost savings that nobody else did. Even Saks management, who were bidders themselves, were not able to compile the numbers we did.

Ultimately bidding against four competitors, we acquired Saks in May for $1.35 billion. That the Mancom could still mount such a massive team effort was a testament to the enduring strength of our corporate culture.

There were cracks in the façade, however. One was that in

1988 I had hired a PhD in economics to revamp our proprietary trading effort through the relatively new philosophy of 'quantitative trading,' an analytic approach that Elie did not sympathize with. Lee Thomas III was educated at Tulane and seasoned at Chase, Citibank, and Goldman Sachs, where he and other 'quants,' as such trading specialists were called, applied their knowledge of mathematics, physics, and economics to develop computer models for the evaluation of increasingly complex financial products. In 1988, quants were cutting edge – so new that little Investcorp had adopted the idea a full year before a gigantic institution like Deutsche Bank.

But Elie lobbied hard – to me, and I suspect to others on the Mancom – to also keep the conventional approach to trading, and I agreed. For the next few years we operated both quantitatively and conventionally. And even as Lee Thomas demonstrated that impressive profits could be achieved without the risk of short-term response to transitory market sentiments, the Mancom grew increasingly negative toward the experiment. I was surprised, and disturbed, by the conservatism of our people. Where were those intrepid entrepreneurs who had started a company from scratch? Was this timidness, or was it politics? In either case, I began wondering if we were in trouble.

Not that anything new is ever easy. Our company success had brought increased demands on manpower, and to help meet those demands we had added a layer of employees between the executive (Mancom) and staff levels – the principals, we called them. Some thirty-five strong, these young, well-educated, ambitious professionals with big résumés brought a new dynamic of their own to our firm. They were not happy taking orders from the Old Guard; some of them were not happy taking orders period. Standing shoulder to shoulder with Mancom members in examining, acquiring, and placing deals, the principals began wondering aloud why they could not participate in the firm's decision-making, and when they might be admitted to the Mancom. For a CEO, it is crucial to keep a sensitive finger on the pulse of the organization he presides over. I stepped up my efforts at corporate acculturation, trying to convert these recent hires to our thinking before they started influencing the rest with their own way of doing things. But the new faces were showing up faster than I could stare them down, and in the eyes of some I saw a different brand of hunger than I had seen in the first-generation executives.

As an organization, we were entering one of the dangerous phases in our history. Most companies, if they last long enough, go through three phases. The first is the entrepreneurial, the second is the transitional, and the third is the phase of the going concern. People attracted to the entrepreneurial phase tend to be like-minded dreamers who band together for the psychic rewards of creating something from nothing. People attracted to the phase of the going concern tend to be those seeking exciting, secure work in a prestigious, well-established company. But the people in the middle, the ones attracted during the transitional phase, tend to be lone wolves who think they are on the ground floor of something they can take over and bend to their own uses, and through which they can make their fortunes. This is the stage when personal expectations – the twin driving forces of self-aggrandizement and personal enrichment, enemies of institution-building – are the greatest.

My main tool for getting inside Investcorp's collective head is the system of annual appraisals submitted by every Mancom member. Toward the end of each calendar year I send out a memo requesting certain information – a critique of themselves, of me, of the firm, of every Mancom member, of each department and its work. This is the most sensitive stuff imaginable – who is doing well, who is letting the team down, issues of pay, questions about what business should and should not be pursued. The answers run to about forty pages per partner, some six hundred pages in all. I read every line of them, making notes as I go. Usually I do this in the last ten days in December, during my family's Christmas holiday. If we are in Gstaad, say, while the girls ski, shop, and relax, I get up each morning and find a quiet spot in the hotel where I can spend the day reading without interruption. My first aim is to determine the general issues that need attention. If there is a lot of duplication, several people saying the same thing, then it is clearly a serious matter. Once I have that information, I can determine what needs to be addressed in the Mancom's annual meeting in January.

But before that, over the first week of the new year, I meet individually with each Mancom member to discuss the issues raised in his or her appraisal. These meetings are as short or as long as the particular partner requires – some may be ninety minutes, while others have stretched to several hours. Whatever it takes, I am ready to give it. These one-on-one meetings provide me with the raw intelligence I need to lead the company.

Stage three of the process is the annual group meeting. This is – or was, for much of the company's history – a two-week exercise in self-analysis: Who are we? Where do we want to go? How are we going to get there? These meetings have an agenda, but it is not restrictive. We touch on everything that is going on both above and below the surface, and we do not bother much with formal or written presentations. It is a general debate, and anyone who wants to speak gets his say. If we seek opinion, I go around the table. After reading the six hundred pages of appraisals, I am well aware of what the areas of concern are, what we should improve, what is missing, what departments are at fault, so I can bring those issues into the meeting without revealing who said what in the appraisals. Those reports are seen by only Betty and me, so I have to run the meeting in a way that protects the confidentiality of the partners. The process is essentially an effort to make ourselves more competitive. We should leave that room after fifteen days with a clear vision of, and an explicit plan of action for, what we want to achieve. We should know exactly how best to use our time and talent in the year ahead.

Some of the Mancom members find this annual two-week self-cleansing exercise extremely tedious. 'Nemir,' they say, 'how can we spend all that time talking when there's so much to *do*?' My answer is that there is nothing more important than renewing and solidifying our culture. Building, maintaining, and focusing our team is what this process is all about, and planning to acquire Saks was the perfect demonstration of the power of Investcorp's style. To put that deal together, we formed a big team at short notice, pulling people in from every office and function. We are able to make decisions quickly and use group dynamics to multiply our individual strengths because there are no stars at Investcorp. If you are working on a deal and the probability of success is 80 percent while in my deal it is only 30 percent, I will drop my own deal and come to your aid if you need me. We will forgo the 30 percent for the sake of the 80 percent, because that is a better use of my time. And if we succeed, we both get the credit. If five people work on a deal, all five get the credit. There is no premium in winning a deal on your own. The important thing is to win it, no matter how many people you need to bring in, and the worst offense is to lose it because you wanted all the glory for yourself.

This is the philosophy I have preached since the beginning, and the first-generation executives adapted to it easily. The problems started when we began adding the big-résumé people at and below the Mancom level. These new executives all came from corporate cultures marked by profit centers and the consequent internal competition. Altering those attitudes takes a long time, and sometimes it does not work – the instinct for individual credit is too ingrained. The new guys want to be the stars, they want to be out in front, they want to be noticed. They fail to understand that they are getting nowhere, because I see what they are doing.

Some even try to manipulate the Mancom appraisal system. One year I noticed two suspiciously similar criticisms of Savio Tung by people who had served on one of his teams. They were petty, egregious comments, neither fair nor accurate to my mind, and they smacked of collusion. I phoned Savio and told him I wanted to fire both these employees. 'Please, Nemir,' he said, 'that's not necessary.'

'I think it is,' I said. If there is anything I cannot stand, it is office politics. I resent it and fight it wherever I find it. Our organization should play the game as one united team. Like in football, it does not matter who has the ball or makes the pass; what matters is to score.

When we all got together for the Mancom meeting that year, I took each of the offending executives aside and told them they were through. They had violated the sacred code. Both asked for a second chance, and Savio asked me to spare them, so I did. Having learned the hard way, both became valuable members of the team.

We closed the Saks deal on July 2 and were in the second phase of investor placement a month later when Iraq invaded Kuwait. Within a day, the assets of all Kuwaiti banks and Kuwait-controlled banks were frozen nearly worldwide. All Gulf-based banks faced severe funding difficulties due to sharp reductions in, or even the complete elimination of, country risk limits in the region. The Bahrain-based Arab Banking Corporation, the Gulf's largest Arab international bank, was besieged with withdrawals when the shooting began. At the request of the Governor of the Bahrain Monetary Agency (BMA), we were invited to a series of meetings to discuss Investcorp's liquidity position. War and money make for an excitable situation. We, however, were determined to stay cool and manage events rather than let them manage us. As the wider world hurled escalating threats of retaliation against Saddam's Iraq, Investcorp's senior management and lawyers met round the clock to devise a plan ensuring continuity of the company's funding. By August 6, four days after the conflict had started, we had our answer: a new corporate restructuring.

The groundwork for such a restructuring had already been laid, years before, as a reaction to the threats of the 1980–1988 Iran–Iraq war. In 1986 we had chosen from among our shareholders the twenty-five who were the most reliable, the most knowledgeable, the most confident, the most committed, and the most friendly towards Investcorp. Calling them the Group of 25, we had put their shares together in a box. Added to the percentage held by employees, this gave us increased voting power. And we had formed a holding company, owned by these trusted investors and our employees, that was incorporated in Luxembourg instead of Bahrain. So this private Luxembourg company held a majority stake in the public company in Bahrain.

The shift to Luxembourg was a protective device, one not to be activated until and unless it became necessary. If the Gulf continued to be considered at risk as a result of the conflict between Iraq and Iran, we needed an alternative base to continue our international banking relationships. To the international banking community, lending to Investcorp with a Luxembourg base would mean that we were no longer to be considered as a Gulf risk but as a European risk.

In 1989 we restructured the company again. We cancelled the Group of 25 and replaced it with a smaller Group of 20 that owned 15 percent of Investcorp. At the same time, we increased the number of shares reserved for employees, setting an upper limit of 37.5 percent. Add the 15 percent owned by G20 to the 37.5 percent reserved for employees and we had a controlling interest of 52.5 percent.

By creating this super-structure in Luxembourg we achieved three things: We privatized the company, we internationalized the company, and we secured full control. For me, the fundamental importance of this change was to assure the continuity of Investcorp – something I was determined to do.

And, of course, we were lucky, because when the Gulf War broke out in August 1990 we already had a structure in place that could protect the firm against political risk if need be. All we had to do was transfer the ownership of our assets to Luxembourg if it became necessary.

Throughout the fall, amid worldwide saber-rattling, we put the pieces in place for the new structure. In London, we made presentations to the major banks that provided us with funding. We visited the Governor of the BMA and informed him of our intentions, and he indicated his regretful understanding. I met privately with Bahrain's Minister of Finance to explain the restructuring to him, and likewise received his support on our proactive stance. At our September 19 board meeting, we placed the issue on the table for discussion, highlighting the purpose of the reorganization – to shift Investcorp's country risk to Luxembourg while retaining business operations and ultimate economic ownership of all of Investcorp's assets in Investcorp Bank EC, Bahrain. The board heartily approved the move, after which I sent a letter to the BMA Governor informing him of the board's action and attaching a copy of the Restructuring Memorandum.

The corporate restructuring plan was fully implemented on November 1, 1990.

Thinking we had the situation under control, I turned my attention to internal matters. On November 10, I sent out my annual call for Mancom appraisals. The memo was divided into six parts: the manager's rating of his own 1990 tangible results ('Please provide an analytical assessment on how you rate your Return on Time and Return on Expenses'); his evaluation of the performance of the firm during the year ('In your judgment, how do you think the annual bonus pool should be allocated in 1990?'); a peer assessment ('I need your careful assessment of each of your fourteen partners' strengths and weaknesses ...'); the CEO assessment ('Please rate the CEO's effectiveness based on the following criteria ...'); the manager's planned business mission/objectives for the coming year; and, finally, his vision for the company ('What kind of a firm do you want Investcorp to develop into; our corporate mission and corporate character throughout this decade ...?').

A week later, I issued my first memo regarding the annual Mancom meeting, tentatively scheduled for January 13–29, 1991, in Bahrain. That turned out to be wishful thinking. By early December it was clear that the Gulf was too volatile a place to count on, so we changed the venue to Geneva, February 2–18.

In these unsettled circumstances, I regarded the arrival of the Mancom appraisals with the silent comfort one generally associates with predictable events like the changing of the seasons. Reading them, I felt grounded by the issues raised, even though some of them were completely unfounded:

- 'This year's significant achievements must be tempered with caution ...'
- 'On the business side, the major concerns are with risk diversification.'
- 'Because of our lax approach, we have failed to complete our Asset Sales Program ...'
- 'The firm is divided within itself and it has never been more poised for a fall.'
- 'Some partners cannot sublimate their egos and they are stepping all over other partners.'
- 'We are understaffed in four of our most strategic areas.'
- 'I feel that we continue to be weak as a firm, and vulnerable, in the area of post-acquisition management.'
- 'I am concerned about the growing size of the firm.'
- 'I recommend that we not add additional positions to the Management Committee.'
- 'There seem to be two separate Management Committees in the firm: the broad Mancom of 14 members, and then an inner-Mancom of Nemir, Mike, and Elie.'
- 'Our administrative functions seem to continue to grow.'
- 'We seem to be less bottom-up and more top-down oriented than we were in the past.'
- 'I would like to make a comment on the method by which executives depart the firm. In the past, most of the departures have been under strained circumstances ...'
- 'During the realization process we discovered how badly some of our deals were structured and how poorly some of them were managed.'
- 'So far we have been lucky, but we shouldn't depend on Mother Luck.'
- 'Overheads and expenses are still high.'
- 'Communication has weakened this year.'
- 'There should be a system of distributing vital information at the dealmakers level ...'
- 'We're overconfident ... referring to our past success as "the

recipe" without realizing that the real world and economy are ever changing ...'
- 'Lack of common goals and thoughts ...'

For a moment, this totally extraordinary year felt like business as usual.

As I say, I welcomed receiving such views and comments from Mancom members year after year, irrespective of whether the content was positive or negative, accurate or inaccurate. I was happy that everyone had had a chance to express himself candidly, bluntly, and without fear or restriction. At my one-on-one meeting with each member, I would discuss each point and make sure that inaccuracies and misconceptions were completely removed. On the other hand, any point that had validity was dealt with at the general, all-hands meetings so that we could make the necessary changes or improvements going forward. Most important – always – was that everyone left those annual meetings fully convinced, fully satisfied, fully committed. As John Thompson said, 'When we leave these meetings, everyone's tank is full in terms of culture, enthusiasm, and commitment.' And that was exactly the purpose of those long sessions. I always felt that this annual process, unique to Investcorp, was well worth the effort. It certainly reinforced our corporate culture.

In the early hours of January 17, 1991, Baghdad time, the US-led coalition unleashed a massive air attack against Iraqi targets. Saddam had failed to pull his troops out of Kuwait by the UN's January 15 deadline, so the coalition was given the green light to force them out. The mission was called Operation Desert Storm.

I was in London, now unable to travel internationally because of my Iraqi passport, but Mike and a skeleton crew were holding the fort at the Bahrain office. On January 17 they published the first of what would become weeks of Situation Reports, or 'Sitreps':

I Personnel. Essential staff only worked today. General Services coverage this afternoon: Faisal & Saleh. Tomorrow: Jaffar & Mohamed.

Ed, Toni, Eden Underwood and Zahid Zakiuddin left Bahrain last night as confirmed early this morning. Current status: MIA. No news received in Bahrain or London office.

II Premises/Equipment: All OK. Computer A/C temporarily out this morning.

III Positions: Spot FX and Money Market squared today and tomorrow. Monday is a holiday in New York. I will be in Friday around 12:30 to confirm activity and balances for EC accounts with BTC NY and MHT NY.

IV Airport: Closed

V US Embassy Advisory: Unchanged.

I holed up at the London office monitoring events in Bahrain – and effects in New York – while coalition jets and Scud missiles fought it out on CNN in the background. But for all this intense focus on Operation Desert Storm, the war I expected was not the one I got.

On January 16, the day before the coalition retaliation on Iraq, a letter from the Director of Banking Controls of the Bahrain Monetary Agency, addressed to me, was received at my Bahrain office. The Director insisted that the BMA had given no approvals regarding Investcorp's restructuring and, furthermore, the BMA threatened to impose 'all relevant sanctions' on Investcorp because of the transfer of assets without the Agency's approval. In closing, the Director 'strongly urge[d]' us to suspend any further action on the restructuring and to get in touch with the BMA immediately to discuss the matter.

Informed of the letter by Mike and Sal Abbasi, general manager of the Bahrain office, I made calls to the board and arranged for Mike and Sal to meet with several board members to get their input and advice. In the meantime, on January 18, I wrote to the BMA's Governor acknowledging receipt of the Director's letter, which I criticized harshly: 'The form, the tone and the substance of the letter unfortunately is shocking and disappointing. We are accused of incorrect actions. We feel that such an accusation is regrettable, most unfair, and inappropriate ...'

The ensuing events remain one of the most baffling episodes in Investcorp's history. Mike and Sal and other representatives of the firm increasingly found themselves in meetings with badgering, accusatory BMA officials who demonstrated no interest in hearing Investcorp's defense of itself or, in fact, even in spelling out the Agency's specific grievances against us.

All the while, I was marooned in London and the Bahrain office was besieged by the fallout from a real shooting war.

Sitrep for January 20, 1991:

I Personnel: ELU & family, and ZZ surfaced in London after being detoured via Nairobi ...

IV Airport: Continues to be closed indefinitely. No news on resumption of commercial flights.

V US Embassy Advisory: Gas masks issued Saturday to US passport holders …

VI Air raid warnings: Two Friday, two Saturday …

On January 23, I issued another note to the Mancom: 'Given the prevailing circumstances, the Management Committee meeting previously scheduled to occur in Geneva between February 2 and February 18 is cancelled. The current plan is for the Mancom to conduct a three-day meeting in London on February 8–10 …'

I also wrote again to the Governor, this time taking exception to the BMA's tone and substance in the first meeting between the Agency and representatives of Investcorp. The Governor responded, granting a second meeting to be held a few days later.

Sitrep for January 23, 1991:

I Personnel: Following people successfully departed Bahrain aboard Gulf Air flight to Muscat: Andrew Osmond, Tony D'Souza's family, Betty Pires's two children accompanied by Loy D'Souza.

II Premises/Equipment: New front door lock installed …

IV Airport: Gulf Air reportedly expanding daily flights in/out of Bahrain to three.

V US Embassy Advisory: 9 more US citizens elected to fly out via military transport this evening, totaling 16 to date.

VI Scud Missile Warning: 17:50 yesterday. Staff still at Investcorp House followed emergency retreat procedures until 'all clear' signal sounded on Radio Bahrain …

The next meeting with the BMA was, if anything, more aggressive than the one before. The Director of Banking Controls complained of supposed instances of our non-compliance going back to 1987. When we objected – the charges were both untrue and irrelevant to the current matter – he threatened a vague series of 'investigative' meetings.

Once again I wrote to the Governor, telling him how and why the meeting had been unproductive, and asking him to please let us know exactly what the BMA needed from us in regard to the reorganization. We also flew in our legal adviser for the restructuring, Peter Baumbusch of the Washington office of Gibson, Dunn & Crutcher. He would be in Bahrain for weeks.

On and on it went like this, letters flying back and forth like missiles, lawyers conferring, officials speaking in circular logic. The episode lasted longer than Operation Desert Storm, well into spring, and resulted in a seemingly malicious on-site audit requiring documents previously flown out of the country at the outbreak of war. Once the papers were returned to Bahrain, at great effort and expense, no one from the BMA showed much interest in seeing them.

Sitrep for February 7, 1991:

II Premises/Equipment: Nine small gas masks were obtained for staff dependants aged 10 through 16, and distributed this afternoon. Smaller masks for younger dependants are still on order but not yet available …

After a winter of combat, the healing power of the English countryside is especially welcome. On a late April day in 1991 we left the noise of London behind and drove south-west into the New Forest, the motorway becoming a tunnel of oak and beech before opening out into green rolling farm-land. As we approached the south coast, we veered sharply left and were soon passing through wrought-iron gates to an ivy-clad manor house set in immaculate grounds. This was Chewton Glen, for the next twelve days our home away from home. This was where the Mancom – and, on day nine, the principals as well – would gather en masse to review the extraordinary events of the year just past.

As I said earlier, we had Mancom meetings every year; I include details of this one at Chewton Glen by way of offering an inside view of our annual process. Chewton Glen itself was no more or less important than any other in our history – unless you consider that it took place at the height of the pressure exerted on the organization by the principals, and it was the first Mancom meeting to which the principals were invited. In that sense, it might be viewed as a turning point.

Our meetings always begin with cocktails and then a long, lively dinner. With spirited storytelling and hearty laughter, it always has the sound of a family get-together. At my end of the table at Chewton Glen, Bill Flanz – my former boss at Chase, now a member of the Mancom – was telling me about the whitewater rafting program offered by Outward Bound: self-awareness for business executives, no books, no radio, no human contact for eight whole days, just the rafting instructor and an onboard psychiatrist. 'I want all our people to do this!' I said. 'We spend all our time in offices, we need a wider perspective!'

I will admit that I sometimes like to stir things up, but an element of this struck a real chord. Were we becoming complacent? A little too fat and comfortable? People were starting to pay attention, so I turned it up a notch. 'We're getting too wise, too experienced. I don't like all this *wisdom*! We know the ropes now so we tend to play it safe. I want us to be bolder, take risks, go where we've never been before! Too much knowledge, too much analysis – this can hold you back, you end up going nowhere. If we'd been wise enough to see all the problems, we'd never have started this company!'

From down the table Elie muttered, 'I am *not* going on a raft.' Everyone laughed.

At a certain point in these evenings, I stand and clink my glass to get everyone's attention. This is the moment I love, this instant of boundless promise when all these colleagues are first together again from the far corners. In the days ahead, there will inevitably be disagreement and the occasional harsh word, but not tonight. Tonight, this moment, is for celebrating the common bond that has brought us together, year after year for nearly a decade, around a bounteous table just such as this.

'Let's be open and frank with each other,' I said that first night at Chewton Glen, setting what I hoped would be the tone of the days to come. 'Let's renew our friendship. As usual, there'll be no agenda. Let's discuss everything, and draw on each other for support and advice. That's how we can use our collective strength. This year profits may be down. Nevertheless, the important thing is to know where we're going, decide what we want to achieve, and make it happen. Now let's go around the table. Everyone say what they expect from this meeting.'

This is and always has been the process for Mancom meetings: Everyone gets a say on every issue, and nobody interrupts until everyone has spoken. You cannot opt out, you cannot pass your turn to the next person. Once everyone has said his piece, if there are wide differences of opinion I will throw it open to general discussion and then we will go around the table again ... and again ... and again, if necessary. I never go by majority rule; I want everyone to realize the facts, to see eye to eye. You cannot go forward as a house divided.

On this first night at Chewton Glen, the bedrock sentiment about the coming sessions was: It's about time. Many spoke eloquently on the subject, but John Thompson spun out a metaphor after my own heart: 'These meetings,' he said, 'are our refueling station. This is where we pump some gas into the motor. But we've been running on empty for months, we're way out in the desert and the last gas station is a hundred miles back. If we don't fill up now, we'll break down.'

I could not have agreed more. And now it was time to wrap it up, to give them something to sleep on. 'Remember,' I said, 'this week we meet as owners. I will coordinate and not dictate. I'll bow to logic. Let's speak up and not be afraid to disagree. But on Friday, when the principals join us, there must be unity. As owners we can debate or even disagree, but when we leave this place we must act as executives. We must assume responsibilities and carry them out.'

At Investcorp's inception, I used to say that starting a company requires four talents: vision (someone has to have the idea in the first place); foundation (some founder must translate the original idea into reality); management (someone needs to take responsibility for that company's operation, setting goals and marshaling resources to achieve them, ensuring growth and profitability); and leadership (someone must point the way and steer that company into the future, ensuring its constant evolution so it remains strong and viable, assuming acceptable risks for achieving target results).

The culture of a company is its essence. Once a company exists, a visionary CEO must look both forward and backward – must always keep in mind the total picture of his organization's past and future. To me, the key challenge is how to keep our fundamental mission and culture unchanged while being flexible and opportunistic enough to evolve and progress and maintain our competitive advantage.

Over the days of our Chewton Glen meetings, we discussed many topics, including the hard issues that surfaced in the corporate assessments. The recession was a constant backdrop to our talks. It had hurt several of our acquisitions and there were divergent views on what to do about – and how long to stay with – those troubled companies. I made an impassioned case for staying the course. 'So this is a difficult year,' I began. 'But is it more difficult than 1984? Then we had nothing, now we're strong. Every year since we began has been difficult, but we've gone on doing better and better. A difficulty, to us, is a challenge to be overcome. Remember, we're businessmen. We're entrepreneurs. We take risks. Most of us, it's true, once used to be employees, but we gave up that quiet life in favor of this one. Why? Because we like to assume risks and solve problems.

'So some of our companies are sick. Are we going to complain about that? A doctor doesn't complain because he has patients. If no one got sick, he'd be out of business. And that's what we are, a corporate doctor. In fact, we at Investcorp are *surgeons*. We're famous, we're the best, so we get the most difficult cases. Some of the patients do not survive – that can't be helped. Others, like Tiffany, make spectacular recoveries. Their cure is headline news, like the latest feat in heart surgery.

'Right now, some of our patients are in intensive care. They might make it, they might not. To help them pull through, we're giving them our entire focus and attention, and they aren't ready to leave our care. But others are showing improvements, and some are as well as they'll ever be. There's not much more we can do for them, so we should send them on their way, whether their health is perfect or not.

'This is our situation today, in 1991. And it will always be so, because this is the business we chose to be in. We're surgeons. Our patients are the unwell.'

It was a speech from the heart. It reflected exactly how I feel about our business.

We also talked about the principals. Their impending arrival at this session was in itself an acknowledgment that things were different, that Investcorp was growing much more complex. We had to deal with that fact in any number of ways, including managerially, financially, and emotionally.

At the Chewton Glen meeting, Linda Cates was the only person hired as a principal who had been promoted and welcomed into the Mancom. In fact, this was her first official Mancom meeting, and now the morale of the principals was the subject on the table. Spirits were said to be low among them, due to their burning desire to also be admitted to the Mancom. But the Mancom was already too big. 'I'll deal with it when they get here,' I said.

Managing expectations is a big part of a CEO's job – in my case, both with staff *and* clients. Once, on one of my periodic goodwill trips through the Gulf to touch base with clients, I heard about an ex-client of ours who was so unhappy with Investcorp that he had become the main source of adverse publicity against us. I decided to go and visit him. My colleagues, afraid I might face an unhappy confrontation, tried to dissuade me. Undeterred, I insisted on paying the man a visit.

My partners and I were cordially received with tea and polite talk. When I saw that the man did not wish to open the subject, I initiated the conversation, saying I had heard he was unhappy with Investcorp. The gentleman responded that of course he was unhappy – he had invested with us in four deals and all had ended in losses.

Whereupon I explained our model to him: We did not offer a general fund, I said, only investments on a deal-by-deal basis. Each deal is presented to the client, who chooses whether or not to invest and if so by what amount. I then explained that by that time Investcorp had completed approximately forty deals, of which some had ended up as stars, with internal rates of return of 40 percent per annum or more. Others had achieved average results, generally 15 to 25 percent per annum. And then, yes, we had lost in almost eight transactions.

When we acquire an investment, I said, we study its past and make predictions on its future based on certain assumptions. We do our best to protect the investment during the post-acquisition management. Inevitably, at the time of realization and exit, some deals turn out to be better than expected, and others worse.

I then turned to our host. 'Sir,' I said, 'if you chose only to invest in four deals that ended up in losses, you must be a very gifted person. We should review with you every deal, and if you like it, we should avoid that investment, given your talent to choose the worst.'

Naturally, the man was not happy to hear this, but I thought it was exactly what he needed to hear. The next time he started to say bad things about Investcorp, maybe he would remember that his losses had been *his* choice.

Now it was time for the principals to receive their own dose of reality. When they arrived, I told them the story of starting the company, the exhilarating experience of building the bridge between investors in the Gulf and investment opportunities in the West. I told them of the sacrifices and risks we all took. I told them Investcorp was like a fine watch that works because every piece in it, no matter how tiny, does its job, and if it stops doing that job the watch stops working. I told them teamwork was our core belief and if that did not suit them they should not stay, because they would only be unhappy. I told them I never wanted to hear anyone say 'I did it' rather than 'We did it.' I told them about the important balance between financial and psychic income, the latter being growth as a person – both of which Investcorp was prepared to offer, but which they had to earn. I told them Linda Cates had not been waiting around hoping to be promoted; a slot opened and I had a need for someone with just her skills to help advise me. I told them never to ask me for titles, but rather for the tools to do the jobs they had – that was the kind of talk I understood and responded to. I told them I hoped Investcorp would not get much bigger in size and that we should be extremely careful with each new appointment, because a large organization would risk our culture. I told them no good firm would ever under-use its resources. I told them to enjoy the reflected glory of the firm. 'We,' I said, 'all of us, are the stars.'

Was this meeting successful? Yes, in several important ways. Some principals, now realizing they were unsuited to Investcorp's culture, left the firm. For the ones who stayed, we made adjustments to buttress their roles. We pushed the decision-making process as far down in the organization as possible, sometimes to the Mancom subcommittees on which principals also sat. The business units began holding their own first-of-the-year meetings, and their Mancom members then attended the Mancom as representatives of those business units. Perhaps most helpful, we took the example of Chewton Glen and formalized the inclusion of the principals for a few days at some of the future Mancom meetings. With this came their own one-on-one with the

CEO prior to the open meeting, just as the Mancom members had always had.

Those were the official results of the principals' coming to Chewton Glen. But by far the most important development was something nobody saw, at least for a while. These new people had come in with their blazing energy and burning desire at the precise time I was feeling a sense of weariness – not just personally, though that was certainly the case, but also in terms of the firm itself. I had been half serious about Outward Bound and whitewater rafting. I knew we needed something, anything, to revitalize and reinvent us, to make us fresh and unproven again, to challenge us anew.

9
IL MONDO DEL BELLO

At the heart of every business is a story about people and their aspirations. But in no case I know of has the raw parade of human emotions, including pride, jealousy, self-delusion, arrogance, revenge, deceit – as well as true brilliance and vision – matched that of the famous Italian luxury-goods company Gucci. We acquired half of Gucci in 1987 and for the next eight years found ourselves playing parts in a melodrama worthy of Puccini. I've chosen to present the story of the Gucci deal in some detail because of its impact on Investcorp and our investing clients – and also because I had to devote my full-time energy to directing this deal to its conclusion. While at one point it was considered by some to be a write-off, it ended among our most significant winners. But not without becoming a true test of nerves.

The Gucci story begins in England in the waning years of the nineteenth century. A young Italian immigrant from Florence named Guccio Gucci manages to land a job at London's chic Savoy Hotel, and there he has an epiphany. Even from his own low-paid position, Guccio cannot help noticing the finery of the hotel's well-heeled guests – the elegant fabrics of their clothing, the sensuous silk of their scarves and cravats, and especially (since Guccio hails from one of the leatherworking capitals of Europe) the unmistakable presence of their luggage. With every new arrival, bellboys roll in carts groaning with massive embossed steamer trunks, suitcases hand-tooled with monograms and family crests, and hatboxes stacked like so many wedding cakes. But Guccio's epiphany goes beyond recognizing that wealthy people like nice things. His real insight, the one that would launch a legendary brand, is that possessions can be advertisements for affluence and high taste.

After a few more years abroad – during which he also worked for Wagons-Lits, the sleeping car company, refining his knowledge of wealthy travelers and the things they carry to tell others who they are when they are away from home – Guccio Gucci returned to Florence, got married, and started a family. He and his wife, Aida, had three sons together: Aldo (born in 1905), Vasco (1907), and Rodolfo (1912).

Guccio eventually entered the leather business and began learning the basics. In time his company promoted him to manager. After World War I he moved to a leather-crafts firm called Franzi, where he was to receive the equivalent of an advanced degree in the fine art of leatherwork – selecting, curing, tanning, and cutting different types and grades of leather. When Franzi asked Guccio to run their Rome store, he went alone because Aida did not want to leave Florence with her young boys. But Guccio kept his eye peeled for a chance to open his own business back home. In 1921, during a Sunday walk with Aida, he found the perfect space – a vacant store for rent in one of the best areas of Florence. Soon Valigeria Guccio Gucci, the first store in the company's complex history, was open for business.

Guccio's strategy was to buy or commission fine leather pieces from Tuscan, English, and German manufacturers and sell them to the wealthy tourists who regularly arrived to soak up Florence's classical ambience. Guccio likely thought of his products as an extension of this world of art, beauty, and refinement. As Sara Gay Forden says in her comprehensive book *The House of Gucci* – for which several Investcorp executives, including me, were interviewed at length – Guccio Gucci 'aspired to elegance himself and was always impeccably dressed in fine shirts and crisply pressed suits.' Forden quotes his son Aldo as saying, 'He was a man of great taste, which we all inherited. His imprint was on every item he sold.'

This, then, was the template – beautiful things for beautiful people – that Guccio Gucci devised for the luxury-goods firm that carried his name. Some six decades later it was the template Guccio's grandson Maurizio yearned to return to after his cousins had cheapened the brand by stamping the hallowed GG logo on key chains and coffee mugs the world over. '*Il mondo del bello*,' Maurizio would say, describing to us at Investcorp that ephemeral place where *his* beloved Gucci belonged: '*Il mondo del bello*' – 'the world of the beautiful.' And he was absolutely right.

The Gucci story is so convoluted that it requires volumes to do it justice. Between Guccio Gucci's founding of the company and Investcorp's involvement with Maurizio Gucci in resurrecting it, the narrative reads like something from that other famous Florentine, Niccolò Machiavelli: Guccio's three sons go into the business, the dreamer Rodolfo only after trying his hand at movie acting (with the screen name Maurizio D'Ancora). Aldo becomes the second-generation business mastermind, spearheading the growth of Gucci outlets in Europe, America, and Asia, while Vasco oversees production and Rodolfo runs the Milan store and designs the company's most expensive handbags. Aldo fathers three sons – Giorgio, Paolo, and Roberto; Vasco has no children; Rodolfo has a single son, to whom he gives the name that had carried his dreams of stardom – Maurizio. Aldo moves to New York, leaving his brothers back in Italy sometimes rolling their eyes at his increasingly grandiose ideas (and expenditure) for growing the company. Guccio dies, followed by Vasco, leaving Aldo and Rodolfo as fifty-fifty owners of the company.

As Aldo's sons come of age, he carves out 10 percent of his stake and gives each boy 3.333 percent; Maurizio, much younger than Aldo's sons, is still in school. The company starts creating separate divisions to keep each of Aldo's sons gainfully employed – a perfume division, a 'boutique' division (with lower-priced products designed by Giorgio and his wife), a watch division, an 'accessories' division, a wholesale division. Aldo and his sons become resentful of Rodolfo's 50 percent ownership in the 'mother company,' and Aldo devises a plan to steer more and more profits through the perfume division, of which Rodolfo owns only 20 percent. Paolo, reporting to Rodolfo in Italy, feels creatively stifled by Rodolfo and launches a barrage of written critiques that prompts Rodolfo to fire Paolo and send him to New York to work with his father. Paolo and the increasingly autocratic Aldo soon have their own falling-out, which leads to lawsuits – lawsuits to go along with the scores of other lawsuits Gucci must file annually against counterfeiters, who find the pens and lighters and tote bags of the accessories division easy pickings. (As Forden writes in *The House of Gucci,* the launch of Gucci's accessories collection 'represents the moment Gucci lost control over the "quality" factor in the business.')

In one lawsuit Paolo accuses Aldo of income tax evasion – a charge the authorities find is true – and the dapper Aldo, by now in his early eighties, goes to prison for a year and a day.

Against this backdrop enters, finally, a grown-up Maurizio Gucci. When we first met him, Maurizio, age thirty-nine, had inherited his late father's 50 percent of Guccio Gucci – the Italian part of the empire, not to be confused with Gucci America. Gucci America was separate – except that it bought all its products from the Italian Gucci. This would one day become a pivotal distinction in our dealings with Maurizio, but for the moment that was all in the hazy, far-off future.

We met in London in September 1987, thrown together by a mutual friend at Morgan Stanley, Andrea Morante, who knew that (a) Maurizio wanted someone to help him buy out his uncle and cousins, and (b) we were the only investment firm on the planet likely to even consider such a mission. We took this as a high compliment. We tend to put a premium on 'heart' both in our company and in those we acquire. And Maurizio Gucci had nothing if not heart.

In fact he wore it on the sleeve of his impeccably tailored Italian jackets. There was always something mesmerizingly childlike about Maurizio, an unabashed dreamer who spun whole worlds out of wishes and hopes – and who had charm enough to entangle even hard-nosed realists in his visions. He was not dishonest – that was my conviction. Others at Investcorp were not so sure, but I think their uncertainty stemmed from their inability to understand a man of artistic talent and vision. Maurizio was someone who had always lived with his head in the clouds. Before Rodolfo, his father, died, he asked his lawyer and longtime confidant Domenico De Sole to assume stewardship of Maurizio's Gucci shares. Rodolfo felt sure his son would squander it all and end up bankrupt. De Sole declined to take on that task per se, though he did agree to Maurizio's request that he move to New York and run Gucci America when all the fighting with the cousins was going on. Few people knew Maurizio like Domenico De Sole did. At a particularly tough time in our own Maurizio dealings, De Sole told us, 'You don't understand the life he's had and his perception of the world. He grew up with so much money that he has no real sense of value.'

Maurizio looked like a movie star – tall and trim, chiseled chin, longish hair, perennial tan. When he walked into our office that first time, his charisma was palpable. Perhaps we were somewhat star-struck – here was the personification of a legendary name, an elegant brand in the elegant flesh. He got right to the point: He wanted to acquire the other 50 percent owned by his uncle and cousins, which would have to be done in secret because 'they would rather burn their shares than sell them to me.' Almost physically sickened by the cheapening of the Gucci image, Maurizio outlined both a clear vision for a revived Gucci and a solid strategy for making it happen. In product lines, he would return to the company's traditional strengths – bags; ties, scarves, and silk products; ready-to-wear men's clothing; women's gifts and accessories; and those famous Gucci shoes – but updated for a new era.

Beyond that, Maurizio preached the importance of consistency. From the atmosphere in the shops to the way the products were presented to the manner in which they were sold to the customer, everything had to be consistent – all around the world. Each of the cousins, given his own territory and allowed to do his own thing, had done it inconsistently. So there were different advertising campaigns and different merchandising strategies, and, of course, each cousin had become a 'designer' in his own right. As a result, the overall collection had completely lost focus and common identity.

It all made perfect sense to us. Then Maurizio said, essentially: 'By the way, there are some things you should know . . .' And he proceeded to tick off a few facts that could have made us run for the nearest exit. His shares in Gucci Italy had been sequestered by the courts because his cousins had accused him of forging his name on his father's will to avoid paying taxes (Maurizio had no doubt that he would eventually get his shares back). Another problem was that he could not set foot in Italy at the moment because there was a warrant out for his arrest – something about a boat he had bought, on which one of his advisers had told him to fly the

Panamanian flag, which turned out to be an infringement of the rules for the export of capital. In his absence, Gucci Italy was ostensibly being run by court-appointed custodians, but in fact 'I have my insiders there who're really running the business for me.' Also, Maurizio and his cousins were presently engaged in about ten cross-lawsuits going in every imaginable direction. As for the Gucci group worldwide – this umbrella name covering some half a dozen individual companies – 'there are no consolidated financial statements.'

The only good news we heard was that Maurizio had approached his cousin Paolo about selling his shares, and they had a deal. 'Within that context,' Maurizio said, 'would you be prepared to help me?'

Incredibly, inexplicably, we would. Our justification was our gut belief in the viability of the Gucci brand. All the other problems aside, Maurizio's strategy was sound – to streamline the product range dramatically, to give it more depth and less breadth, to unify the Gucci message around its historic strengths. 'Unless we do that,' he told us, 'Gucci will die. In fact, the GG symbol is so debased it's already dying. On the other hand, I am convinced the world will move back to the "pleasure of possession" in the decades ahead. That's what will drive the customer.'

In the ensuing months, working in secret under the in-house code name 'Project Saddle' (so named for the myth, created by Aldo, that his Gucci ancestors had been saddle makers to medieval courts – hence the products evoking such 'horsey' symbols as linked stirrup and horse-bit hardware, and green-and-red webbing from girth straps), we set out to forge basic agreements with Maurizio and devise a plan for acquiring the desired shares. Paul Dimitruk headed up the team, supported by Rick Swanson. For Cem, whom I had reassigned to London in mid-1986 in order to spearhead a Corporate Investment Europe (CIE) effort to match the already successful Corporate Investment North America (CINA), Gucci was a major piece of business, though he was not engaged in the day-to-day activities. On the other hand, Elie, as our Chief Financial Officer, was very involved in the Gucci decision-making.

I too found myself more involved in this deal than usual, and Rick Swanson later shared his observations on this with an in-house interviewer: 'Maurizio had a very strange relationship with his father, who was perhaps too domineering, too protective of him. Then for some reason that I cannot explain, Nemir assumed a sort of father-figure role in his life. Anyway, Maurizio felt a very close kinship with Nemir. He felt above all else that he could always trust him.'

Mutual trust was vital, and in the beginning we each made gestures to strengthen that trust. With Maurizio the Investcorp team hammered out a Security Agreement providing for his buying back the first two tranches of shares from us if we failed to acquire the entire 50 percent – but after the first two tranches, we were unprotected. On the other hand, he showed his trust of us by tendering his shares in Gucci America, worth some $100 million, for security. He actually handed us the shares and we put them in our own safe. We also signed a Heads of Agreement covering two main principles: One, once we had acquired the shares, both parties would consolidate joint shareholdings within a single global holding company; and two, we would eventually take the company public. This was our preferred exit strategy.

It took us eighteen months to buy the first 15 percent from the cousins. Paul, a skillful tactician in whom I had great faith, managed to maintain secrecy even while involving some forty-five people in ten or fifteen outside firms to help us. We used Morgan Stanley as a front in buying, sometimes having both Maurizio and Morgan Stanley bidding at the same time. Because he was Italian, Andrea Morante did most of the bargaining for us, and Morgan Stanley actually bought the shares – another instance of trust. While we indemnified them against risk, there was precious little indemnification for ourselves. In 1987, our net worth was around $150 million, and here we were paying $40 million for the first tranche of shares and another $40 million for the second. But we also trusted ourselves – trusted that somehow we would find a way to make this turn out all right.

The day we bought Aldo's shares was a momentous occasion, and a little sad as well. The meeting took place in Geneva, and Paul, Rick, and our attorneys from Gibson, Dunn & Crutcher took the same plane from New York as Aldo and his advisers (though they went first class while our people sat in business). Rick said the flight was kind of awkward: Here was Aldo, this intensely proud man who could not understand why his sons had sold the shares he had given them, but they had left him no choice. Now here he was on the same plane with the people who were about to buy out his life's work.

Aldo had insisted that before he released his shares, the money had to be wired to his account and confirmation given to him over the phone. So the two sides were sitting at a long table facing each another, and there, between them, were Aldo's shares. Our lawyers were nervous, fearing that once the phone call came saying the money was in the bank, Aldo's men would grab the shares and run. The atmosphere was that tense. The shares had not been signed over yet, and in Italy one does not get actual title until the signature is on the paper.

The phone rang. Rick picked it up and was told the money had arrived. He handed the phone to Aldo's adviser, who listened and then said to Aldo, 'The money's there.' For a moment there was dead silence. Nobody seemed to know what to do. Suddenly Aldo reached toward the shares – at which point one of our lawyers, an ex-football player, launched himself across the table, but not fast enough to stop Aldo from picking up the shares. Aldo stepped back somewhat surprised, then walked over to Paul Dimitruk and handed him the shares. Aldo then made a speech about a man and his life, about building a company, about how he was giving away his child and trusted that it was now in good hands.

Champagne was popped and everyone had a glass. Then Paul also made a speech in which he talked about Aldo in the warmest and most generous terms. By this time Aldo was in tears, because this really was the end of his life. After the toasts and the speeches, he and his advisers put on their black hats and overcoats and walked in silence out through the big oak door.

Our people stood for a long moment looking at one another, not quite knowing what to say. For them too, this was an end – the end of the beginning.

Suddenly they heard a knock at the door. They opened it and there, again, was Aldo. 'The taxi hasn't turned up,' he said, taking off his hat. 'May I come in and make a phone call?'

If we had known then what we know now, we would have recognized this as an example of what might be called Gucci's Law: Whenever you think something is over, you had better think again.

Maurizio got his shares back in the fall of 1989, and then in short order three things happened. First, at a meeting at Investcorp, I waived the clause in the Heads of Agreement that said Maurizio would be owner while a professional CEO was brought in to run the business. At the end of that meeting, Maurizio was effectively Gucci's CEO. There were some people inside Investcorp who thought I had caved in to Maurizio's considerable charm, but I believed in Maurizio's vision and told people to let him do what he wanted. Not only did I trust his instincts for revitalizing the company, I felt that if his name was on the door Gucci would be in better hands than ever before.

The second thing that happened was that I had to pull Paul Dimitruk off the Gucci assignment. After Investcorp bought the cousins' shares and we and Maurizio each owned 50 percent of the company, Paul tried to introduce some corporate governance into the deal in order to define each party's rights. It was soon brought to my attention that in the course of these negotiations Paul had made what I considered to be errors in judgment that resulted in Investcorp's losing leverage. I liked Paul and wanted to save both him and Investcorp. He had done a great job in negotiating the purchase of the shares, but now he was becoming emotionally involved in Gucci, so I took him off it.

Paul later told Rick Swanson that he had perhaps 'gone native,' meaning that he had started identifying too much with the culture he was supposed to be overseeing. It turned out that Maurizio had even asked Paul to come to work for him – always a dangerous sign. During our meeting, Paul asked if he could work for Maurizio as vice chairman on a secondment basis. Absolutely not, I said. I then assigned him to a project in Geneva, but in a matter of months he decided to leave the firm. To take care of Gucci, I appointed Andrea Morante, who had since come to work for Investcorp. Then Andrea wanted to go to work for Gucci, too – everyone was falling in love with Maurizio. My ultimate solution was to assign our toughest, most hard-nosed, most no-nonsense negotiator to the case: Bob Glaser.

After a couple months of working with Bob, Maurizio came to see me in New York. 'These guys of yours are driving me nuts,' he said. 'The recession is coming, sales are poor, and our expenses are rising. What can I do?'

'Look, Maurizio,' I said, having listened to all his reasons for the skyrocketing expenses, 'deep in my heart I trust and like you, but I have an institution I have to run as a business, and I must work through my people. We want to get out, so why not buy us out? You'll then own one hundred percent of the company and can run it the way you want.' I told him I agreed with his vision of taking the company's image upscale again, but it would take five years or more to achieve it. If I was his private partner, I would see it out to the end.

But Investcorp had invested its clients' money in Gucci, and those clients were not happy seeing their investment declining in value. They wanted a return.

Maurizio very much liked the idea of 100 percent ownership and agreed to buy Investcorp's half of the company. This was the third big thing that happened. We settled on a price of $300 million, plus a $25-million fee – a nice profit on the $200 million we had spent on the cousins' shares and our expenses in acquiring them. Maurizio and I both signed off on those numbers. It was December 1989.

I was satisfied with this turn of events, and the following month I called a meeting in Bahrain with Bob, Elie, and Rick. Our first and foremost priority, I told them, was helping Maurizio buy us out. We immediately dispatched Rick Swanson to New York to search for financing. He was to stay there for as long as it took.

The problem with selling 50 percent of Gucci was that the big banks were not swayed by Maurizio Gucci's name or charm or vision; they wanted to see hard numbers, projections based on facts, a serious business plan – none of which existed. So before we could generate interest, we first had to fill in the blanks.

Rick spent months in the New York office preparing what is called a Bank Information Memorandum – essentially a complete dossier of a company being offered for sale. Preparing it involved collecting information from all around the world and piecing everything together – the history, the operations, and so on – in order to present Gucci to the banking community as the global group of Maurizio's intentions. The finished Memorandum reached four hundred pages, which was probably much too long to be useful.

We never could secure the financing for Maurizio to buy us out. His projections seemed optimistic, and his management decisions – such as shutting down wholesale and all the downmarket products and outlets before building up something to replace them – struck bankers as suspicious at best. 'Interesting strategy,' a guy at Bankers Trust said to Rick. 'But why would you want to cut so much of your sales?'

As a result of the failure of achieving the financing with the help of Investcorp, Maurizio decided he would secure the financing himself – but first he insisted on a contract committing Investcorp to sell him the company on the terms previously agreed upon. A new agreement, incorporating what would turn out to be crucial changes, was signed between Investcorp and Maurizio in January 1991.

When Maurizio's efforts at securing the financing also collapsed, he tried to backpedal out of the new contract – the situation had changed since we had signed it, he argued. But Bob stood his ground. 'We're joint owners now,' he told Maurizio, 'and both sides must act according to our original Heads of Agreement. We will now put all our shares – yours and ours – into one vehicle.' Maurizio was livid. To him, the idea of sharing power with a bunch of investment bankers was almost as bad as working with his cousins.

Forming a single holding company – the Gucci Group – out of Gucci's haphazardly organized global units would have been a massive, maddening job in the best of situations. We had to put in corporate governance for each company, changing all their charters and by-laws and establishing their legal and accounting values. All this cost us a couple of million dollars in lawyer's fees. But that was nothing compared to the cost to our relationship with Maurizio. Across the table from one another sat two sides with seemingly nothing in common, fighting over the details of a common future. Bob, backed by his bevy of New York attorneys, was inherently compelled to go to the mat over every point. Maurizio, backed by his bevy of Italian attorneys, could hardly focus his elegant mind on such mundane issues. A mutual suspicion sprang up between the two sides, each one writing in protective clauses in the event of bad faith by the other. Maurizio nicknamed Bob 'What If,' because as soon as Maurizio agreed to do anything, Bob would say, 'Yes, but what if you don't carry it out?' And he would insert some wording to protect Investcorp in that eventuality.

At times, when the lawyers' battle grew too intense, Maurizio would ask to take a break and come see me. At my house in London we would sit by the fire and talk it out. 'Tell me, Maurizio, what is the problem?' I would say.

'Nemir, they are being too harsh,' he would reply.

'It's not our intent to be harsh,' I would tell him. 'If that is too harsh, let's change it. I'm not trying to attack you or trick you. My lawyers aren't either. They're just doing their job.' Reassured, Maurizio would then return to Italy until the next crisis.

By March 1991 the new ownership agreement was in force. Not long after that, Bob told me he thought it was time I assigned someone else to Gucci. 'I've used up a lot of goodwill with Maurizio, sitting across a very confrontational table.' It was true, he had – but it was necessary, despite the cost to the relationship. Here was poor little rich boy Maurizio, who had lived his life under attack. He could never really trust anyone. Now, all of a sudden, the comfort he had taken in Investcorp turns into another nightmare of people he fears want to take advantage of him.

Like it or not, however, we were yoked together just as tightly as those linked Gs on a pair of Gucci loafers. The best thing for both Maurizio and Investcorp was for us to learn to walk, calmly and purposefully, in the same direction.

To that end, I decided that to follow Bob Glaser I needed a consummate diplomat. I found him in Bill Flanz, my wise former boss at Chase and a calming influence on Investcorp's Mancom. Bill took over in the summer of 1991, and it was not long before his diplomatic abilities were sorely tested. Early on, we had agreed with Maurizio to eventually leverage Gucci, putting debt into the holding company and taking out some $150 million for each side. Having shelved that plan in lieu of Maurizio's aborted buyout, we now wanted to proceed with the leveraging as fast as possible. Maurizio, however, was no longer so interested. He resisted the plan in every possible way: ignored it, condemned it, sidestepped it. In the end, over seven long years, we never put a single dollar of debt into Gucci. It was all equity, all the time, a risk that grew more perilous with every passing day.

Even so, we decided – this time as full co-owners – that we would support Maurizio's vision and go along with his strategy. That was my order; I still believed in Maurizio and told our guys to let him run. And indeed there were some good things happening. To fulfill his dream of a renewed Gucci, Maurizio had wooed and finally hired Dawn Mello from

Bergdorf Goodman as creative director of Guccio Gucci, and she had brought on a hot young American designer named Tom Ford to help her reinvent the Gucci classics. Dawn and Tom had gone through the Gucci archives and selected classic items – leather goods, handbags and shoes, scarves and ties – to update for a thoroughly modern audience. These new products were introduced with a major advertising campaign, and the fashion magazines were positively gushing. Maurizio's reinvention of Gucci was actually happening. All over the world, the Gucci name was again being pronounced with pride.

Maurizio was not about to let his momentum slip, and in the spring of 1991 he announced he was moving the company's headquarters from Florence to Milan. While this came as a shock to us, there was a certain undeniable business sense to it. Milan had become, along with Paris, one of the true fashion capitals of the world. Paris was still the center of haute couture, but Milan was the hot spot for trendy ready-to-wear. Several times a year the world's fashion elite descended on Milan, and Maurizio felt it was vital for Gucci to have a presence there.

With the help of a decorator friend, he had found and rented a five-story jewel of a building nestled in a piazza surrounded by La Scala, the Duomo, and the imposing Palazzo Marino, Milan's city hall. It was a perfect location, and Maurizio had the renovations and decorations done at warp speed – five months, from start to finish. No expense was spared: walnut wainscoting, parquet floors, forest green fabric on the walls in the executive offices, antiques and classical statuary, a state-of-the-art audiovisual system. In

September Maurizio hosted a gala staff dinner and cocktail party on the rooftop terrace, overlooking the glittering lights of his new city.

But that was not all. After announcing the establishment of task forces for each product area, to assess and make recommendations on Gucci's relaunch, Maurizio introduced his people to his latest dream; a 'Gucci School' in which all employees the world over would come for instruction in a unified Gucci approach to design, to fashion, to *il mondo del bello*. To house the school, Maurizio had bought a sprawling sixteenth-century villa in the Tuscan countryside, Villa Bellosguardo, that had once belonged to the opera star Enrico Caruso. On top of the $7 million purchase price, which we had approved, he had earmarked some $10 million for renovations. He saw this villa also being used as a cultural, conference, and exhibition center. It was a grand vision, but achieving it required a lot of money up front.

At the beginning of 1991 Gucci had $60 million in cash and no debt, but by now the recession had started and Maurizio could not manage his expenses. Meanwhile, our people kept pressing him for information, which he regularly complained about to me. I told him it was perfectly fair in the circumstances, because we were trying to protect our clients' investment. Unfortunately, his financial reporting systems were very unsophisticated. Whenever Rick or Bill quizzed him about the financial situation, Maurizio would toss out some selective statistic to paint a generally hopeful picture: 'My God,' he might say, 'sales of handbags are up thirty-two percent!'

For me, the moment of reckoning came in a devastating

meeting in London in May 1992. Our team – which now included Bill Flanz, Rick Swanson, and Philip Buscombe, accompanied by Elie Hallak – gave me a twenty-page presentation on 'The State of Gucci,' complete with bullet points, color graphs, and lots and lots of red ink. From having $60 million in cash just a year or so earlier, the Gucci Group was now $30 million in debt. It had sold off valuable real estate to pay some of its losses, but it was still bleeding to the tune of $30 million per annum. This was more than a meeting, it was an intervention: 'The capital is draining away,' they told me, 'and our shareholders have no value left. Whether you like the guy or not, this is your investors' money. What are you going to do about it?'

To say I was stunned would be a gross understatement. But I have always told my people I will bow to logic, and once they had laid the evidence before me I agreed to follow the logical course. 'Okay,' I said. 'You've alerted me to the problem. We must take action.'

We immediately summoned Maurizio to London. On the day he arrived, he found himself facing a very tough room – the Gucci team, plus Mike, Elie, and me, all probably looking to him like executioners-in-waiting. Philip Buscombe stood up and calmly began walking Maurizio through the mess that was his family company. 'See this red line going upwards,' Philip said, pointing to a slide projected on to a screen. 'That, Maurizio, was your original forecast of sales over five years. Now see the green line way below it. That's Rick Swanson's revised five-year projection, based on his having sat down with your management team and reworked the model to incorporate your latest forecast.'

Maurizio kept his focus firmly on the charts, studiously avoiding making eye contact with anyone. In a joint history of uncomfortable meetings, we were setting a new standard with this one.

'Now this next line,' Philip continued, indicating a yellow line pointing sharply south, 'shows actual sales for the last two years. In reality Gucci is running at a loss.'

When Philip got to the final slide, I stood and went to the screen myself. I gave a nod to Mike, who pressed the button and projected this message on to the screen:

THERE ARE ONLY TWO SOLUTIONS:

1. RESTORE SALES GROWTH.
2. REDUCE EXPENSES.

The obviousness of the words apparently struck Maurizio as absurd. 'Good idea,' he said, with more than a hint of sarcasm. 'But how do you want me to do it?'

'Maurizio, that's for you to figure out,' I said. 'But you must do something, and you must do it fast.'

He promised to go back home and produce a real business plan. I doubt that any of us believed we would ever see such a thing.

Shortly after the London confrontation, Maurizio invited us to come to Italy. Ostensibly we were going for a meeting, but his real purpose seemed to be an evening of pull-out-all-the-stops seduction. Elie, Bill, Philip, Rick, and I flew to Florence, where Maurizio had his people put on a fashion show in our honor. Then we drove out into the hills to Villa Bellosguardo for dinner on the veranda. It was a lovely evening, Tuscany in the full bloom of springtime, and we dined in true Gucci style watching the sun set behind Enrico Caruso's cypress trees. Maybe Maurizio hoped we would become so caught up in his vision of *il mondo del bello* that we would overlook his excesses in achieving it.

I could not let that happen. At a certain point in the evening, I stood and raised my glass to our host. 'We at Investcorp believe in your vision, Maurizio,' I said, 'and we subscribe to it. We'll do everything we can to help you. But in order to reach the light at the end of the tunnel, you must first enter the tunnel.' In hindsight, I now see that Maurizio was already in a tunnel of his own, a parallel universe in which the only reality was the beauty of his vision. Investment bankers do not often encounter artists like Maurizio, and we kept trying to bend him to our way of thinking.

At this point, we were still committed to a non-confrontational approach. After the Italian extravaganza, our Gucci team began spending several days of every week in Italy working with Maurizio and his product task forces, the units designed to take responsibility for each business sector. We had brought in Gucci managers from all over the world to be involved in these task forces, and they were all enthusiastic and full of good ideas. And Maurizio too seemed engaged, upbeat and committed to the task-force plan – as long as our people were in town. Later, I would phone Andrea Morante, by now Gucci's Vice Chairman, to ask if the problems had been sorted out, and he would say, 'Not really.' Apparently, Maurizio would revert to traditional autocratic form as soon as we left, cutting his task-force managers out of any decision-making. They would not even know what was going on in their product areas. 'Maurizio respects you a lot and looks on you as a father figure,' Andrea told me, 'but he's not happy with what you agreed with him.'

So we tried another plan – management by executive committee. Both owners would have seats on this committee and would share power. Gucci's management teams would report to the committee and take decisions from it; the committee would also make sure the decisions got implemented. Maurizio agreed, but his modus operandi remained the same. In our presence, he would put on a most convincing performance. But as soon as we left, he lost his enthusiasm for this form of managing.

Our next tack was to suggest hiring an experienced chief operating officer to implement Maurizio's vision. Of course when our people raised that idea, Maurizio rejected it out of hand. I then invited him to London to discuss it face-to-face. 'Look, Maurizio,' I said, 'why put yourself under all this stress? Why not allow someone else to deal with all the hassles? You remain in charge, but let someone else do the day-to-day work. We're both men of vision; let's use our vision wisely.'

For a moment, it seemed to work. He agreed to let us begin a search, but nothing came of it. Maurizio was a master at dragging his feet, at obfuscating, at saying what we wanted to hear and then doing the opposite. He saw us as merely 'numbers people.' 'Numbers come from the brain,' he would say, 'but the company's sales and its image – those are things that come from the heart. The heart comes first, numbers only follow.'

When we countered that there needed to be a balance, he would dismiss it with a shrug. 'All I need to do,' he'd say, 'is buy myself some time. It'll happen, you'll see. Meanwhile, I'll come back to you and give you a business plan.' We volunteered to give him all the resources he needed to produce it.

A month passed, then another. Then one day, to our eternal surprise, Maurizio came to Rick Swanson and handed him his business plan. He seemed very proud of it. But when we began reading it, we found it to be a chaos of numbers without any basis in reality. There were no comparisons, no figures from previous years. It was just a mass of projections straight out of Maurizio's head.

But it did seem to prove one thing: We were asking Maurizio to do the impossible. No matter how right his vision was, we now became doubtful that he or his people were capable of achieving it.

In early 1993, the situation was inexorably coming to a head. Gucci was some $60 million in debt and the banks were starting to apply pressure. By February we were hearing that Maurizio was borrowing from one bank to pay down a note at another, then borrowing from a third to pay the second note. Suppliers were beginning to withhold shipments. Many of Gucci's managers approached us in secret to request that we take some kind of action. Maurizio, meanwhile, seemed to be circling his wagons – he was said to be spending a considerable amount of time holed up at Villa Bellosguardo, which our people had started calling The Mausoleum. Anybody from Gucci headquarters who wanted to see Maurizio had to get in a car and drive three hours one way, then turn around and make the trek back to Milan.

The time, we knew, was here: One way or another, Maurizio had to be relieved of his executive power. The only question was how.

For a moment we saw an opportunity when an Italian Guccio Gucci board member secretly implored us to intervene. He was deeply concerned, he told us. Maurizio was despondent, acting irrationally. Something had to be done, and this board member would work with us however we thought best. His vote would give us control on the board, so after consulting with our lawyers we decided to call a board meeting in which Maurizio would be voted out. But just before the appointed day, Maurizio heard about the plan and cancelled the meeting. Any trust Maurizio still had in us was now obliterated.

Then we heard news that provided another opening. We had been making the rounds of the banks, doing all we could to shore up their confidence. During one of those meetings, we were told that not only was Guccio Gucci in deep financial trouble, but Maurizio was too. All but broke, he was scrambling to raise cash. He had even put his beloved yacht up for sale. His personal debts reportedly amounted to some $40 million. To pay off some of it, he had borrowed money from a Swiss bank using his Gucci shares as collateral. That was patently against our agreement with him; he was not allowed to pledge his shares to anyone else.

While we were trying to figure out how to respond to this,

the Swiss bank foreclosed on Maurizio's note and seized his shares. The bank then contacted us to say that if we did not want to buy them, they would stage a public auction and sell the shares to the highest bidder. We certainly did not want those shares in anyone else's hands, but we decided time was on our side. So instead of buying Maurizio's shares outright from the bank, we made plans to attend the auction just in case. And I began mulling a strategy that could both save Maurizio and give us the control we needed.

The offer I came up with was this: We would buy 5 percent of his shares for $10 million; at the same time, we would make him an interest-free loan of $40 million, of which no repayment of principal would be due for three years. Through this plan, he could clear all his personal debts and still have $10 million. He would remain chairman of the company with 45 percent ownership, but we would have executive control. In time, we would either sell Gucci or take it public, and Maurizio would again become a very rich man.

In March 1993 I dispatched Elie Hallak and Bill Flanz to Florence to present the offer to Maurizio in person. I felt very satisfied with this plan, which was intended to do good while doing well. I had no desire to see Maurizio ruined. On the contrary, all any of us had ever wanted was for him to be wildly successful. We had tried our best to help him achieve that, but his pride – or his inability to trust – had always gotten in the way. If he had just accepted being the visionary while someone else implemented his vision, we would not be confronting the difficulties now before us.

To my great relief, Maurizio did not reject our offer. Instead, he asked that we put it in writing, which we were happy to do. We were working on that when, suddenly, Maurizio seemed to vanish into thin air. One day he was in Florence at the Villa, and the next he was nowhere to be found. His secretary refused to tell us where he was. A day passed, then two, then three. We heard he was in Switzerland, then Italy, then California. It was maddening.

After a week of invisibility – and the day before the scheduled auction – he phoned us out of the blue with a message that made our stomachs drop: 'I've found the money, I've paid my debts, I've got my shares back.'

Besides being flabbergasted, we had an uneasy feeling that he had borrowed from someone using the shares as collateral. I sent Bill and Rick to Milan immediately to confront Maurizio about it.

They were ushered into his sumptuous executive conference room and made to wait for half an hour. Then the door opened and there was Maurizio, back from the dead. No longer was he morose and withdrawn with his head in the sand; now he had his old style back, in spades. 'Rick, Bill, how *nice* to see you!' he gushed. 'So you've heard the news? I know you guys have your spies everywhere!' He was beaming – really enjoying the moment.

He had tea brought in for the three of them, and finally Bill put down his cup and got to the point. 'Maurizio,' he said, 'where did you get the money?'

'Well, Bill,' he said, 'that is an *incredible* story. I was trying to fall asleep in my home in St. Moritz and I was worrying about everything and what I was going to do, and I had a dream. And my father came to me in my dream and said, "Maurizio, the solution to all your problems is in the parlor.

Just look over there by the window, one of the floorboards is loose; pull it up, and underneath you will see." So when I woke up, I looked under the loose board and it was incredible! There was more money than I could ever know what to do with there, under the floor! I didn't want to be greedy, so I took just enough to pay off my shares!'

Bill and Rick listened in disbelief, and not just at the preposterous story; they were astounded at how blatantly Maurizio was thumbing his nose at them – at us. When they returned to London and told me everything Maurizio had said, I could feel my blood boil. Such disrespect, such lack of appreciation. 'This time,' I said, 'we're going to show him Investcorp in all its strength.'

My first act was to form a team to defeat Maurizio Gucci. I chose my men for their unique talents: Elie Hallak for the money; Bill Flanz and Rick Swanson for their intimate knowledge of Gucci; our in-house attorney, Larry Kessler, for the law; and Bob Glaser because he was the only one at Investcorp Maurizio was afraid of. When they were all assembled, I laid down the ground rules. 'You have only one responsibility,' I told them. 'You're to sit in that boardroom downstairs, day in, day out. You will eat, sleep, and breathe Gucci. You will do nothing else until you have resolved the situation and acquired this man's shares.'

There were some misgivings. Elie worried how an all-out war might be viewed by our clients and bankers, and I agreed that we should send them all a letter telling them what we were doing and why. And Bob Glaser, who had always thought I was too lenient with Maurizio, wanted to make sure I was prepared for what was in store. 'You have to be willing to go to the brink,' he said to me in front of the others, 'and you have to be willing to back us up. Maurizio is going to sue us, he's going to embarrass us in the press, and he's going to push the company to the point of bankruptcy. We have to make him believe we will go to the edge. Otherwise you shouldn't go down this path.'

I nodded. 'Let's go,' I said.

Money was no object. We began by hiring a prestigious lawyer in Italy, and then we all started digging into Maurizio's business affairs to find out where he had actually gotten the 'dream' money. While we were investigating, Maurizio fired the first salvo in the war with the help of a euphoric media: 'The Arabs,' Maurizio told the press, 'are taking over Italy's heritage and national asset.' Soon we were front-page news all around the world. Our response was to repeat to the media Maurizio's story to us about the money: 'I dreamed my father told me it was under the floorboards in St. Moritz.' Of course the media loved it, and Maurizio – who hated looking silly – was furious.

In the meantime, we discovered that he had borrowed the money from some obscure people in Switzerland – a 'shelf' company with virtually no assets – and indeed had used his Gucci stock as collateral. All the money had been paid out on his debts, and now he had no cash left. The loan was for six months. If he did not pay it all back in that time, he lost his shares. Maurizio was under enormous pressure, and we intended to turn up the heat in every way possible. We knew that if we were ever going to succeed in buying his shares, two things had to happen: Guccio Gucci had to go bankrupt, or be on the brink of it. And Maurizio himself had to be in the same condition.

First we sued him for breach of contract. Then Maurizio shocked us by having Guccio Gucci sue Gucci America for non-payment of some $63.9 million in products the American company had ordered from the Italian parent. We were stunned by this move, and the press had the proverbial field day with it. Gucci suing itself! Bob Glaser began looking into the matter and determined that the prices had been inflated as a means of sucking the assets out of Gucci America in order to benefit the troubled Italian company.

As Bob began devising a strategy for confronting Maurizio about it, Maurizio floated a plan to bring $20 million into Gucci America in a virtual give-away of a twenty-year supplier licensing contract. The contract required board approval, and here we saw a chance to strike both hard and deep. The key was Domenico De Sole, lifelong confidante of Maurizio and his father before him, as well as Maurizio's trusted, handpicked CEO of the now-embattled Gucci America. We went to Domenico and enlisted him to vote with us against Maurizio at the next board meeting. While Domenico was heartsick at having to make this choice, he had already concluded that Gucci could not survive with Maurizio at the helm. His decision was all the more noble in light of the fact that Maurizio still owed him $4 million from a personal loan.

This particular board meeting was held in Maurizio's top-floor office in Milan. Chairs were brought in, cappuccino was served, and Maurizio presided over the event from behind his enormous desk, sitting in a chair with carved lions on the arms. Before the $20-million contract was on the table, Bob Glaser began questioning a surprised Domenico De Sole about the prices Gucci America paid to the mother company. 'What do you do when you get a product that in your view is overpriced?' Glaser demanded.

'There is nothing I can do,' said De Sole, feeling put upon. 'I complain all the time. We are a captive company and you guys' – meaning Investcorp – 'have never supported us. All you've ever done is just try to get along with Maurizio!'

Maurizio, his face purple, turned to Domenico. 'Are you saying that Gucci America overpays for the merchandise?'

'Yes, I've been saying that for years!' Domenico said. 'You are overcharging Gucci America just to support your cost structure. Look at this building! What do we really need this building for?'

Maurizio got up and began pacing the room, clearly furious at this on-the-record challenge to his authority. But the real blow came when Domenico voted with Investcorp on the issue of the supplier contract. Visibly stunned by this sudden change in the accepted order, Maurizio glared at Domenico. 'Look, Maurizio,' his old friend said, 'this is what I have to do. I am voting for the company, it is my duty. We can't simply give away a license because we're running out of money ...'

That vote eventually won the war. Without an infusion of new cash, Guccio Gucci, like a dying body, gradually began to shut down. By mid-summer it could no longer meet its employee payroll. It failed to pay its monthly social security tax obligation. It could not pay its suppliers, who quit shipping. Finally the banks put stops on the company's lines of credit.

Maurizio became a crazy man, threatening to take down the ship with everyone on it. As a last-gasp effort, this visionary – this idealist who had abhorred the cheap plastic and canvas products with which his cousins had so debased the Gucci logo – began commissioning those very products in an effort to bring in quick money. He sold off some inventory in China and was giving away the license to distribute it. In short, he was repudiating everything he had done over three years to promote the image of his company.

By August, however, we began receiving subtle overtures from Maurizio, and the two sides entered into a period of gentle negotiation – against a loudly ticking clock. Gucci was headed for bankruptcy, and the deadline for Maurizio to turn over his shares was just days away. He was acting erratically, and we did not know until the last second whether he would negotiate in earnest or let the whole thing go up in smoke. We could not help recalling the Italian proverb Domenico De Sole had so often quoted apropos Maurizio: 'It's better to burn down the house than to admit a stranger.'

Then, suddenly, for whatever blessed reason, Maurizio agreed to sell us his shares for $125 million. The deal was to be consummated on September 23 at the offices of UBS in Lugano, and we sent Rick Swanson and one of our attorneys from Gibson, Dunn & Crutcher to do the honors.

As a gesture of goodwill, Rick waited outside the bank to meet Maurizio when he arrived, but Maurizio somehow slipped past him. When Rick went upstairs for the meeting, he found that Maurizio had locked himself in a conference room separate from the one our people were in. So there both parties were, shut off from each other, with advisers going back and forth down the hall asking questions.

In the end, Rick coaxed Maurizio into a single conference room, and they ended this long, difficult episode sitting side by side at a table, copies of the agreements before them, pens in hand. There, perhaps relieved that it was all over, Maurizio reached inside himself and found the charmer we had first met all those years before.

'Okay, Rick,' he said, 'this is a race. The guy who finishes first wins two million dollars.'

'Okay,' Rick said, 'let's go!'

Maurizio finished signing first. 'Well, Rick, that's two million you owe me.'

'Fair enough, Maurizio,' Rick said. 'But look, we're very good friends, so I'm sure you'd be willing to go double or nothing on the next document.'

'For you, Rick, of course.' But as Maurizio started to sign, Rick flipped to the end of his copy and signed the last page.

'Maurizio,' he said, 'it looks like you owe me four million dollars.'

'That's very clever of you, Rick,' said Maurizio. 'Please tell Elie Hallak that I owe you four million – but he owes me six million dollars because you cheated!'

I was to see Maurizio only twice more before his tragic death. At the time of the sale, I had not spoken with him for quite a while. The hostile letters between us had put paid to our personal relationship, so my guys were delegated the task, and I had been advised not to contact him. But when the lawyers told me he had agreed to sell, I decided to call him. He was dumbfounded when he heard my voice.

'Maurizio,' I said, 'I would like you to come over and have lunch with me.'

'Are you sure I'll be safe?' he asked jokingly.

When we met for lunch I gave him a big bear hug. 'Look,' I said, 'the past is the past and the money is now yours. Let me tell you something. If we can save this company, I would like to keep a relationship with you. Who knows? One day we might sell the company to you, or you might join it in some capacity!'

That never happened. We invited him to become an adviser, but he turned us down. He was busy building a boat, he said. To our surprise, he never started another business of his own.

With Investcorp's guidance and support, Gucci became a resounding success. Bill Flanz moved to Italy to run the business day-to-day, and his calming manner succeeded in winning over both employees and suppliers. In 1994, we brought Domenico De Sole in as Chief Operating Officer of the mother company. He would later move up to CEO.

The last time I saw Maurizio was on a New Year's Eve – the final hours of 1994. We both happened to be at the Palace Hotel in St Moritiz, and Maurizio spotted me across the lobby and came over to say hello. We chatted for a few minutes socially amid the revelers, then we hugged and went our separate ways. Less than three months later he would be shot dead on the stairs of his building. His ex-wife was later convicted of ordering his murder.

Maurizio used to tell us that, one of these days, Gucci

sales 'are going to explode.' I never doubted him. By mid-1995 his prediction had come true. With 1995 sales on track to reach $500 million, we decided the time was right to take Gucci to the next stage in the cycle. Most of our people wanted to sell the company outright – there were several suitors – but I overruled them. I knew we could get more in an initial public offering.

On the morning of the IPO, as Domenico De Sole and I arrived at the New York Stock Exchange with other executives from Gucci and Investcorp, we were met by a huge Italian flag hanging outside, next to the Stars and Stripes. Inside, as we waited for the opening bell to begin trading, a giant blinking digital banner proclaimed HOT STOCK TO WATCH: GUCCI. And hot it was – in two offerings, Investcorp would receive some $2.1 billion for Gucci, on an initial investment of just $246 million.

Maurizio would not have been the least bit surprised. Certainly it was his vision that created the success that ultimately translated to such financial value. No one more than Maurizio Gucci deserves the credit for the final outcome of this incredible story. I will always remember Maurizio with the highest admiration and respect.

10
A SEA CHANGE

Since my early childhood years, my aspiration was to pursue a career in public service and engage in national and international affairs. My aptitude and interest was evident and was encouraged by my father, who himself spent his entire life in public service. But my relocation out of Iraq closed that door for me. In the early 1990s, however, Investcorp opened another.

In the Western world, corporate leaders have traditionally assumed active roles outside of their business engagements. These might include philanthropy or involvement in such worthy causes as educational institutions or public policy organizations. An American or European CEO undertakes such activities as a way of 'giving back' and therefore fulfilling social responsibilities.

When I worked for Chase Manhattan Bank, I had the privilege of watching one of the most distinguished US corporate leaders, David Rockefeller, as he devoted significant time and energy to world affairs, among his many other interests. This enabled him to be recognized as a global statesman. Wherever he traveled, he was received with displays of respect generally reserved for heads of state. Of course, the magnet of his last name was an undeniable factor. But it was also David Rockefeller's intense interest in and deep knowledge of world affairs that provided him with a special welcome by leaders around the globe.

From the very start of Investcorp, our ambition was to build the firm into a world-class organization. This required careful strategic attention to cultivating its brand name internationally, not only for its tangible business performance but also for its exemplary social responsibility. Earning such recognition in the West would, I knew, attract special attention and admiration from Gulf leaders, thereby distinguishing Investcorp from other Gulf-based financial institutions. I felt I was naturally suited to play, over time, an effective role in serving Investcorp's interest and realizing its goal of achieving international recognition. Thus what I had not been able to practice through public service in Iraq in the past, I should be able to demonstrate in my current capacity as CEO of Investcorp.

At the firm's inception, we promised the founding shareholders that our objective was to build an institution that was bigger than any one of us and which would last indefinitely. Naturally, I had to take a more internal hands-on role in the early years, but by the end of the 1980s Investcorp was up and running and I found myself faced with two challenges. First, how could I reduce my direct involvement in dealmaking and thus allow the firm to gradually fulfill its destiny as a true institution? Second, how could I upgrade my effectiveness as a more sophisticated CEO by increasing my engagement in international forums and platforms?

By this time Investcorp had become a very complex organization relative to its size and objectives. It operated as a bank in Bahrain and was therefore subject to the strict compliance requirements of the Bahraini banking regulations, which are considered the most demanding and sophisticated in the Gulf. It also engaged in business in the USA and Europe and therefore was subject to taxes that required a level of efficiency and legal structuring that offered clients maximum efficiency and advantages. Furthermore, in order to attract superior investment opportunities on both sides of the Atlantic, Investcorp had to be well recognized and respected by those who were the sources and providers of those opportunities as well as by the banks that extended acquisition financing for those transactions. All of those and more needed huge, targeted efforts.

The founding nucleus composed of three key partners who had joined me to create Investcorp had been absolutely essential to build the firm's foundation, but now we needed to add an additional pool of talent and skills to form the body of the firm and deliver its business activities. Thus we intensified our efforts to expand the base of professionals who could earn the respect of our clients and bankers, and the sources of our investment products. The loyalty and dedication of the original founding group was obviously critical. The professional productivity of the second was becoming more and more vital. Yet, adding professionals based on perceived skill and talents created unexpected incremental challenges and complexities within the firm.

In the early 1990s, then, in order for us to expand our activities, earn greater recognition, and deal more effectively with the increased complexity of our firm, I decided that a new administrative position had become necessary within Investcorp: that of Chief Operating Officer. I saw my role as CEO and leader as continuing to deal with the firm's architecture, strategy, and direction, thus making decisions on consequential issues. The COO would oversee and ensure the implementation of the strategy in the most effective manner and focus on the firm's day-to-day management requirements.

But this position could not – at that time – be filled from the outside. It needed someone who understood Investcorp and could ensure the continuity of its culture. It was also imperative that the existing body would accept our injection of a boss between the Mancom and their CEO. Given the complementary skills between Mike and Elie and their mutual respect for each other, as well as the high esteem by everyone at Investcorp for both of those two individuals, I decided to appoint them jointly to fill the position – as co-Chief Operating Officers. They were the ideal team for the job.

I made the announcement in January 1993. Mike, formerly in charge of administration, would henceforth become co-COO overseeing investment placement and administration in all three offices. He would be based in Bahrain. Elie, formerly in charge of finance, would oversee finance and all investments and acquisitions activity from London. I instructed him to replace himself as CFO as soon as possible.

I had also extracted a promise from each man that he would give Investcorp another five years – but no longer. By then Mike and Elie would have been at the firm fifteen years, and it would be time to step aside for someone else. The essence of an institution is that it is self-perpetuating.

As I expected, the staff received the news enthusiastically – with a hint of relief, even. Some people – Savio Tung, for example – had been concerned about me personally, about how thinly stretched I had become. Others were probably just happy imagining how much faster and smoother everything would run now that it did not all have to go through me.

For a while, life at the firm did seem better. I assumed a supervisory role, making myself available to provide leadership when needed but otherwise concerning myself with long-range strategy, marketing, internal appointments, the Board of Directors, and the cultivation of high-level external contacts. By the early nineties I had met and developed relationships with international statesmen. I had forged connections at Harvard, and was an active supporter of the Center for Contemporary Arab Studies at Georgetown University. Some of the Mancom members grumbled about the time I spent away from the office on such 'outside' activities, but I countered that it was time well spent for Investcorp. We of all people should understand leveraging, and my twenty-five outside days a year – this was my estimate in 1992 – would accrue to Investcorp's benefit many times over.

Mike and Elie appeared to take well to their new duties too. All in all, this major change – for a culture that eschewed strict hierarchy – seemed to have been effected with remarkable ease.

*

Cem was the third founder, and though I did not feel that he would fit into a similar capacity to that of Mike and Elie, he had his own exceptional qualities for continuing to play a critical role.

A Turkish citizen brought up in France and educated in Switzerland, Cem was an exemplary diplomat. Highly sophisticated, very articulate, and extraordinarily presentable, he was the perfect person to represent Investcorp to bankers, clients, and government officials. His command of languages – English, French, and Turkish – was flawless. He could excel in any culture. One of his earliest mandates had been to establish the London office as Investcorp's European headquarters. Moreover, he had established the network of Investcorp's international banking relationships on both sides of the Atlantic. Finally, in the mid-1980s, I handed Cem the very tough job of initiating our European dealmaking capability.

It was a tough job for many reasons, mostly due to intrinsic business difficulties in Europe. Even today you can talk about 'the European Union,' but the truth of the matter is that each country has its own legal system, its own tax code, its own language, and – still in some cases – its own currency. In Europe, the rules governing the buying and selling of businesses vary greatly from country to country. The US, on the other hand, has a single language, currency, banking system, and tax structure, as well as unified fiscal and monetary policies. Culturally, in the late 1980s the US was a veritable marketplace for the buying and selling of businesses, while in Europe selling a family business was considered unusual.

Cem tackled his new assignment in his own inimitable way. I had given him a year to study the situation and come up with a European strategy to present to the partners, but as Cem later told an in-house interviewer, 'I'm not much of a strategy man. I thought the best way to prove that the European market was viable was to go out and do transactions there.' That he did, but our first few European deals did not go as well as intended. There often seemed to be some exceptional difficulty with them, and returns for our investors failed to meet our expectations. After 1989, we did not make another European acquisition for three years.

They were long and lonely years for Cem. Increasingly isolated, he was repeatedly forced to defend himself and his unit from the criticism of the other Mancom members. Some argued that we should discontinue our European efforts and focus entirely on the US. That, so the argument went, would reduce our costs and increase our effectiveness where the market was more developed.

I refused to consider such a move, insisting that our original promise to shareholders had been to present the Gulf investors with Western investment opportunities. In the long run, I said, Investcorp would gain an advantage by being the first on both sides of the Atlantic. Investment opportunities should be available in all traditional industrialized countries where grandfathers had built businesses and the grandchildren who inherited them had eventually decided to sell them.

Cem was encouraged by my optimistic long-term view and argued with conviction, confirming that we should not abandon our efforts in Europe based on our short-term experience. Our objective in Europe was to be well positioned, with a preferential access to key traditional institutions that could be our sources for future deals.

Despite my belief in both Cem and our European expansion, I had to give him some harsh performance reviews those last couple of years. Inevitably, the situation brought a cooling in our relationship. But what he probably never realized is that I began feeling that any failure was partly my responsibility. What qualifications did Cem have to buy companies? None – and yet I had placed him in that situation. He was a banker, and while my hunch had always been to put him in marketing, I had veered from that course. Spending money is not the key to our business; the real key is raising money. Cem could have been great at marketing Investcorp to sources of capital.

But while I came to wonder if I had put him in the wrong job, the question was larger than that of Cem and European dealmaking. Accepting assignments for which we had not a shred of qualification had been the Investcorp way from day one, and it was a model that had served us well for years. But had our business now become too complex for that?

It was not until later in 1993 that I got my first inkling of internal problems stemming from Mike and Elie's promotion. Announcing that both of them would be joining me in reading the personal end-of-year Mancom appraisals, I received the clear message that this was distasteful to some members. When I added that the co-COOs would also sit in on each staffer's year-end clear-the-air interview with me, there was an immediate backlash. That these two former 'equals' would now be occupying positions of judgment over them made the other Mancom members very, very uneasy. But I insisted we try it, which we did for two uncomfortable years before giving it up and going back to the old way.

By then, many formerly unseen problems were now crystal clear. Mike, a solid soldier with an ironclad sense of self – he had often exasperated me by struggling against my exhortations to reach for new heights beyond his comfort zone – had approached me less than a year after the promotion and asked to be relieved of his five-year commitment. Despite notable successes in his work with the placement team – whom he had won over by becoming not their master but their supporter, providing them with better research, better intelligence, better computer models, and better facilities – he had decided it was time for him to shift his attention from Investcorp to his family. His children were getting older, he said, and needed to be someplace besides Bahrain for their education. I reluctantly accepted his decision but asked him to stay one more year, until January 1995. Mike, being Mike, agreed to this extended tour of duty. We told no one of this arrangement. He would devote his remaining year largely to corporate cost-cutting – his kind of management job.

Perhaps another factor in Mike's disenchantment was the subtle competitive tension that had sprung up between him and Elie. While never erupting into overt nastiness, it nevertheless was a new and unseemly specter hovering over the firm. Part of it may have been caused by their individual personalities. There was also much in-house speculation over whether Elie could bear to cede his CFO power to someone else. With no formal training, he had combined his innate work ethic and his God-given facility with numbers and willed himself into becoming one of the world's most astute financial experts. He was such a stickler, and had made the job of CFO so much his own, that few on the Mancom could imagine him giving it up. And so, over a year and a half, as candidate after candidate arrived for the requisite round of interviews, Elie's partners began developing the uneasy feeling that the interviewing would go on forever.

Then, in the summer of 1994, Elie surprised everyone by announcing his successor – or at least his successor-in-waiting. Gary Long, a trained accountant who was a Senior Vice President at American Express, would in time become a pivotal player in Investcorp's second fifteen years. But for the moment he was brought on to work with Elie as his understudy.

During the firm's first decade I had allowed Elie – in his capacity as CFO – final approval over any deal, based on his reading of the risk and the effect on the company's bottom line. Since January 1993, however, he had been the overseer of all deals from start to finish, with a final say over acquisition, funding, post-acquisition management, and exit strategy. He embraced his new power with every bit of his considerable energy.

In our world a lot of damage can be done in a short time, and by mid-1994 there was an increasing sense within certain pockets of Investcorp that our investments had gone off track. Elie's tendency to play his cards close to the vest made matters worse. In the absence of real information, backstair whispering stepped in to fill the vacuum. From Bahrain to London to New York, gossip and rumor ran rampant.

Unfortunately, in my efforts to promote Investcorp on the international stage, I had taken myself out of position to know exactly what was going on at the backstair level.

I began reconnecting in September, when Cem came to me to discuss his desire to exit the firm. He said he wanted to pursue business ideas of his own. He would not leave immediately, however, as he was still intimately involved in several of our acquisitions. He would complete those jobs before beginning this next chapter in his life.

To replace Cem as head of Corporate Investment Europe, I reached into the New York corporate investment team and tapped Paul Soldatos to take over in London. Less than a year later, it would be Paul who managed the wildly successful Gucci IPO.

On the other hand, I also saw Paul's move as my opportunity to strengthen the New York office. I had not been pleased with his handling of Saks Fifth Avenue, which appeared to be headed in the wrong direction. Although I had engineered the acquisition, I left its post-acquisition management primarily to Paul. Looking back on it today, I rank that as among my mistakes at Investcorp.

Saks was not on the right track for two reasons: The recession hit just as we acquired Saks, and consumer confidence dropped like a stone. I could not fault us for that, but I could fault us for Saks' management turmoil. Melvin Jacobs, Saks' longtime Chairman, was 'Mr Saks,' and it was crucial that we keep him in place. We acquired the company from British Tobacco, which was represented in the negotiations by its Executive Vice President, Arthur Martinez. I was impressed with Martinez and thought he would be a good number two for Jacobs.

But Paul Soldatos had another idea, post acquisition. He had heard that Philip Miller, the ex-Chairman of Marshall Field Department Store in Chicago, was the brightest star in the industry, and Paul was eager to attract Miller to run Saks.

My solution was to keep Mel Jacobs as Chairman and appoint Martinez and Miller as his two vice-chairmen. I proposed a bonus system that would satisfy all three. I then left Paul to oversee our interest in Saks by interacting with the new management team of three.

While still under Paul, we took Saks public through an initial public offering. It was a successful move but we could not liquidate investors' interest in Saks and the market turned against us. As time went by, Mel Jacobs got discouraged and decided to leave. Paul insisted that Phil Miller be given total authority as Chairman and CEO, which displeased Arthur Martinez, who submitted his resignation. It was a mess, and we would eventually – in 1998 – sell Saks in a disappointing outcome. Of course, I did not know that at this point. I just knew we had problems at Saks, and for that and other reasons I was happy to move Paul to London and put someone else in charge of New York.

The man I brought in was Garrett (Gar) Bewkes, head of investment banking at Bear Stearns. Gar had worked with us on various financing transactions and we had been impressed with him. His greatest assets were his engaging personality, powerful presence, and extraordinary persuasiveness. Besides those personal traits, his professional credentials looked every bit as stellar. At Bear Stearns he'd had some four hundred people reporting to him.

Cem leaving ... Mike scheduled to go ... Gary Long poised to become the firm's next CFO ... Paul Soldatos running London ... Gar Bewkes leading New York: All were threads of a theme I felt emerging throughout that autumn. A good CEO instinctively reads the world around him and discerns the patterns in it. This, I realized, was a design I had long foreseen. And now felt like the perfect time to move us to the next stage of our institutional development.

This was a hard decision in many ways. People who were very dear to me, who had helped put this company on the map, would need to retire to make way for the next wave. Bringing this about required an especially delicate touch. Paramount in my thinking was that they be allowed a graceful exit.

By the end of the year, I had made the necessary arrangements. The results were announced to the entire firm in my summary memo following the Mancom meeting of January 1995. Instead of emblazoning them at the top of the note, I chose to place them – under the heading 'Management' – near the bottom of the second page:

> ... The smooth, efficient transfer of senior management responsibility and authority is a mark of any truly institutionalized organization. At Investcorp, we are dedicated to building an organization that considers management development and transition of the utmost importance....
>
> Therefore, this year will be a significant management transition year for Investcorp. Seven of the eighteen-member Management Committee will be retiring or will be leaving by the end of 1995, while ten principals have been upgraded to fill these Management Committee vacancies. This is an

exciting development because it demonstrates our ability to 'pass the torch' from those who carried it in the past to those who will carry it in the future.

The management changes are summarized below.

- Those retiring include Mike Merritt, John Thompson, Bob Glaser, Linda Cates and Abboud Jallad. Bill Flanz has been seconded on a full-time basis to Gucci, where he serves as acting Chief Executive Officer.
- The Principals appointed to the Management Committee, effective immediately, are: Marwan Hayek, Jon Hedley, Johannes Huth, Rick Lukens, Khalil Nooruddin, Chris O'Brien, Nezar Al-Saie, Rick Warner, Talal Al-Zain and Zahid Zakiuddin. As you know, those who have joined the Management Committee from the outside over the last several months include Gar Bewkes, Charlie Philippin, Gary Long and Ed Lord . . .

Elsewhere in that same memo I also announced the end of our experiment with quantitative trading and Lee Thomas's consequent departure from the firm.

Throughout the company, news of the management changes was received in various ways, and by all as a bombshell. For the principals – even those not appointed to the Mancom – it was like the breaking of a dam. For the Mancom, it was a stunning repudiation of any concept they may have held of 'status quo.' As in Mike's case, Linda Cates and John Thompson had already confided their wishes to retire, but others were shocked when I told them it was time for them to go.

Despite my deep personal affection for each of these longtime colleagues, I had to do what was required for the good of the firm. And for Investcorp, the moment was right for our first great sea change. I made it clear – as I had between the lines a year earlier at the 1994 Mancom meeting – that this was normal, that there would inevitably be sea changes to come. 'When we started this firm,' I told the partners then, 'we were in no position to hire in ready-made professional skills. Instead, we looked for smart, adaptable, hard-working and dedicated risk-takers. Once we had some capital and an office, we set about turning those smart and dedicated people into entrepreneurs. The skills they acquired as they went along, plus the fact that the timing was good, were enough to see us through our second five years.

'But we shall need more than that to see us through our third five years, because this is an industry in which the bar is constantly rising. Not only must we recruit some top-level professionals from outside with a proven track record, each Mancom member here must also strive to improve their skills, just as I have had to do over the years as CEO.

'Nobody at this table has a fixed job. Its demands are constantly rising.'

Like Cem before him, Elie began to feel uneasy. He and Gar Bewkes, especially, seemed at loggerheads over the management of various acquisitions. At the beginning of 1995 I made several changes that I hoped would help.

With Mike about to retire, I asked him for yet another extension – to the end of the year. He graciously agreed, postponing the next stage of his life to help me with various internal matters. I then transferred Mike's co-COO responsibility over placement and administration to Elie, who, though now acting singly, retained his co-COO title. At the same time, I relieved Elie of sole power over Investments, creating instead a committee that would review and approve all transactions. This new team, called the Investment Committee, consisted of Elie as co-COO; Gar Bewkes and Paul Soldatos as operational heads of New York and London, respectively; and our economic adviser Professor Geoffrey Maynard.

It did not work. Removing Elie's power over deals injured his pride, while handing him Mike's duties – which I had thought might compensate for the loss of Investments – simply stretched his capacities. Meanwhile, Elie and Gar continued their squabbling across the table in the Investment Committee. I was able to quell the battling when I was there; when I could not be, the two adversaries went at each other like schoolboys whose teacher has left the room. Professor Maynard tried to impose peace, but did not have the power to make it stick.

Throughout the firm, disagreements at the top created an unhealthy atmosphere. I later learned that a senior partner was telling people that Investcorp had no money on its balance sheet and its losses would be more than it could ever recoup. A sense of alarm spread through the firm.

It reached its peak that July at our summer Mancom meeting, a two-day conference held at a hotel in upstate New York. Gary Long, who was still working as Elie's understudy, had prepared a paper I had asked for on how our financial reporting could be improved: budgeting, capital position, monitoring our expenses, valuation of our investments, and so on. Gary's heart must have pounded as he tiptoed through the issues like a man traversing a mine field.

When I started to read his report, I was shocked. It was very diplomatically written, tactfully suggesting various areas where we could make improvements, but it contained no figures, nor did it cover our exposures and provisions against losses (those were recommendations Gary would make later, after he took over from Elie). Shaking my head at the loss of our traditional candor, I went ahead and distributed copies of the report to everyone at the meeting.

This Mancom summit took place when we were at a crossroads. Gar was hinting that Investcorp could go belly-up, which made Elie furious. Elie was feeling depressed, not knowing where he stood with me. Prior to the meeting, he had come to see me about the whole mess. 'Why are you distancing yourself from me?' he had asked. 'We were such good friends, and you always trusted me.' But now I had gone and brought in Gar, who was causing so much damage. Elie was attacking Gar, Gar was blaming Elie, and I was caught in the middle.

The meeting sessions were very tense. With rumors flying around, as soon as anybody asked a question Elie would shut them up. And so would I, because I knew such poison could destroy the company. Suddenly Nick Bryan, one of the just-promoted principals, stood up at his first-ever Mancom meeting and put a very blunt question directly to me: 'Is our balance sheet accurate? What are these rumors about losses? Would you please explain?'

Amazingly, this was the first time anybody had asked me that question. I got to my feet and said, 'Right – I'm going to give you the answer.' Going to the writing board, I drew a couple of boxes. The larger one was black, and next to it

I drew a smaller box in red. 'This black box represents our assets, everything we own,' I said. 'This red box represents those companies in our balance sheet that aren't doing well. So our net worth today is this,' and I pointed to the area of the black box minus the mass of the red box.

'We have two jobs, gentlemen. The job for the post-acquisition people – Nick Bryan, Charlie Philippin, and their teams – is to improve the problem companies and gradually reduce this red box to nothing. Meanwhile, the job for the dealmakers is to increase the size of the black box by doing better deals and adding more value.'

Later Gar came to me and said, 'You did a great job there. It was just what the young guys wanted to hear.'

Whether it was or was not what they wanted to hear, I was tired of not hearing from 'the young guys' what *I* wanted to hear. Instead of getting down to the business of overcoming the obstacles of doing business – of being part of the solution – they were too busy second-guessing and finger-pointing at others about problems. Problems are normal; without problems to solve, why are we employed?

But I had no idea of the extent of our problems.

My wake-up call came one night a few weeks after the summer Mancom meeting. In New York for a gathering of the Group of 50 – the latest incarnation of our elite shareholder body – I had been to a working session at the Waldorf Astoria. The meeting had finished at about 6 p.m., but one of the members had invited several of us, plus our wives, to dinner afterwards.

Stopping off at the office to leave some papers and see what was going on, I was met by Gar, who looked pale and worried. He told me I had to attend an emergency meeting. When I entered the room, I found lots of long-faced people there, including Jon Hedley and Charlie Marquis from the New York office (Charlie had joined us from Gibson Dunn by that time) and, of course, Elie. I was told it would be a long meeting, so I phoned to cancel my dinner. Our dinner host was very upset with me and later pulled out of the Group.

'So what's this about?' I said. Whereupon Gar proceeded to tell me that two of our portfolio companies, Color Tile and Camelot Music, were bleeding money and could not be saved. Both were about to declare bankruptcy.

I could not believe it. Never in our thirteen years of business had we allowed any of our corporate acquisitions to go under. Nor had we pulled the plug, even though, when the going got tough, some people had urged me to write off several companies, including Gucci – Gucci, which would become one of our most spectacular success stories. Where was the old Investcorp spirit and will to prevail?

I was livid. 'What kind of system do we have here?' I said, searching the room but finding only hangdog expressions and averted eyes. 'You wait till the patient is dead *and then you call me*?' Then I turned to the senior members in the room and asked, 'What, are you running the show on your own?'

That night I learned about the losses in these two companies. In 1989 we had bought Color Tile, America's largest retailer of floor and wall coverings, for $450 million, our largest purchase to that time. Both Paul Soldatos and Gar Bewkes – then at Bear Stearns – had worked hard to recapitalize the company and eliminate the debt that was dragging it down. At the time, Gar called the recapitalization 'a leading-edge transaction, and a very successful one.'

From then on, Color Tile embarked on a five-year plan of growth. Even as recently as mid-1994, there was no cause for anxiety. The company had weathered the recession well and even increased its market share, growing from 700 to 800 stores and becoming the second-largest American carpet retailer.

Suddenly Color Tile's growth began to wane, and then stopped. This was later attributed to a sharp drop in US house sales in the first half of 1995. By the time I heard this sad tale, the company had suspended dividend payments and was in default to the banks.

Camelot's story was one of changing times. When we acquired it in 1993, it was the third-largest retailer of recorded music in the US. It had steadily been gaining in market share. But by 1995, Camelot was blindsided by a perfect storm in the music business. First, to boost their sales of electronic hardware, the big-box national chains began selling recorded music at deep discount; second, this coincided with the rapid rise of mail-order music clubs, which sold CDs for a pittance through their vast catalogs. The effect on specialty music retailers like Camelot was an instantaneous disaster. In shopping malls all across America, dinosaur music stores saw their margins reduce and their profits shrink.

I was dismayed by this news and ordered infusions of cash to try to save these critical patients. But it was too little too late. By January 1996, Color Tile had filed for Chapter 11 protection; the following September, Camelot did the same.

After thirteen years of business, to have two acquisitions go bankrupt in a nine-month period was very concerning and, indeed, hugely disappointing.

After that momentous meeting I took Gar aside and told him that I felt he was responsible. 'For the last two years you've been running the New York office,' I said. 'Two years ago the value of Color Tile was high, now it's zero. Why didn't we get out at eighty cents or seventy cents or sixty cents? Why did you wait until now to tell me about it?'

He was doing a bad job, I told him, and in particular I criticized him for spreading rumors in the corridors. 'Why do you think I hired you?' I said. 'You were meant to clear the whole thing up, but what have you done?'

Two weeks later, in early August, he told me he was resigning. 'No,' I said, 'the noble thing would be to stay and clear up this mess.' I told him I would give him more authority to get the job done if he decided to stay. 'But right now I'm going on vacation. I'll talk to you when I come back.'

When I returned in September, he told me he was going to leave. I accepted his resignation immediately.

Then Elie resigned, too.

And all these months I thought we had experienced a sea change. But we had not seen anything yet.

By October of 1995 I found myself confronting a formidable challenge. The Investment Committee was a bust, Gar was gone, Mike would be out in three months, and Elie had given notice. And yet companies do not compliantly stand still and wait while problems get magically solved.

I asked Elie to withdraw his resignation. I sat down with him and we agreed, amicably, on a timetable for his retirement: January 1997, one year after Mike's departure. Then I rolled up my sleeves and got to work, to correct what was needed. My inclination was to start fresh – no retrofitting of existing teams, in fact no retrofitting at all. This was my opportunity to look ahead, to mastermind a brand-new governing process designed to take us safely into the future. Of the many lessons I had learned from the co-COO debacle, one of the most important was that the culture we had created in nearly fourteen years at Investcorp was strongly averse to hierarchy. With that thought foremost in mind, I gathered around me my most experienced, most trusted people; then I set about molding them into a body that could help me run the company with a minimum of formality or hierarchy.

These people would not be given new titles. Instead, they would be coordinators, handpicked representatives from each area of the company whose job description was to keep the CEO informed and assist him in the direct management of the firm. That would be their sole job as members of the Coordinators Committee – nothing less and nothing more.

The initial incarnation of the Coordinators Committee included Sal Abbasi from investment placement; Lawrence Kessler, our in-house attorney and Mike's successor as head of administration; Gary Long from finance; Paul Soldatos as head of investment in Europe; and Savio Tung, whom I had put in charge of investment in North America, replacing Gar.

With these five people, all the facets of the business were presented in full. The group's main function was to spin a web of communication, linking me to the activities and concerns of each group and each group to the other. Once a week, each Coordinator reported in writing to me, copying the other Coordinators. Each Coordinator also phoned me weekly to discuss his report. Finally, we all came together face-to-face one day a month to sort out problems, monitor performance, address questions, and decide on direction.

Within weeks, we all felt this was a system with legs – as indeed it turned out to be, carrying the firm comfortably and profitably into the new millennium. The key was transparency. The system not only forced each Coordinator to report the slightest nuances of his own area, it also gave him a reassuring sense of how the other parts of the business were being run. Each man passed pertinent information from his Committee interactions down to the people who worked under him. The result: no more darkness, no more rumors, no more backstair politicking.

As for me, I felt an unexpected new energy. The five Coordinators were, for me, a recreation of the spirit of the original team. We were all in it together, and there was nothing we could not accomplish as long as we stayed together. With this core group in place, I could remain involved with the daily life of Investcorp while being free to take my own role to the next level. Though I would never have predicted it at the start of the year, I found myself happier than I had been since the first five years of the company's existence.

We held Mike's retirement dinner in January 1996, during the Mancom meeting in the South of France. It was a bittersweet evening, full of tears and laughter and generous, heartfelt words. For most people in attendance that night, the snapshot moment was of me pulling Mike and Elie into a big group bear hug. As I would for Elie a year later, I presented Mike with a silver dhow, the traditional Arab sailing vessel, as a symbol of our journey together.

11
THE INTERNATIONALIST

Investcorp's fifteenth anniversary was celebrated in a moonlit desert oasis, where flickering flames of candles and torches danced on the face of a midnight blue lake. Palm trees rustled in the breeze. Musicians played both Arab and Western music, and tables were laden with foods from all cultures. Surrounding it all were flowers, more flowers than anyone in Bahrain had ever seen in one place at one time. Some thousand important guests attended, and all readily agreed it was a spectacular evening.

And it was all the more spectacular considering that the event took place in a vast museum space in the diplomatic area of Manama, Bahrain. But while the oasis itself was a clever illusion, the occasion it celebrated was solid and very, very real. On February 24, 1998, the day after the party, I addressed, via electronic hook-up, the entire staff of Investcorp:

> This morning I just wanted to say, thank you, thank you, thank you.
>
> You have built up this company and raised it to a premier level – and the secret, as always, is teamwork. It has been, and still is, a team effort ...
>
> I am being congratulated by many people this morning,

> and I wanted to pass this praise on to you. We have shown the world what we can do. The story is not over, of course. But . . . a company's life goes through stages, and for us now the developmental stage is complete.
>
> Investcorp is now a recognized brand in the US, in Europe, and in the Gulf. In all these places, your company has achieved significant position and become a highly respected organization.
>
> For example, look at the attention we attracted in Davos this year, where fifteen hundred of the world's leaders – in media, business, politics, and academia – assemble annually.
>
> Attendance was optional, but many came to the seminar on globalization where I – representing Investcorp – was on a panel with representatives of Hewlett Packard, Deloitte Touche, the Dean of the Harvard Business School, the Editor of *Fortune* magazine, and the big Swiss firm Asea Brown Boveri.
>
> I told them: You don't have to be big to be global. We operate on three continents from three linked headquarters. Decisions are taken by group dynamics from two hundred and twenty people representing twenty-two nationalities.
>
> We never were a one-location company. We sprang from Bahrain to become a global business.

Further recognition of our status came when Investcorp was one of four companies selected by Deloitte Touche to feature as an example of globalization – the others being the global giants Hewlett Packard, DuPont and Asea Brown Boveri.

This was the new message I wanted to drill into everyone in the company: After fifteen years, we had turned a corner, around which waited a larger, more challenging, even more rewarding world than the one we had been operating in up to now. More than a mere buzzword, *globalization* was, at best, a new way of thinking, of doing, even of being. The term I preferred for us was 'internationalists,' a company of professionals who moved through the world easily, creating an indelible presence in it. While we might choose to focus our business in certain geographic areas, we would be comfortable everywhere, with everyone – and everyone would see it and know it. World class was our rightful class.

This meant making absolutely certain that we were every bit as good as the world's perception of us. Excellence is always a work in progress, and so, beginning with the great sea change of 1995, we had embarked on a two-pronged campaign to raise the bar both inside and outside the firm.

The questions pressed by the new Mancom members at mid-year 1995 had cut right to the heart of what I considered some lingering weaknesses. Risk management, improved procedures, more transparency, greater diversification of assets – these were among the challenges Gary Long faced as he dug into his new role of CFO. I informed him of my priority, which, if achieved, could address more than one of these issues. In our London basement, the dead eyes of shutdown trading machines stood as reminders that after some thirteen years we still did not have a viable third line of business. That had to change. An asset management arm could generate short-term income with acceptable risk, providing us a cushion against the volatility of corporate investments and real estate. For various reasons we had never found the right way to make a trading business work. Now I handed that task to Gary.

Real estate too was due for a renewal. One of the major problems that had dogged both Lee Thomas and John

Thompson was that each was alone at the helm of a line of business. Nobody else was an equally qualified expert – in Lee's case, nobody even understood his work enough to challenge him, much less help him. It was a lonely road for both of them, and in a company whose culture is based on group dynamics and participatory management, it was inexcusable. About a year before John left, I decreed that every line of business should have at least two Mancom members in it, or else we should not be in that business. The result was the recruiting of an international real estate professional, Edward Lord III, to partner with John. Among many other achievements, Ed Lord had managed the $3 billion real estate portfolio for Dean Witter Realty. He knew both North America and the Middle East, having worked for part of his career in Saudi Arabia and Iran. Ed took over the real estate operation in New York in November 1994.

At the end of that same year, we made the decision to withdraw from real estate investments in Europe and to close down the London operation. With that, John Thompson elected to leave the company and Ed Lord set about reviving our real estate arm from New York. He had two priorities: First, to dig our existing properties out of the problems they were in as a result of the real estate business turndown, and exit them – but not in a fire sale. We wanted to get the best possible price for all our holdings. Second, he was to rebuild the link between real estate and corporate investment that had been there in our early days.

Our next challenge was to figure out that third line of business – some form of asset management. To that end, at one of our mid-1990s annual Mancom meetings I divided the

Mancom into three teams. The mandate was that each team would come up with recommendations based on debate and collective concern.

Once the reports were in, we hired the consulting firm McKinsey & Company to study each proposal and give us their choice based on external factors: the market, the global competitive landscape, the need in the Gulf. They were also to address how we should position ourselves to generate incremental net income and gain market share.

The product that won the day was 'a fund of hedge funds.' While being overseen internally, this fund would be the result of trading by various external hedge fund managers following different strategies and adhering to parameters established by Investcorp. With the goal now identified, I asked Gary to coordinate a team charged with establishing this line of business. To help him, I selected three Mancom members to dedicate themselves full time to the task – Deepak Gurnani, who, until his recent retirement, was head of our hedge fund line of business; Ibrahim Gharghour, who acted as co-head of the business until he resigned in 2008; and Jon Hedley, who was involved at the establishment phase and then left the firm.

Their first task was to research the hedge fund industry and interview individual managers. This part of the process took six months and produced feedback from some two hundred US and UK fund managers. The purpose of all this interviewing was to choose people we could work with: We also needed to feel comfortable about entrusting our clients' money to them. We assessed them from two angles: One, the quantitative side (how was their track record?), and, two, the qualitative side (did they swing from one method to another, or could they be relied upon to stay within certain parameters of risk?). We were looking for a balanced stable of people, each of whom could be counted on to be consistent in their methods.

Once we found our fund managers, we tried them out for a year in the task of managing our own liquid assets. The results were stellar, and in October 1997 the Investcorp Asset Management Program was opened to clients.

In addition to overseeing the introduction of this important line of business, Gary brought real practical accounting experience to the position of Investcorp CFO. He instituted consolidated P&Ls and balance sheets and made certain we were tracking the key financial figures and key indicators on a monthly basis, against the previous year and against budget. With his expertise, he was able to institute five-year projections – revised several times a year – based on the types of deals we were doing and the sort of liquidity we had in place. He also conducted an efficiency study, looking at the head count to determine whether we were optimally staffed, particularly in the back office. This allowed us to smooth out the operation and eliminate considerable overtime. Finally, he raised the level of expertise in our treasury operation, allowing us to positively influence our balance sheet through the systematic management of interest rates and foreign-exchange rates.

Such improvements, while perhaps not as glamorous as going toe-to-toe with Maurizio Gucci, are nevertheless the kind of grown-up details that banks and rating agencies thrive on. In mid-1998, we were duly rewarded for all our efforts: Investcorp's credit ratings, from all four of the world's leading rating agencies, were raised to International Investment Grade. We had indeed turned a corner.

Or, to return to one of my favorite images, we had built another bridge – this time from the past to the future.

From the very beginning, bridge-building has been the defining metaphor of Investcorp. Our very existence was a 'bridge' linking the Middle East and the West. Now, in these exciting years of our increasing maturity, I found myself thinking more and more about bridges. As the new team worked to create a new infrastructure inside the company, I was finally free again to focus on the external bridge-building front.

I have often described my external involvements as 'burnishing the Investcorp brand.' To clarify how I view that activity, I should differentiate between 'name recognition' and establishing a 'brand.' Advertising will create name recognition, whereas a 'brand' is established in the consumer's mind as a deep psychological affinity with a product or service. All brands must be preceded by name recognition. But not all name recognition will necessarily end up as a brand. A company can spend millions on advertising and never achieve a brand. A brand is establishing a mindset in a customer so they will want to own or be associated with the product or service. To the consumer, that product or service is synonymous with quality, prestige, creativity, and differentiation, and he feels proud to be connected to it. A brand, then, is public recognition of and admiration for the strategy of a company, its products, its vision, and its status.

As a roving ambassador for Investcorp, I have sought

to build bridges between us and people and issues of true substance and import in this changing world. I have attended the IMF and World Economic Forum meetings, the annual summit in Davos, and other conferences important to Investcorp's world. I participate in several political–economic forums and strategic think-tanks. I am involved – sometimes personally, sometimes as a representative of the firm – in the arts and in a variety of charitable and philanthropic causes.

Such an international life requires a first-rate support system. I am able to travel between Investcorp's three offices and tend to all these external activities because of Betty Pires and the people she has put in place in the office of the CEO. Betty has organized my life and time for thirty years now. Wherever I am in the world, I am preceded by the papers I need to read and the decisions I need to make. In each headquarters I have an office that looks essentially the same, with the same desk situated in the same place. Whenever I arrive in Bahrain from London, or in New York from Bahrain, the letters that were awaiting my review at the last office will be sitting in my in-box in the new office. I respond to correspondence from wherever I happen to be operating. My movements around the world have been described as 'cyclonic,' and sometimes it feels that way even to me. But if that is the case, then Betty and her staff have become top-notch 'corporate meteorologists,' bringing a level of almost scientific predictability to a peripatetic existence.

This allows me to focus on the issues that are important to me, and to Investcorp. In my outside work, education has been a major theme. I have had the great honor of addressing audiences at such universities as Columbia, the University of Chicago, Fordham, Harvard, Georgetown, the University of the Pacific and Bilkent University in Ankara. I have spoken to students throughout the Middle East, stressing – as I did in the following words delivered in Morocco – that education is the key to a successful future, and not just for them, but for their region of the world:

> It is enormously inspiring for me to be here in this wonderful country, not too far from the seat of an Islamic empire in its golden age, a civilization that led the world of its time in almost every educational field, from science and mathematics to astronomy and philosophy – a strong reminder of what the Middle East is not today and what it still, hopefully, could be.
>
> But that will never materialize until we revolutionize our educational foundation and adopt a total change in our mindset and outlook ...

Occasionally, I get the chance to put my money where my mouth is. One of my longest-running outside involvements – dating from the mid-1980s – has been with the Center for Contemporary Arab Studies (CCAS) at Georgetown University, in Washington, DC. My first contact with the Center was through two people on Georgetown's staff, Barbara Stowasser and Michael Hudson, who had participated in an exchange program with the University of Ankara in Turkey and on their way back to the States had made a stopover in London to see me. I was fascinated by their descriptions of – and their dream for – the Arab Studies Center at the university, which at the time was some ten years old. It was, they said, the only academic center in the United States devoted to the study of the contemporary Arab world. It was also the only academic center with a graduate teaching program focused solely on the Arab world, which Georgetown presciently felt was under-studied, under-known, and under-appreciated in the world of American higher education.

At some point after that initial meeting, Michael Hudson – by then Director of CCAS – told me they wanted to form a board that would be advisory, but that they needed advice, guidance, and support in getting that board established. He asked if I would be willing to become Chairman and help form such a board. I told him I would be honored to be associated with Georgetown University, given both its preeminent position in Washington and the fact that my own high school education in Iraq had been at Baghdad College, run by American Jesuits.

On my first subsequent trip to Washington I visited Georgetown and asked to see the CCAS. I was very surprised – indeed distressed – to find out that the Center had no home. Professors were scattered in several different locations. My first reaction was: The Center needs its own headquarters. My second was: This would become my first mission as Chairman.

To work with me on a plan for building the new CCAS headquarters, I commissioned the same Boston architect who had redesigned Investcorp's Bahrain headquarters. Over many months we got the necessary permissions from the university for locating the building on the Georgetown Campus. We also received estimates of the cost, and I dedicated myself to raising the necessary funds. Finally, in the fall of 1999, it was my great pleasure to welcome His

Majesty King Abdullah II of Jordan – a Georgetown alumnus – to preside over the grand opening of the new CCAS headquarters.

'Before the building was completed,' said Barbara Stowasser, who became the Center's Director in 1993, 'we were in a little place on the fourth floor. We had only three offices, plus a tiny hallway, and were practically sitting on each other's laps. It was really very difficult. But this has created a whole new relationship among people, and between people and their jobs. Indeed, it has started a whole new chapter. Today, because our environment is so elegant compared to everybody else's, we are perceived within the university in a whole new light. Until then, I wasn't fully aware of the enormous importance of image – even in the university where everybody professes to deny it. Anyway, image is a very comfortable thing if it's on your side.'

As Chairman, I also worked to help CCAS reorganize and strengthen their board, which had been apathetic and inactive. We thanked the old board for their service and replaced them with energetic business people – people who could also help attract the financing the Center would continue to need going forward. Today, no other US university can equal Georgetown's coverage of the modern Arab world. The Center offers more courses in this field, and attracts more students to them, than any academic institution outside the Middle East. Moreover, in addition to its academic mission, it acts as an intellectual bridge between the thinkers and the leaders of that part of the world and their counterparts in this country – a valuable mission indeed.

*

One of the joys of being an internationalist is that you have friends everywhere. The world becomes your neighborhood. And thanks to Investcorp's reputation and prestige, I have had the great good fortune of meeting presidents and kings, princes and prime ministers, as well as the brightest political and business lights in the international sphere.

As I have mentioned earlier, not every one of my colleagues was instantly able to see the value of my devoting time and energy to such efforts outside of Investcorp. But as time went by, no one in the firm remained in any doubt of the importance of those connections. In particular, the attention that I have received from top government and corporate leaders as a result of those activities has propelled the Investcorp name to the highest levels.

And there was another, more immediate, advantage that both I and Investcorp derived from those international involvements. Having access to the wisest and brightest thinkers, the directors of those organizations, has allowed me to expand my scope and outlook. Thus, upon returning to my duties inside Investcorp, I hope I am a better leader, one who can bring a sharper focus and a more sophisticated approach to problem-solving. In contrast to someone who is locked within his firm, the leader who is more exposed will obviously generate a higher quality of output and value. Again, my colleagues at Investcorp today acknowledge such a conclusion with no doubt or hesitation. In the long run, access to important thinkers and distinguished individuals can only be assets to the firm.

While it is a privilege to be in the presence of greatness, and I have enjoyed that privilege many times in my life, three moments nevertheless stand out among the rest. The first was in July 1996, when Investcorp's management team was invited by the Prince of Wales to have dinner and a lively discussion at St. James's Palace. On this truly international, multicultural occasion, I had the honor of introducing Prince Charles to the assembled guests. I stressed the importance of his global vision and philosophy, particularly his courageously expressed views on the need for greater understanding between the Islamic World and the West at a time when the technological revolution is shrinking the world.

'As a result,' I said, 'our differences are becoming more and more visible and if we cannot learn how to tolerate them, we will end up in more and more conflicts and confrontations.

'Therefore, the challenge facing mankind is how to accept our differences and capitalize on our similarities to establish the basis for mutually beneficial cooperation. I am proud to say that Investcorp believes in your principles ...'

That was a spectacular night. But while it is a special thrill to be invited into the home of one of the world's most important leaders, it is perhaps even more special to welcome such a person into your own home. I have had that experience with Prince Charles, who has become a friend; I have also had the distinct honor of welcoming American president George Herbert Walker Bush.

Nada and I first met President Bush and his wife, Barbara, when we accompanied His Majesty, the late King Hussein, to the White House in 1989. After that, we enjoyed the Bushes' hospitality both at the White House and at their fabulous summer mansion in Kennebunkport – a piece of heaven which I hope they will enjoy in good health for many more years.

For Nada and me, however, the high point of this warm friendship came in the spring of 1999, when George and Barbara Bush paid us the very great compliment of visiting us at our home in the South of France. One evening during their stay, we hosted a gala dinner in their honor. Again, this world leader was gracious enough to share his thoughts on the international situation with Investcorp's management team and other distinguished attendees. And, again, I was proud to be the one to introduce our special guests. It is for me, once more, a memory that will never dim.

But in the quiet moments, when I am soaring above the clouds on my way to yet another conference or meeting, I have to pause and remember that none of this might have happened to me had it not been for one very special man who, by his example, showed me the way. He was not a president of government, nor was he a prince, though he certainly traveled in those circles. He was an extraordinary man who just happened to notice me when I was young and gave me a chance to learn and grow. I am speaking, of course, of David Rockefeller of Chase Manhattan Bank. And that is why my third indelible memory is of a dinner Nada and I hosted in New York for David Rockefeller in March of 2005. He was just shy of turning ninety years old, and I was unspeakably proud to be able to publicly thank him for the life that I have been so fortunate to have.

It was significant to me that this dinner took place in New York City. For Nada and me, this will always be the city where our life was transformed. It was in 1969 that we decided to leave Iraq with our ten-month-old daughter, Rena. This meant leaving behind our home and belongings, and all our assets and inherited property, to start a new life from scratch. But in New York we found freedom, hope, promise, enthusiasm, and energy. Even more importantly, coming to New York brought a further transformation. We were no longer citizens of just one nation. We became citizens of the world.

I did not actually say all of that to David Rockefeller on that special evening. Strangely, in fact, I was much less wordy in paying tribute to this man who had once been my boss than I had been when introducing President Bush and Prince Charles. I guess great bosses forever occupy a special, almost unapproachable, place in our hearts and minds.

When I think of David Rockefeller I naturally drift back to thoughts of my own beginnings in the business world. It was, I have to say now, a long time ago. As I write these words, Investcorp has been in existence thirty years. On many levels we have been extraordinarily successful – for one measure, our asset base has grown from $50 million at inception to $11.5 billion; for another, we have realized client returns of 14 percent IRR on corporate investments since inception; for yet another, we have been profitable in every one of our thirty years except one. That – profitability – is the prime criterion of success for a lot of people, but I tend to measure success in more qualitative ways. Are we yet the Ideal House that I set out to build? Have we become the institution that I always envisioned?

From time to time, and especially during the good periods,

I am pressed by various members of the Mancom on the subject known internally as The Succession. This has been happening for nearly my whole tenure at Investcorp, but it has been most pronounced since the early nineties, about the time of the firm's tenth anniversary. I was certainly feeling weary and thinly stretched back then, and in the nearly two decades since I have had my ups and downs. But a man of principle cannot quit before the job is done.

Whenever I have been asked about my successor, I have usually given the same answer: I have not actually identified any potential candidate to be my future replacement, but there are two different circumstances in which my departure might take place. First, there might come a time when I leave of my own accord, in which case I would obviously not do so before being able to recommend a successor to the board for consideration. If selected by the board, he would then take over; and if I were asked, I would certainly agree to remain and serve on the board. That is one possibility.

The other possibility is a sudden vacancy because of some accident. If that were the case, there would be no immediate cause for concern on the part of the board, as day-to-day activities would be handled by the senior managers. They would meet, and so would the board, who would see that the company was in safe hands until the board formally appointed a successor. I would venture to say that the job would attract people of the highest quality. Investcorp has a superior brand and a golden reputation. It has excellent people and a strong client base. The job of CEO pays well, is fun to do, and is extremely gratifying. It carries a lot of authority, together with the scope to grow and become an international statesman. The firm should not short-change itself and move too hastily to appoint a successor.

While that has traditionally been my standard response, I confess that The Succession and its attendant questions have largely defined the last decade for me, and not just because I have been asked so often about it. The thornier questions are the ones I am forced to ask myself: Why is it that whenever I start thinking I have the right people and processes in place, something always seems to go awry? Has my goal of a selfless corporate culture been a pipe dream? Am I expecting the impossible of mere humans? Have I been too much the idealist?

For the second half of the 1990s, all seemed to be going exceptionally well at Investcorp. From the pivotal year 1995 to the end of the decade, earnings rose to new levels. Not only was there a surge in the number of new corporate and real estate acquisitions, but a series of successful exits also helped shore up the bottom line. I felt good about where we were – felt that we had successfully reinvented ourselves after the mid-1990s difficulties. I continued my globe-trotting with a clear mind and the energy of a man half my age.

Then came the millennium decade.

Looking back, we can see the themes of these roller-coaster years beginning in the late nineties, with the burgeoning worldwide craze for technology and telecommunications companies – a sector of the market that some touted as 'the new economy.' I use the word *craze* pointedly: People seemed to lose their minds. If I thought I was flying high above the clouds in a jet plane, others – both our clients and our competitors – were over the moon. Gravity no longer existed. Suddenly when we went to our clients to place a solid corporate acquisition, they asked why we were bringing them these old deals yielding 20 percent instead of a dot.com deal with a 40 percent return. We felt the technology sector was too volatile and told our clients so, but they would not be dissuaded.

One of our biggest problems with dot.com companies was how to apply due diligence to something that was only months old, or that had not yet earned a single dollar. Too many people were throwing big money at start-ups whose only recommendation was an IPO dream – and yet, just enough dot.com companies were making overnight killings to keep the big money coming. Private equity firms were circling these start-ups, and I began to see that we had to get involved somehow or be left behind.

But I imposed two conditions: First, we would only invest modest sums at the beginning; and, second, not a single dime would be invested until our key people had a firm understanding of this market. In our usual methodical way, we turned to an outside expert – an English-born technology consultant in Boston named Richard Fuller, who came in on a temporary basis to tutor us. In short order he joined us full time, remaining with Investcorp until 2005. (He is now an elected member of the UK House of Commons.)

The upshot of all of this was that, in January 2000, we started a technology investment fund, headed up by Savio Tung in New York. By then I had become more favorable toward technology and regarded this fund as a fourth line of business. Fortunately for us, we were still getting set up when the bottom dropped out of the dot.com market in the summer of 2000, so we did not lose as much as others did. All of us, however, became quickly reacquainted with the concept of gravity.

Gravity pulled surprisingly hard in the early years of the decade. As the US and other Western nations slid into recession, we began seeing problems with some of our portfolio companies. By the start of 2001, at least one of our holdings had filed for bankruptcy and another appeared headed that way. Still others were finding the going exceptionally rough.

In the firm's early years I had been directly involved with several of our corporate acquisitions, and almost all of those had turned out to be spectacular deals – among the very best Investcorp has done. They generated excellent results for our investors and helped to build our brand name. But, starting in the mid-1990s, I pulled back from direct involvement in dealmaking; and did not participate in the approval process of acquisitions under consideration. The reason was my commitment to institutionalizing the firm and not allowing it to become dependent on one person. If I kept participating in the approval process, my instinctive likes and dislikes might influence the rest of the members involved in the approval system. For me it was a leadership call: On the one hand, I was of course eager for our investors to have access to the best combined judgment of the firm; on the other hand, if my participation in the approval process discouraged the development of skills necessary to the long-range good of the firm, then my involvement would essentially be derailing Investcorp from future institutionalization. I had to take the long view.

At the January 2001 Mancom meeting I directed that

everything possible should be done to shore up our weaker portfolio companies, including supporting them with additional capital if needed. By May, Gary Long was wrestling hard with his own long-held beliefs about asset allocation and risk management. He and I spent many hours discussing the pros and cons of supporting portfolio companies or leaving them to their fate. What impact would it have on our client franchise if we let them go? If we supported them, how should we go about it? Gary advocated asking our clients to invest additional amounts while we put in our portion.

I saw it differently. To me, the client franchise was the prime consideration. We had to protect that at all costs, despite the strain that a huge exposure to individual companies – admittedly not good risk management – would place on our balance sheet. As always, I had to see the bigger picture. Unless we as a firm provide the necessary support, we could end up having to write off companies over time. That would impact our placement ability – which is to say, it would disturb the very core of our business.

But Gary was not going to set aside his opinion easily. That summer, before we went on vacation, he wrote me a fifteen-page letter detailing the likely effects of both courses. It was one of the toughest documents I have ever read. Injecting more money into these companies, he said, could result in rating downgrades and difficulty persuading banks to lend us money in the future.

I resolved not to worry about it for the few weeks of my August holiday with my family, but the issues seeped into my head anyway. In early September, as Gary was wrapping up his vacation in Hawaii, I sent word for him to fly directly to the South of France to meet with me at my home. A couple of days later he arrived and we spent the next twenty-four hours going over the points of his note in exhaustive detail. As before, Gary argued his case cogently and effectively. I listened to everything he had to say, and then I made my decision, explaining why we had to use our balance sheet to support companies that were capable of survival. At the end of the day, Gary accepted my argument.

On September 11, 2001, I was hosting two of our board members, Mr Abdul Aziz Kanoo and Mr Abdul Aziz Al Suliman, for lunch at our London offices. Before we finished our coffee following the meal, a paper was slipped to me on the table, which meant it was urgent. When I stepped out, Betty informed me that a major plane crash in New York had caused a horrific fire in an office tower. At first I did not understand – I thought the tower was the one where our offices were located, at 280 Park Avenue. After being told that it was the World Trade Center, and that downtown Manhattan was on fire, I returned to my dining room and turned on the TV so my guest and I could watch the news on CNN. In a few minutes we were dumbfounded to see a second plane targeting the WTC towers. It was clear then that the first was no accident.

Before the end of the working day I called our New York office and was told that, while everyone was in a state of shock, there was no personal injury to the staff or physical damage to the building. I promised I would be with them just as soon as I could manage it. By now it had been announced that all US airports were closed and no flights were permitted.

A week later I was finally allowed to fly. In New York I called a staff meeting and expressed my horror, disgust, and deep condolences. At a later date, when contributions were being made by leading business entities to support the victims and the firefighters, Investcorp gave $1 million. We and our Board of Directors felt strongly that since New York had long been our most vital area of product generation, Investcorp should be among the top contributors.

Following the tragic events of September 11, 2001, the business climate became extremely cautious, but this was nevertheless the period during which Gary was spearheading the drive to raise capital for our portfolio companies. Throughout the remainder of 2001 and into 2002 we battled, saving some and still losing others.

As an internationalist – and a man born in Iraq – I also watched with great interest the ways in which September 11 changed the political climate in the United States. The invasion of Afghanistan and then Iraq were profound undertakings with serious consequences, but believing deeply in Iraq's enormous potential for good in its conflict-prone region, I welcomed the removal of the brutal dictatorship of Saddam Hussein. My hope was that the ousting of Saddam would be followed by a grand effort of nation-building similar to that of Germany or Japan at the end of World War II; after a half-century of successive dictatorships, Iraq desperately needed to enter into a rebuilding process. But as I write this, we all know that did not happen. Consequently, in 2009 I was moved to express my feelings in my first book, *Saving Iraq* – a portrait of my home country past, present, and future. It is my fervent hope that the Iraq of tomorrow can again become a beacon of democracy, stability, and prosperity. I wrote the book in the spirit not just of the internationalist I had become, but of the public servant I was supposed to be.

At the February 2002 Mancom meeting, The Succession came up once again. Instead of giving my usual answer, this time I took the opportunity to hold forth on the kind of qualities that would be required by my successor: 'He must be a businessman by mindset and experience,' I said. 'He must have a global outlook and international recognition. He must know and be known in both the US and Europe, and have a strong standing in the Gulf.'

In that same meeting, I announced a major change in the corporate investment structure. Effective immediately, the North American and European efforts would be combined under a single head Christopher O'Brien (who has since left us). He would be assisted by lieutenants both in New York and London.

But in a period of pronounced difficulty for our core business, I felt we had to do more than just rearrange our management structure. It was high time we took a good, hard look in the mirror. How could we reduce our number of unsuccessful acquisitions? How could we improve our batting average?

Even before the Mancom meeting, I had turned this question over to the management consulting firm McKinsey & Company. They tore into it in their usual comprehensive fashion, interviewing every partner in Investcorp and looking at every deal we had done in both the US and Europe from 1984 to 2001. The idea was to search for common elements that might explain success or failure. They also sat in on many of our meetings to see if they could spot problems in our internal methods of operation. The McKinsey study took a year, and after that Chris O'Brien headed up a task force to brainstorm an action plan. Their recommendations – good ideas all – nevertheless involved hiring more people, forming more teams, holding more meetings, and applying more rigorous approval processes. These good ideas included the value-enhancement model which is discussed later in this book.

By 2003, the worst appeared to be over. Gravity did not seem inclined to pull as hard as before. Business – private equity, real estate, asset management, technology – picked up across the board, and as it did we were reorganized, recapitalized, and revitalized to meet the world on better terms. There was only one thing lacking.

In July of 2003, a few days after our fiscal year ended, I phoned Gary Long from my house in the South of France. He was in Bahrain, closing the books on the twelve months just past. I asked him to fly up to see me. Later Gary said he thought I wanted to talk about how to present the previous year's results to our shareholders. But I was more concerned with the years to come.

Gary arrived during yet another beautiful day on the Cap d'Antibes, and I suggested we take a walk in the garden. As we strolled along pathways winding down to the sea, I told him I had been impressed with his good work as Chief Financial Officer. He had helped the firm immensely. I was not planning on leaving, I said, but I wanted to concentrate on my big-picture work – forging contacts, participating in the larger discussion, setting strategy, pointing the way. Consequently, I was asking Gary to become Investcorp's Chief Operating Officer, in which capacity he would take charge of all day-to-day operations. He was speechless. When he returned to Bahrain, he sent me a letter thanking me for my faith in him.

Gary's appointment was well received throughout the firm, as I knew it would be. He was perceived to be highly qualified to oversee day-to-day operations – the right man to execute strategy set in motion by the CEO. Gary's successor as Chief Financial Officer was Rishi Kapoor, one of our ablest 'home- grown' financial executives. With Gary as COO and Rishi as CFO, we entered a new and exciting phase marked by sophisticated accounting expertise at the top. Gary and Rishi worked well together, and I felt confident that our balance sheet was in excellent hands.

In the year 2006, Investcorp needed to increase its capital following several write-offs. As we were now in internationalist mode, an idea arose that seemed quite promising.

While Investcorp had originally been established in the expectation that the firm would be owned by prominent Gulf nationals and leading merchant families in the Gulf region, more than two decades later our profile had increased significantly – both throughout the Gulf states and beyond. Consequently, in 2006, we decided that to meet our growing need for capital we should target the international capital market through a listing on the London Stock Exchange.

The listing was intended to meet three objectives: to raise capital in support of our growth plans; to provide a sophisticated and objective platform for the valuation and trading of our shares; and to enhance Investcorp's standing and brand awareness around the world.

Two weeks before the listing we undertook an exhaustive road show, meeting with leading financial organizations in London, Frankfurt, Rotterdam, Boston, and New York. These institutions expressed keen interest in our firm and its shares and wanted to know everything about Investcorp, including its financial position, its past accomplishments, and its future plans. As a result, when we became officially listed on the London Stock Exchange in December 2006, twenty leading international institutional investors participated in the base offering, purchasing 145,000 shares at $2900 per share and generating $421 million in new capital for Investcorp. This represented a 23 percent increase over the quoted price of $2360 per share on the Bahrain Stock Exchange at that time.

I was extremely proud of Rishi Kapoor, who had spearheaded this drive, and of Gary Long, who had overseen it. It was a pleasure for me to share the good news about our new international status with our stockholders, who had the potential to profit handsomely from our London listing. 'Investcorp's evolution has moved on,' I told them. 'The initial identification of a market need was followed by the establishment of a sophisticated, world-class operating platform. Next came our process of institutionalization. Now, finally, we have achieved Investcorp's internationalization ...'

12
YEAR OF THE TUNNEL

In 2007, we proudly celebrated our twenty-fifth year in business. To mark the occasion, I sent a glowing note to shareholders, clients, and friends of the firm. Here is part of what I said:

> ... Our record over the past 25 years speaks for itself. Investcorp has been profitable, and has paid dividends, in every fiscal year. The average annual return on equity is more than 19%. The original shareholders have received back over 400% of their initial investment through cash dividends, resulting in an overall return to ordinary shareholders of 20% per annum.
>
> The firm has shown consistent ability to grow organically by introducing new products and widening its client base. Established with initial capital of $50 million, Investcorp's market value is now $2 billion ...
>
> For all the achievements of its first 25 years, there is great potential ahead and the prospects are brighter than ever ...

Entering our second quarter-century, we were gearing up for even more dynamic growth. Just nine months earlier, we had launched our listing on the London Stock Exchange. Now, one of the projects I was most excited about was the creation of what I called a 'European Advisory Board (EAB)' to help us build our business on the Continent. Although Investcorp had enjoyed some notable success in Europe, I had become convinced that a higher profile in the UK, Germany, Spain, France, Scandinavia, Italy, Austria, and Switzerland would accelerate our ability to capitalize on the potential of this part of the world. Unlike the US, which we can cover effectively from New York, Europe is more diverse and complex. We needed assistance in creating a higher profile.

For much of the first half of 2008, then, I dedicated myself to creating this impressive body. Generating business would be Investcorp's responsibility, but the EAB would be expected to provide wisdom, introductions, advice, and profile. It would comprise individuals who enjoy a recognizable, respected, and prestigious stature, and who have access to business leaders and governments. The EAB members would have no legal or corporate governance obligations – their only functions would be to provide guidance and generate goodwill. Formation of this group would, to my mind, provide the firm with two advantages: First, Investcorp would have a 'good friend' in each of the principal countries in which it sought to operate – someone who in turn could network with and attract other senior opinion leaders; and, second, it would help us strengthen our Gulf-based position at a time when Gulf countries and companies were increasingly eager to expand into European markets.

But what a difference a year makes. In the fall of 2008, a little over twelve months after sending that triumphant twenty-fifth anniversary letter to our stakeholders – and just as I was preparing to welcome a stellar line-up of European Advisory Board members (list on page 372) to their first meeting at our London headquarters – I learned that Investcorp was facing, in its 2009 fiscal year, a very large loss. Suddenly our priorities changed. The European Advisory Board and other brilliant growth strategies had to be put aside for the moment. Survival was the most important item on our agenda.

I must warn my readers: This chapter contains an inordinate number of internal memos – too many, according to some of my early readers. But I still feel they communicate critical messages at a crucial and decisive period in Investcorp's history. Fiscal year 2009 was an extraordinary year in the life of the firm. Never had I been more prolific – out of necessity – in my written communication with my staff, my board, and my shareholders.

The collapse of asset values worldwide as a result of the global financial crisis of mid-2008 left no financial institution unharmed. What had started as an excess in the US housing and mortgage markets – the desire for every American to own his home, regardless of his ability to service and pay back the mortgage – had led to a full-blown world banking crisis and credit crunch and a problem of over-leverage. Some institutions ceased to exist. Others had to merge for survival. Some were bailed out, or nationalized, or acquired, or had to undergo a major overhaul of their business model, and almost every other organization needed infusions of additional capital. For those of us in the industry, there was, in addition to the practical challenges of getting through these days intact, a decidedly psychological challenge as well: It was horrifying to watch firms that had been respected household names for our entire lifetimes now simply cease to exist: Bear Stearns, founded 1923; Merrill Lynch, founded 1914; Lehman Brothers, founded *1850.* If the 2008 global financial crisis had been a flood, or a tornado, or a hurricane, it would now be designated 'A One Hundred-Year Storm.'

And indeed the banking system in the West at that time was critically over-leveraged – the $650 billion of new capital now raised by banks was simply compensating for almost $700 billion in losses. Reducing leverage required capital over and above that. For the top twenty global banks to reduce their leverage to the levels of the year 2000, they needed to shed $4 trillion of assets. On the other hand, hedge funds – which added up to a $2 trillion pool – had leverage controlling more than $10 trillion of assets. All this caused a massive meltdown in asset value. It reduced confidence and spread fear through the leading financial centers of the world.

Upon learning that Investcorp was not immune to the losses being experienced throughout the industry, I likened our situation to being inside a long, dark tunnel. We were looking for the light, but visibility was almost non-existent. I did see one thing very clearly, however: To blame this disastrous result at Investcorp solely on the world financial crisis would be a deceptively easy response.

My priority was to find out why we had been so vulnerable. In that way, a crisis can be an opportunity for the kind of self-evaluation that leads to improvement.

My instinct was to report our impending loss immediately and widely. According to Bahraini law, we are required to release our results every six months by – minimally – posting our numbers in two Bahraini newspapers. Anything we do over and above that is entirely up to us. In late October of 2008, when I began to learn that we could potentially have a large loss, we could have chosen to be quiet for a while. I considered this not only shortsighted, but just plain wrong: To my mind, we had a moral as well as a legal obligation to report this adverse development right away and in prominent fashion. In the months since my upbeat twenty-fifth anniversary message to shareholders, clients, and friends, we had learned that the picture had changed dramatically. To go forward without divulging this drastic downturn to our stakeholders was, to me, a breach of trust, and there was nothing – not even capital losses – that would hurt us more in the long run than that. It contradicted the very grain of our principle and foundation.

We took space in all of the prominent newspapers in the Gulf to advertise that we had lost money and published the following mid-year letter laying out what exactly had happened:

> Dear Shareholders, Clients and Friends:
>
> Investcorp was established to be a world-class financial institution. It was built to last. That has always been, and will continue to be, our mission.
>
> Investcorp has generated profits and paid out cash dividends to our shareholders in every single fiscal year since our inception. However, in the last six months of 2008, which comprise the first half of our current fiscal year ending

June 2009, we made a net loss.

We continued to be profitable in our fee-generating activities by providing and managing investment products for our clients, although we had a decline of more than $526 million on our balance sheet co-investments, a significant amount of which are unrealized and driven by mark-to-market accounting requirements. While this in itself is not surprising given the unprecedented and horrific crash in the world financial markets, our duty to you is to explain clearly what has happened, where the business now stands, and how we plan to move forward. Open communication in current markets is vital, and our half-year results statement today, together with the accompanying discussion and analysis of performance, is consistent with our customary practice of providing open disclosure and full transparency of which we are always proud.

We all know that the last six months have seen extraordinarily devastated financial markets and an unprecedented downturn across asset classes, fueled by a dramatic loss of liquidity. Along with other financial institutions around the world, Investcorp's asset portfolio has been equally impacted. In normal periods, an alternative investment firm such as Investcorp seeks to outperform traditional asset classes and provide superior risk-adjusted and generally positive absolute returns. While the past six months has shown that alternative asset classes do, in fact, comprehensively outperform traditional assets in the global and local equities and fixed-income markets, the scale of recent market turmoil was such that, notwithstanding this relative out-performance, all alternative assets became co-related and witnessed unprecedented levels of value declines over a very short period of time. Although this is a disappointing result, we can confidently demonstrate that we have taken swift action to mitigate its impact.

There is absolutely no question that Investcorp remains

strong and is fully equipped to seize the new investment opportunities being offered by current market dislocations. We have already seen results as we broaden our array of alternative investment products to leverage our expertise and distribution network in new ways. For example, our real estate credit fund has made $175 million of investments in distressed loans over the last eight months. Our Gulf private equity business has its second significant acquisition poised to close imminently. Our buyouts business closed a new acquisition in Europe in November, and several of our portfolio companies made accretive add-on acquisitions over the period.

In terms of current trading, we are cautiously optimistic about the outlook for the coming six months. In spite of the disappointments of the last six months, we hope to be able to draw a line against the past, and we are looking forward to the future. Overall, based upon publicly available information, our private equity portfolio is in better shape than that of many competitors and our long practiced private equity value-enhancement model will likely prove to be the key to success in this difficult environment. In hedge funds, we have refocused our portfolio with continued emphasis on risk management in every aspect of the business, and we are encouraged by its strongly positive performance in December and January across our hedge fund products.

Investcorp remains strongly capitalized with our capital adequacy ratio of more than 13% exceeding the international BIS minimum requirements by $292 million and the Central Bank of Bahrain's target levels by more than $90 million. We maintain high levels of liquidity with over $1.5 billion of cash and liquid co-investments. A significant proportion of our debt is on a long-term basis which means we are well-armed for difficult conditions over a prolonged period and refinancing needs over the next 12 months are fully covered

> through available liquidity. Evidence of the importance we place on balance sheet strength is demonstrated by the fact that we have taken the opportunity to reinforce it further through a preference share capital increase, currently under way. We have also taken firm action to manage costs, lowering fixed expenses by almost 25%. We fully understand and are prepared to face these challenging times.
>
> Over the past 26 years, Investcorp has lived through a number of economic and geo-political crises. It is true that the current economic crisis is unprecedented in scope, but I believe that our experience in managing through many market cycles, our strong franchise and brand in the Gulf, our disciplined investment approach, and the prudent management of our balance sheet, will enable us to emerge stronger and more competitive. Challenging times provide opportunities for those who understand the market and are well positioned to act. Our driving force has always been, and will remain, our clients' interests.
>
> I take this opportunity to thank our clients, shareholders and many other supporters of this great firm, starting of course with our capable and dedicated staff. We have had you at our side as we have successfully navigated our way through past crises, and we are blessed to have you alongside to guide and support us at this time.

With the major reduction of capital as a result of the reported half-yearly losses, we were faced with two choices: either to reduce the size of our firm drastically and change our business model to match our new diminished capital; or to inject new external capital in order to keep the firm operating within the framework of its traditional lines of business. Of course we decided on the latter. In the meantime, we took the steps necessary to reduce the number of staff wherever we could without hurting the core of our business activities.

In determining the amount and form of the required incremental capital, our able Chief Financial Officer, Rishi Kapoor, advised me that we needed a total sum of US $500 million in preference shares that are considered tier-one capital. Ironically, Investcorp had had $200 million of such capital on its books until 2007, when we paid off the entire amount because it was costing us 10 percent per annum at a time when we had excessive liquidity and high earnings and did not need to carry such a burden. Now, only a year later, we were forced by the collapse of the financial markets to go raise $500 million at who-knew-what annual percentage cost.

Normally, fund raising for the firm's investments is conducted by our placement and relationship managers. They are the ones who maintain contact with our institutional as well as our private clients. But while it would be those same sources that we needed to contact for our new capital requirement, given the monumental magnitude and gravity of this particular task, and under the prevailing depressing circumstances, I did not think it would be appropriate to follow our standard channel. As raising the new preference shares became our most important corporate objective, it was very clear to me that there was no one to delegate this critical task to but myself. Indeed, Investcorp's survival in its current form was at stake.

The outlook was extremely gloomy. With capital sources in the Gulf being targeted by the most prime of prime banks from both sides of the Atlantic, the Gulf-based sovereign wealth funds were being offered 14 percent or more for preference shares, sweetened by warrants that could be converted to common shares at maturity. On the other hand the bureaucrats running those sovereign funds were themselves under attack by their own government officials, who were questioning the choices that had led to such enormous losses in their portfolios. Thus none of the fund managers were enthusiastic about even *considering* acquiring additional assets, irrespective of the coupon offered. There was too much danger of further loss in the underlying value. I cannot exaggerate or overstate how depressed everyone involved with the banking industry was – whether on the side of seeking funds or providing them.

Having been established to serve the investment needs of the Gulf region, Investcorp had an additional pressure. Our entire energy since inception had been directed at becoming one of the most trusted and respected institutions in the Gulf. Now, with giant global financial organizations rushing to the region to raise capital, we could not be seen as being incapable of fulfilling our needs in our own backyard.

'Lonely at the top' has become a business cliché, but I must admit that I felt extremely alone in dealing with this challenge. It reminded me of 1995, when the breakdown of our collaborative teamwork at the senior management level threatened the culture and direction of the entire organization. I remember feeling quite alone then too, as our most experienced professionals departed and a younger group stepped up to preserve the Investcorp culture. That happened this time, too, as Savio Tung – our longest-serving executive besides me – selflessly volunteered to resign in order to help us cut costs and preserve the resources with which to hold onto our best young people.

But this time the challenge was far more serious. Failing to raise the required capital meant the loss of our image and stature in the marketplace. Moreover, it risked the defection and loss of skilled and talented members of the firm. While I was acutely aware of the heavy weight on my shoulders, I knew I could not let that be detected by others. I had to look positive, confident, self-assured, and optimistic.

And in truth, deep in my heart I believed that if there was any possible solution, we had what it would take to achieve it. Never did I feel short of determination or resolve. I rested on the belief that our reputation of integrity and our years invested in building trust and goodwill would help us win this battle – eventually.

For the first time in Investcorp's twenty-six-year history, I called an extraordinary meeting of the Board of Directors. I shared with them the gravity of the challenge we were facing and presented them with my strategy to navigate the firm to safety. The board expressed admiration and 100 percent moral support. Two of the members helped directly – our Chairman, Mr Al-Ateeqi, and a board member from Oman, Mr Al Ardhi. The former initiated a call to a Gulf-based sovereign wealth fund, which, as you will see, made a huge difference. The latter both arranged and accompanied me in my meeting with the Crown Prince of Abu Dhabi, which also led to a successful outcome.

But at the beginning the situation looked extremely bleak. For about seven months of 2009 I did not visit my home in London but operated out of hotel rooms in the Gulf. In Bahrain, where our Gulf business activities are headquartered, I kept my base at the Ritz Carlton Hotel. During those months I ate, slept, and drank Investcorp, pondering our problems 24/7, mulling solutions, and several times a week traveling to wherever our capital-raising objective sent me. Echoes of the year I criss-crossed the Gulf trying to launch this firm were not lost on me. Now I was flying around trying to save it in its current form.

The re-capitalization logjam was finally broken when a large and prestigious Gulf institutional investor commissioned an international consulting firm to perform a feasibility audit on Investcorp. We welcomed this development with open arms and open books. Finding nothing at all disturbing, they reported back to this investor, upon which the latter agreed to participate in our preference shares in the amount of US $100 million. Against stiff competition offering more attractive terms, Investcorp stood its ground for a 12 percent coupon with no options for conversion to ordinary shares. We could not allow ourselves to do anything to reduce our credit standing. In the end, we got our preference shares at 12 percent in a straightforward, no-warrants deal – in five years' time we would have the right to repay the money. And with that precedent established, from then on we could refer to our agreement with this large Gulf institutional investor as our strict standard.

By June 30, 2009, when our twenty-sixth operating year ended with a huge reported loss, the task of raising the preference shares fortunately ended up successfully. In fact, the amount raised exceeded our target of $500 million. Top sovereign wealth funds from Kuwait, Bahrain, Abu Dhabi, Dubai, and Oman provided $425 million. Additionally, certain board members as well as several prominent clients from the private sector also wanted to show a vote of confidence by participating, investing a total of US $109 million.

The spectacular roster of official institutional names that funded our preference shares was a remarkable testament to Investcorp's prominence in that vital region. It reinvigorated our firm in the minds and hearts of everyone throughout the Gulf, and our image once again shot up as a vibrant and dynamic institution. Also, it energized every one of our staff members on three continents.

On August 3, 2009, I sent the following memorandum to the Board of Directors, informing them of the successful completion of our capital increase:

> I am pleased to inform you that, as expected, we have received subscriptions exceeding $500 million for our preference shares from Gulf institutions and individuals. As you know, our publicly stated minimum capital raising target was $250 million ...
>
> Thank you for your support and I wish you a pleasant and relaxing summer.

By May 2009, with the capital increase looking secured, I was able to shift my attention to what needed repairing within the firm. While I would never have suspected it when I started my capital-raising campaign across the Gulf, the extreme difficulty of that mission had turned out to be a hidden benefit. Because of this long grind, I got to visit, in depth, with a lot of influential contacts. From them I gradually began hearing things about Investcorp that raised issues of concern – but I needed to hear about them in order to fix them.

In general, I learned that the perception in the marketplace was that we had lost a step or two in the quality of our products and our ability to meet increasing waves of competition. We were still admired for our absolute integrity and high values, but we were no longer seen as being as dynamic as we once had been. In so many words, what I heard was that this firm that had always prided itself on being cutting edge was in danger of becoming an organization of the past.

It was frightening to me to think of what would have happened if the first person I had called on had handed me a check for $500 million. I might have been tempted to ignore my instincts and proceed on the blissfully ignorant assumption that our troubles were all a result of the worldwide economic collapse. Fortunately, however, I had heard the truth, and this information led me to probe more deeply into the firm.

Among the problems I discovered was that considerable 'siloing' – separation into vertical groups throughout the company – was occurring. Also, our compensation program had gone awry, compromising the logic and balance among our areas of business. These are serious problems in any company, but they are especially critical issues in one like Investcorp. We are a firm built on the idea of collaborative teamwork. Anything that prevents that – either structurally or from an internal competition point of view – is a breakdown in the corporate culture.

At my hotel in Bahrain, I added these concerns to the mix.

One of my tasks during that period was to secure a new head of administration, since Larry Kessler was slated to retire at the end of the year. I had been talking for months with a very strong candidate. Now, in light of the issues that I had learned about, I began broadening my thinking about our general management structure. For countless hours I was filling a series of yellow pads with copious notes about Investcorp's past and future, and diagrams denoting various methods of reorganization and reporting.

Occasionally I took a walk on the little spit of manicured land jutting out from my hotel. Across the cove was Manama, where our blue-cube Gulf headquarters stood. Contemplating it from this external vantage point, I defined my goals as twofold: first, to see us to the end of this tunnel with a minimum of damage; and second, to identify and repair any existing defects that might have changed investors' perception of us – so that when we did emerge into the light, we would be ready to take off without being weighed down with old baggage. Mine, at that stage, was a mission of renewal.

Throughout the winter and into spring I had burrowed into Investcorp's problems, emerging with a comprehensive decision. Now I needed to figure out the precise steps I should take to implement it. Looking for an environment in which to think more clearly, at one point I flew to the Seychelles Islands in the Indian Ocean. My program was to play golf in the mornings for a total of three days and then work on my Investcorp restructuring in the afternoons and late into the night. On the fourth day I flew back to Bahrain with a full plan of action.

What I realized was that the way we had been set up, with all the business heads reporting to COO Gary Long and Gary reporting to me, was no longer the optimal situation. All I knew was what Gary told me, and clearly that was not good enough. On my yellow pads I had sketched out a bold new plan for Investcorp's future. I divided our company into four parts:

- The Gulf, which included product placement and investor relations;
- Product Management, including corporate investments, real estate, technology investments, and hedge funds;
- Administration, encompassing legal, operations, and strategic planning;
- and Financial Management.

In the past, Gary had had to deal with and worry about each one of those areas, and that was why some discrepancies were arising. I now decided to break his job into four parts, each section being run by an executive giving it 100 percent of his time and attention. With each section head reporting directly to me, I would have a complete and in-depth picture of what was happening in the firm.

But that was only half the plan. The other half was to find the four best people in the world to run those divisions.

This plan, I felt, was absolutely key to Investcorp's future. It was time for me to arrange for the long-anticipated succession. But to me that did not mean naming a successor as CEO; in this fragile economic environment I could not step down yet. It would not be right. What I could do, however, was to upgrade and fine-tune the corporate machinery that, hopefully, would remain in place after my future departure. It would be up to the board to eventually select a new CEO, but in the context of this new management framework, the future CEO should operate with some comfort. He would be like the driver of a modern automobile, pointing the car in a direction and turning the wheel to steer it. But in fact this state-of-the-art corporate mechanism should function smoothly no matter who was chosen to succeed me as CEO.

That is my definition of an institution.

While much of the rest of the corporate world was still groping in the darkness of the tunnel, I was now focused on coming out at the other end. As I continued my calls on investors, I also composed, in my head, the job descriptions of the four individuals who would largely run the new and improved Investcorp. And I began tracking down candidates and inviting them to visit with me.

I took personal charge of the recruitment process. This was not a time to impose even a single layer between me and my perceptions, much less my expectations. With some thirty-five years of international banking under my belt, I had a sense of who the stars were. And yes, after decades of proclaiming a no-stars system, I definitely wanted stars. I also wanted impressive titles. I wanted to wake up the industry to Investcorp's own star power, and the best way to do that was to show that we could still attract the best and the brightest at every level. That was one consideration. But of course the stars I sought had to be capable of working effectively within our corporate culture. They had to have the character, the values, and the skills to become a Dream Team – with heavy emphasis on the second word.

Months before this big-picture plan had registered in my consciousness I had essentially taken the first step in implementing it. Pursuing an administration successor to Larry Kessler, I phoned the office of Mark Slaughter, Chief Operating Officer of Global Banking at Citigroup. An international banking heavyweight who had earlier spent more than twenty years as COO of Goldman Sachs International, Mark was a Harvard-trained lawyer with undergraduate degrees in nuclear engineering and history. To my mind, Mark would bring great expertise – and a unique skill set – in corporate operations, strategic planning, and investment banking to the table.

Mark and I knew each other only by reputation, and later he told me he was impressed that the founder of a firm would personally pick up the telephone and ask for a meeting. We met several times in London before the end of 2008, and later he visited me at my hotel in Bahrain. We each had a lot of feeling-out to do. In his current job, Mark had some six thousand people reporting to him; at Investcorp, the entire company topped out at around four hundred. If he were to join us as Chief Administrative Officer, would he feel a loss of identity? Would he be able to make the transition from global to boutique brand? And why would he want to? Those were some of the topics we explored together over many months.

In the meantime, I began considering who might be best suited for two other positions – product management and finance. This was a particularly gratifying part of my search, because after careful examination of the industry, I decided we had the best operators right there at home.

With a business background at both Mancuso & Company and Manufacturers Hanover Trust, Christopher O'Brien had joined Investcorp as a principal in 1993. He was among that first group of principals to move to the Mancom in 1995, and over the succeeding years I had watched him grow into a consummate manager. Chris was already overseeing corporate investments and real estate on both sides of the Atlantic; his new role as President of US and European Business would add technology and hedge funds to his portfolio.

In the area of finance, Rishi Kapoor had joined Investcorp in 1992 and had seemed to grow up in the company, holding several positions – including Senior Internal Auditor; Head of Applications Development; Head of Business Analysis, Planning, and Reporting; and Head of Financial Management – before stepping up to the job of Chief Financial Officer when Gary Long was promoted to COO in 2003. Rishi had earned a BTech, summa cum laude, in electrical and computer engineering from the Indian Institute of Technology in Kanpur, India, and an MBA – again, summa cum laude – from Duke University in North Carolina. Rishi Kapoor was the walking definition of the phrase 'smart as a whip.'

The trick was going to be the Gulf. This was our base, the home of our investors. One night as I sat at the desk in my hotel suite, I wrote the following words:

> Emphasize the importance of the region. It is one of the world's most promising growth areas and the location of 40 percent of its proven oil reserves. Whatever happens around the world, there will always be demand for energy.

> But it is also a difficult area to penetrate effectively. The way to win recognition and the heart and mind of the region is through trust and respect. It is going to require a very special organization – one built on integrity and competence and held together by an unusual culture – to be accepted, respected, and trusted.
>
> In a global industry driven primarily by financial incentives, sometimes to the point of greed, the marketplace in the Gulf is looking for an organization that is driven by pride, quality, and principle.
>
> The investment needs of the region were never under-served. However, there were certain qualifications that the Gulf required and found to be lacking. Investcorp was created to fill that gap. Its instant success was evidence that clients had found in Investcorp the qualities they were looking for.
>
> Investcorp's culture was based on pride, quality, competence, and principle. Its staff was motivated, excited, and empowered.
>
> Investcorp will continue to thrive if it can hold to that culture – and decline when that culture fades. That has been, and will remain, its most critical challenge ...

From the Gulf I had heard of changing perceptions of Investcorp. So *for* the Gulf, I needed someone whose very name would instill respect and confidence.

This was not a difficult problem from my point of view: Clearly, the person I wanted for Investcorp's President of Gulf Business was Mohammed Al-Shroogi, the one and only Gulf national – he was from Bahrain – to work for an American bank, Citigroup, for more than three decades. He had gone from the lowest, smallest job and risen to the highest ranks. Now he was Citigroup's man in the Gulf. As Citi's Division Executive for the Middle East and North Africa region and CEO for the United Arab Emirates, Mohammed knew everyone and everyone knew him. Among his many achievements at Citigroup was establishing Citibank Bahrain as a major trading room between Asia and Europe. He also served as Chairman of Citi Islamic Investment Bank. He was a member of the Bahrain Economic Development Board; a member of the board of trustees at Bahrain University; a member of the board of the National US-Arab Chamber of Commerce in Washington, DC; and a member of the board of Injaz Al Arab. He held a BA in commerce from Kuwait University and had attended the Executive Program at Harvard Business School.

Mohammed Al-Shroogi fitted into my plan perfectly. The question was whether Investcorp would fit into his. Why should he leave Citigroup at this stage of the game? As with Mark Slaughter, Al-Shroogi presided over an enormous geographic span, and some ten thousand employees throughout the region from Afghanistan to Algeria reported to him. What could tiny Investcorp offer to get him to leave all that behind?

That was my challenge.

Again, I used no executive recruiters. I knew Mohammed, so I phoned him and we started talking. He came to visit me in my hotel. 'You want me to leave Citi after thirty-four years?' he said.

'Think about it,' I said, and I emphasized that Investcorp was not a giant box store; it was a highly distinguished boutique. 'You could do a lot in a place like this.'

In the darkest of these dark economic days, my conversation was all about the light-filled future.

★

On June 11, 2009, I sent out a Memorandum to All Staff at Investcorp worldwide. Excerpts from that memorandum are set out below:

> In the midst of the painful financial and economic crisis that we are currently experiencing, I feel that Investcorp needs to focus on two fundamental objectives in order to reaffirm its stability and engender confidence.
>
> The **first** is to ensure that we survive this dark tunnel with minimal damage.
>
> The **second** is to use the crisis as an opportunity to engage in accurate self-diagnosis and to reshape and reposition the firm for a powerful take-off as soon as we emerge at the other end of the tunnel. Our immediate strategy, therefore, should be to overcome any obstacle, identify and remove any weaknesses, reinforce our strengths and prepare ourselves for a decisive relaunch – all with the aim of re-establishing Investcorp as a vibrant and dynamic institution and regaining our pre-eminence in our target market.
>
> Some of our competitors may not emerge from the tunnel. Others may be less prepared than we are when normal conditions return. On both counts, we must seize the opportunity to regain momentum, take meaningful market share and place ourselves at the head of the pack.
>
> Wherever we have weaknesses at present, we should not be satisfied with piecemeal repairs or partial improvements. The challenge is to focus on any weaknesses with courage and determination in order to turn them into strengths. Our margin for error is minimal. We have to get it right.
>
> **Priorities**
>
> To meet these objectives, we need to pay particular attention to the three fundamental components of our business model.

First, the products we offer to our clients should stand out as best in class as evidenced by their performance. This is as straightforward as it is absolutely essential. We cannot regain market recognition without a fundamental change in our clients' perception of the quality we offer.

Second, we must re-energize our internal culture and the power of our brand. From the very beginning, Investcorp aspired to be a superior organization. Its founding culture was based on pride, quality, competence, trust, and principle, and we hired only those who truly cared about these values. No one in the 1980s joined Investcorp for the compensation alone. They joined because they were proud to be part of this firm. They believed in the culture and knew that its underlying fairness would ensure adequate rewards. In short, the attraction to any newcomer was our environment, our culture, and our dynamism. There was a partnership mentality and a willingness by all those involved to invest their future in the firm.

Today, much of Investcorp's workforce is relatively new to the firm and may or may not be aware of the culture of the earlier period. We must re-emphasize that the people we need to attract and retain are those with passion and integrity whose greatest incentive is the pride of belonging to an outstanding organization.

We must ensure that Investcorp's spirit and culture are as strong today and in the future as they were in the early years. This will mean upholding our commitment to excellence, dedication, creativity, innovation, and principle – all of which are vital for restoring and maintaining our dynamism.

Third, we must substantially enhance Investcorp's position in the marketplace. Investcorp was created to be a Gulf-owned yet world-class-managed investment firm. For 25 years, there was no other organization that came even close to the recognition we had earned in terms of prestige, trust, reliability, respect, and competence.

This was illustrated for me a few years ago in speaking with the CEO of one of the largest private equity firms in the world. He told me in New York how he had visited the Gulf and was amazed when a prominent local business leader explained to him that his organization took care of all its domestic investments in-house but left international investments entirely up to Investcorp. Our competitor was courteously received, but left empty-handed.

The current crisis may have caused a temporary erosion of confidence in investments in general among our clients. But the region in which we specialize has huge hydrocarbon reserves that world markets will continue to demand. As a result, the region will continue to generate surplus funds and these will continue to need credible investment outlets.

Investcorp must act boldly and decisively to re-assert its market leadership and establish itself, once again, as a trusted brand. We must take measures that will increase Investcorp's long-term competitiveness. We must be the most needed and respected investment firm in the region, reliably delivering quality services and products. Our breadth and depth provide a unique opportunity to rise and be perceived as the most prestigious and transparent investment firm in the region.

Organization

These priorities require a well-orchestrated re-direction of our skills and talents to enable Investcorp to maximize the available opportunities.

Organizational structures are not and should never be static. They are vehicles for mobilizing the human resources of the firm to accomplish its objectives at any given point in time. Such structures therefore need to be reviewed periodically to ensure the firm's dynamism. As circumstances and objectives change, organizations must similarly evolve in order to fulfill their purpose. This is essential for sustained success.

Thus, at this stage of our development, we need a new focus and a transformed organization to ensure quality, flexibility, accountability, and speed. The process will require clarity of vision with commensurate courage and know-how in defining our objectives. Our approach should be both diagnostic and aspirational.

Action

Moving forward, the position of Chief Operating Officer at Investcorp will be discontinued.

A new organizational structure will be announced in July. Until then:

Chris O'Brien, Deepak Gurnani, Jim Tanner and Rishi Kapoor will report to me.

I have asked Larry Kessler, whose retirement has been announced, to extend his stay at Investcorp for six more months. Until the new organizational structure is in place, managers of all current support centers (Corporate Communications, Legal/Compliance, Human Resources and Executive Compensation, as well as the Administration Managers in Bahrain, London and New York) will report directly to Larry, who, in turn, will report to me.

The transitional period will end when the final management structure is in place and assumes its full responsibilities in July. At that time, Larry Kessler's role will change from executive to adviser until his departure at the end of December 2009.

For my part, I remain as committed as ever to standing shoulder to shoulder with you all in order to fulfill our mission and reaffirm Investcorp as the successful organization it has always been. The past 26 years have seen numerous ups and downs. We have enjoyed the heights of success and been tested by severe setbacks. But at no time did I lose my

> confidence in Investcorp's potential to be one of the world's most empowering, inspiring and exciting organizations – a firm to which we can all be proud to belong.
>
> Our collective responsibility is to face the new environment with determination and ambition. We need to apply laser-like focus and total attention to our products, markets and capabilities – not only to secure our survival during the present crisis, but, equally, to ensure growth, vitality and prosperity thereafter. We must rise to the challenge as Investcorp has done many times before and reaffirm our robust commitment to succeed.
>
> Each and every member of the Investcorp team is now needed more than ever. Your efforts and dedication are critical and are highly valued and appreciated.
>
> For the first six months of fiscal year 2009, our results saw red ink for the first time. Prior to this, as you know, we demonstrated a consistent record of profitability for over a quarter of a century. Our challenge, now, is to look past the storm and show energy and commitment in re-launching Investcorp as a competitive force, stronger and more robust than ever.
>
> I do believe the best is yet to come for our staff as well as our other stakeholders. I am counting on you to join me in realizing this vision.

The new Senior Management Team came together for the first time in early July. The site was a hotel in the mountains high above Vevey, Switzerland, with blue Lac Léman spread out like a second sky below. Mark and Mohammed had not even officially joined the firm, and none of the four had yet been identified within the company as part of the promised re-organization. This was a bonding session, the cementing of a strong new partnership. My goal for those few days was to establish a common platform of understanding among the five of us. I wanted us to think as one about Investcorp – what it had stood for over the past twenty-five years, and what it should stand for over the next twenty-five.

I talked a lot over those days. I spoke candidly of the shock of a financial loss after a quarter-century of profits. I spoke of the perceived weaknesses this crisis had exposed in our culture. And I especially spoke of my hopes for this new team, both individually and collectively. I had always been the sole architect in the past, I said, leaving to others the job of translating my visions into reality. Now, going forward, I wanted this to be a collective effort. I viewed this group as essentially a team of equals.

I wanted the firm as a whole to be similarly egalitarian, following the principles that the firm's founders had set out to institute. Our culture must ensure fairness for the people we choose, and who choose us, and the deciding factor should be the pride of belonging to a truly special organization. The deciding factor should be the culture itself.

Those were special days that this new management team spent together in Switzerland. While engaging in a spirited give-and-take about strategy and corporate culture and how to attract the best people and create the best products, we five also came to know and appreciate one another. A management team may look excellent on paper, but until those individual participants gather in a room you never know how the chemistry will go. I had taken a big risk in bringing two new people into the company in such senior positions and asking them to form a seamless team with two incumbents – all at a moment of such uncertainty. But when I witnessed this team in action, even in this limited capacity,

I was heartened to see that they were each engaged at the right levels with the right tones and the right message. They were listeners, thinkers, and doers all at once. I felt certain that when this new team went to its first Mancom meeting in London in the fall, they – we – would present an impressive, united, and reassuring front. There were moments during those few days when I felt as though I had gone back in time: a new Team of Four, a new beginning, a new and better future ahead of us.

On July 10, 2009, I sent out a follow-up Memorandum to All Staff at Investcorp worldwide:

> Further to my previous communication in early June, I am pleased to announce Investcorp's new senior organizational structure.
>
> We have established a leadership team of Senior Partners which will be chaired by myself and will comprise four other members, all reporting directly to me. While each of the Senior Management Team members will have specific functional responsibilities, the group will function seamlessly with collective ownership of and accountability for the operation of the entire firm.
>
> Two members of the Senior Management Team are newly appointed and come to Investcorp with splendid credentials as highly accomplished leaders in world-class organizations. The other two are home-grown Investcorp members, also with records of outstanding performance whose responsibilities will be significantly expanded.
>
> Mohammed Al-Shroogi will be President of our Gulf business. In this capacity he will be responsible for all Gulf-based business activities including Placement and Relationship Management, Gulf Growth Capital and the MENA Mezzanine Fund. He will also head any other business that we may

choose to establish in the Gulf in the future.

Chris O'Brien will be President of our US and European lines of business, operating out of New York. Private Equity, Hedge Funds, Real Estate and Technology Investment on both sides of the Atlantic will report to him.

Mark Slaughter will be our new Chief Administrative Officer, coordinating the development of strategy and overseeing the administration of all three offices along with corporate communications, legal and compliance, human resources and compensation.

Rishi Kapoor will continue to be our Chief Financial Officer with responsibility for directing the firm's corporate financial management function. He will oversee Investcorp's relationships with all key financial stakeholders.

Rishi and Chris need no introduction, but I would remind you a little of their backgrounds. Both have highly successful track records with Investcorp. Rishi joined the firm as a Vice President in 1992 and held a number of senior positions in our finance team before being appointed Chief Financial Officer in 2004. Chris joined us in 1993 as a principal in private equity and, as Head of Direct Investment since 2001, has overseen our private equity, real estate and post-acquisition activities across the firm.

I am very pleased to welcome Mohammed Al-Shroogi and Mark Slaughter to the firm. Mohammed Al-Shroogi is one of the most experienced bankers in the Middle East and North Africa having had an exemplary career running Citigroup across the region, latterly as Managing Director for the Middle East and Chief Executive Officer in the UAE. With his unparalleled knowledge of the Gulf, there is no one better to lead the charge to reassert our brand, prestige, and reputation in the region. Mohammed will be based in Bahrain.

Mark Slaughter brings heavyweight international banking experience in operations, strategic planning and investment banking, acquired during a career of senior leadership roles at Goldman Sachs International, where he was Chief Operating Officer, and, most recently, at Citigroup where he was Chief Operating Officer, Global Banking. Mark will be based in London.

I also said when I wrote to you in June that we need to focus on three fundamental components of our business model. First, we must ensure that the products we offer to our clients stand out as best in class in terms of their performance. Second, we must re-energize our internal culture and the power of our brand. Third, we must enhance Investcorp's position in the Gulf marketplace. With its unique mix of skills and experience, this new team will enable us to achieve these objectives.

We have just concluded the first meeting of the Senior Partners in which we covered the following topics:

- Vision: the long-term architecture of the firm.
- A new partnership team to ensure a vibrant corporate spirit and a dynamic management structure.
- A fair, equitable and sustainable corporate culture that ensures commitment and dedication and achieves both immediate targets and long-term objectives.
- Attracting and retaining the required talent.
- Restoring our market pre-eminence.
- Ensuring the superiority of our products from our clients' perspective.
- Planning for fiscal 2010 with a determination to turn our results around and regain our historical upward momentum.

I am proud to report that the team is fully committed and united and will do its utmost, both as a group and within each area of responsibility, to achieve the above objectives …

With the capital raising behind us, each and every member of Investcorp is now needed more than ever to help drive

> the transformation of our business over the next year. Your efforts and dedication are vital and are highly valued and appreciated. I know I can rely on you to give your full support to this new team.

Ever since I had first learned of our potential loss for fiscal 2009, I had been wrestling with what had gone wrong and how to put it right again. I had personally lived in the long dark tunnel. Now I was truly excited by the impending changes I had set in motion. Far broader and deeper than mere personnel adjustments, they were no less than a re-envisioning of Investcorp for the twenty-first century.

With the successful completion of the required capital increase, followed by an effective reorganization of our senior management structure, our corporate attention shifted to rebuilding a robust balance sheet. Our most pressing challenge was to make certain that fiscal 2010 was a success.

One of the fiscal issues we needed to confront was our listing on the London Stock Exchange. We had made the decision to list there at a time when Investcorp's unparalleled profile in the Gulf made the international capital market an attractive new source of equity capital. But everything had changed between 2006 and 2009. In the aftermath of the global financial crisis, every financial institution was in a hurry to de-leverage its balance sheet. As a result, Investcorp's shares had suffered massive sell orders and their value had fallen dramatically. When our shares in London are quoted at substantially less than their intrinsic value, the listing becomes a liability to our reputation and stature. Since the essential objective of Investcorp has been and will continue to be a Gulf-based organization, we now decided that our shares need not be quoted anywhere but in the Gulf. So we spent several months in 2009 organizing to get out of the London Stock Market.

Another major fiscal problem we had to address was hedge funds. In mid-2008, Investcorp's exposure to hedge funds had been $2.2 billion, which got badly hit by the crisis. In 2009, in line with our public disclosures, this exposure was reduced to $1 billion, and the proceeds were applied to prepay loans and reduce liabilities. Thus, we achieved our third corporate objective by de-leveraging the firm.

At the end of June 2009, Investcorp had $1.2 billion in cash on the balance sheet plus more than $600 million of liquid assets. Such abundant liquidity in a total balance sheet of $3.6 billion gave us the ability to withstand the extremely stressed environment in which the overall financial world was still operating. Moreover, it ensured ample capability, allowing us to perform our normal business activities.

Our fourth corporate initiative was directed by Chief Financial Officer Rishi Kapoor, in which several executives, including myself, played an active part. Looking at our debt payments over the next three years, we decided to raise new financing from international banks in order to pay off all those maturities in advance. A new facility of $500 million would effectively refinance and roll over our next two and a half years of debt maturities to early 2013, buying us extra protection at a time when any protection at all was hard to come by. This was a bold move by Investcorp, initiated when banks around the world were under pressure to reduce their balance sheets and curtail cross-border lending. Yet once again we were remarkably successful. Fourteen banks participated in the Investcorp facility, comprising a 'Who's Who' of global blue-chip names. This result is testament to the relationships our firm has developed and nurtured over many years, and to the support we enjoy at all levels in these top institutions.

In a memo thanking his colleagues for their hard work on this initiative, Rishi Kapoor wrote, 'This achievement epitomizes the key qualities that differentiate Investcorp – our ability to come together and work as a single cohesive unit across three continents and our dogged determination to succeed in the face of adversity, no matter what the odds. Successes like these define our institution, and are to be toasted. Cheers!'

Finally, as I put the finishing touches on this chapter, I am able to report that Investcorp posted a fiscal 2010 net income of $102.1 million. This impressive and rapid rebound from the challenges of our previous fiscal year proved the robustness of our business model and the enduring power of our Gulf franchise and relationships, and it also demonstrated the effectiveness of the bold and decisive action we had taken to reshape the firm to meet changing conditions and to exploit rising opportunities in a world economy starting to reset itself. Finally, our 2010 performance underscored the difference that Investcorp's market position and reputation can make in a more difficult investing environment. Our clients recognize, more than ever, the pre-eminent importance of sound advice, first-class service, transparency, and clear alignment of interests.

★

So I can say with confidence that we as a firm have emerged from the dark tunnel. Now we – the Senior Partners with the willing and able participation of every employee at Investcorp – are together working hard to rebuild the firm's value.

To a great extent, we are doing that by rebuilding the firm's *values.* 'You must be needed, you must be respected, you must be trusted,' said my father, and while we drifted somewhat in recent years from the corporate culture that had made us so successful for so long, that period of drifting is over. Now we are systematically re-emphasizing and re-embracing our core values and beliefs.

One of Mark Slaughter's first major assignments was to prepare a 'Strategy and Vision' document, which would be rolled out in company-wide presentations starting in the autumn of 2010. The document begins like this:

> Today, Investcorp is a client-driven financial services firm that is focused on the countries of the Gulf region.
>
> We are a trusted provider of unique, value-added and non-traditional investment opportunities and services to Gulf investors, primarily private individuals and merchant families. We also serve institutional investors and, where it has a positive impact on our Gulf business, we also provide these investment opportunities and services internationally . . .

It is a deceptively simple statement. But the more you read it, the more certain ideas rise to the surface: *client-driven; Gulf region; trusted provider; non-traditional investments.*

In the past few years at Investcorp, there was excited talk

among some of the Mancom about expanding into other parts of the world, such as Asia. No more. We are returning to our roots. For three decades we performed as an effective bridge between non-traditional investment opportunities in the West and the elite of the private-sector business leaders in the Arabian Gulf. Going forward, we will continue to do what we have excelled at in the past.

But not only are we returning to our roots, we are *nurturing* those roots. We will serve our Gulf clients' needs in the West, but we also hope to serve their emerging requirements in the Gulf as well. Investcorp, with its stellar brand name, should gradually build additional lines of business to be the Gulf region's prime merchant bank. We should be active in Gulf investments. We should be at the forefront of equity and fixed-income markets in the Gulf. We should be ready to provide advisory services to family businesses as well as to institutional clients.

In short, in the next twenty years Investcorp should have a track record of a half-century in international investments and nearly a quarter-century of Gulf merchant banking business. Our vision remains clear, our mission unchanged: to excel in every one of our markets, products, and lines of business. We will do whatever is required to be needed, respected, and trusted by anyone who does business with us.

That is the core message of the Strategy and Vision document. I find in it echoes of that long-ago 'concept document' that Mike Merritt distilled from our discussions when Investcorp was still just a dream. As that statement was an affirmation of who we were and who we intended to be as an institution, this one is a reaffirmation for a new generation.

Back to the future was our motto.

PART III

TOWARD A MISSION ACCOMPLISHED

13
A WELL-OILED MACHINE

In the Prologue to this book, I wrote that this is the memoir of a vision – the story of what happens when an ideal meets real life.

There are two certainties about real life – it is unpredictable, and it is filled with obstacles. You will not be surprised to learn, then, that my bold new plan for Investcorp's future has already faced significant challenges. In the fall of 2010, just a year after his arrival, Mark Slaughter informed me that he had reluctantly decided to resign, for personal reasons. This was a matter of regret to both sides, as Mark had keenly appreciated the high expectations we held of him when he joined our Senior Management Team, and he was disappointed that personal circumstances now prevented him from continuing the journey. In my memo to the staff announcing this development, I made a point of saying that Mark 'departs as a good friend of Investcorp, and with our best wishes.'

In the same memo, I proudly announced the return of Mike Merritt, who – being the good soldier he is – immediately agreed to leave his comfortable home near a golf course in heartland America and move once again to Bahrain to serve Investcorp, the firm he played such a momentous role in founding. Replacing Mark Slaughter as Chief Administrative Officer, Mike brought with him – in addition to his deep devotion to a fair and equitable Investcorp – his still-fierce talent for systems that have already made us an even stronger company.

A year later, Chris O'Brien resigned from the firm after nearly two decades of service. By that time I was again in regular discussions with Savio Tung, who for two years had been enjoying his life serving on boards around the world – and also living for a time in China, where he had gone to work on improving his Mandarin. But I missed Savio's experience at assessing deals, not to mention the influence of his presence on our corporate culture – in conversation with his colleagues, he leads by invoking humility as a goal. It is a message we cannot hear enough, and so I asked Savio to put his new life on hold and come back to Investcorp. Like Mike, he again answered the call. Savio is now head of all of the firm's investing lines of business – corporate investments, technology investment, hedge funds, and real estate.

Though Mike and Savio's return was not something I had imagined in the depth of the financial crisis, it nevertheless underscores the 'back to the future' philosophy we were working toward in those dark days, and which we are emphasizing today. As I write these words, we are nearly four years beyond the depth of the global economic crisis. Many of our competitors never emerged from the tunnel, and four years ago I was not one hundred percent certain where our firm would be at this moment. But I am happy to report that we have never been stronger. Where we had allowed our firm to become bloated, whether from misjudgment or inertia, we have cut back – losing nearly 25 percent of our personnel since 2008. We have rebuilt our compensation system to ensure a wider spread of fairness and alignment of interests. Today, we are *all* pulling together in the same direction – something we perhaps have not done since Investcorp's earliest days, when we were a small, tight force unified by a common dream.

Mike Merritt perhaps expressed it best in a recent presentation, when he was contrasting the Investcorp of today with the organization of not too long ago. 'How do you take a bridge?' was the question Mike, the former infantry officer, posed to his audience. Of course, they had no clue. 'From *both sides*,' Mike said – meaning as a team, working together, coordinating the effort – whatever that effort may be.

You know I always love a good bridge metaphor, and this one was absolutely perfect for these new times. But, in fact, the image that most often comes to me to describe the post-crisis iteration of Investcorp is that of 'a well-oiled machine.' What I have in mind is not the concept of the tight, humming mechanism of a fine watch that I used to invoke when describing the smooth running of the company; today I imagine a more robust machine – something between an automobile engine, with its pistons and rods and crankshafts working in concert to create motion, and a modern, fully automated factory in which all the avenues of production are connected and coordinated to the nanosecond – and if one avenue becomes congested or contaminated for any reason, the system corrects itself without missing a beat.

The five members of the Coordinators Committee (which was formerly referred to as the Senior Partners Group) are the linchpins of the operation. Yes, five: In addition to the four I initially penciled in during my crisis planning in 2009 – Chief Administrative Officer (Mike Merritt), Chief Financial Officer (Rishi Kapoor), President of Gulf Business (Mohammed Al-Shroogi), and President of our US and European lines of business – now called Chief Executive Officer, North America, and held by Savio Tung – I have since added the position of Chief Executive Officer, Europe, a slot filled by Scott Freidheim. Scott had been Global Head of Strategy for Lehman Brothers, among other prominent positions there, and we had known each other for twenty years – staying in touch, occasionally having dinner together when I was in New York. Scott shared my feeling that Europe, despite its problems, was a region of vast opportunity for us, and in 2011 I invited him to come be our point man on the Continent.

So the five Coordinators are the people who oversee Investcorp's corporate performance in total. Communication channels from them are designed to go up, down, and sideways – up to me, down to the various business enterprises each Coordinator supervises, and sideways to one another, so nobody operates in either a vacuum or a silo, as the case may be. Three Coordinators are based in Bahrain, one in London, and one in New York, and we meet formally twice a month – once in person, and once by video conference. Not only does everyone know what everyone else is doing, he is expected to pass the relevant information on to those who work for him, including any instruction in, or reinforcement of, the corporate culture. And those receiving this information from the Coordinators are obliged to pass it on to *their* people, and so on down the line. It has proved to be a solid system.

Think of the Coordinators as five powerful engines setting in motion the activities of scores of experts engaged in dozens of tasks around the world. At the level immediately below the Coordinators are the heads of all the firm's lines of business. And yet these lines are not totally separate, or even straight. Like the electronic tracks on your computer's motherboard, Investcorp's lines of business go this way and that, connecting to one another here and there, up and down, in and out: real estate intersects with corporate investment when appropriate; our technology investment fund includes a focus on private equity (what we call corporate investment); Scott Freidheim plans his European forays around ways he can help drive his partners' businesses; corporate investment draws from all the firm's talent to assemble management teams according to the project at hand; real estate and corporate investment coordinate with the placement team in the Gulf (overseen by Mohammed Al-Shroogi), because an acquisition without investor placement is only part of the process; and *everyone* is connected on many levels with Mike's administrative systems and Rishi's financial oversight. In this well-oiled machine, you might say that Mike is in charge of allocating the oil, and Rishi makes sure we can afford all the oil we require.

This, then, is the state-of-the-art, self-evolving machine that my colleagues and I have spent three decades building. It is a machine with a soul.

★

To many people, especially those outside our industry, Investcorp is still best known for the glamour businesses we acquired in our earlier corporate investment days – Tiffany, Saks, Gucci. We are extremely proud of our association with those fine companies, but, then as now, Investcorp has always focused less on marquee names and more on the opportunity a given deal presents for our investors. We are just as proud of rescuing Circle K – America's number-two convenience store chain – from bankruptcy, turning it into a healthy company, and finally taking it public, or of acquiring Thorn Lighting, a UK manufacturer of light fittings, and later watching it debut on the London Stock Exchange. In our thirty-year history there have been any number of similar success stories – companies like Jostens, a producer of school-related products such as class rings and yearbooks; American Tire, a leading tire distributor; and Hilding Anders, a Swedish bed and mattress manufacturer. These and other mid-size companies like them have always been the bedrock of our business, and that is precisely how we intend to keep it. Our philosophy is to concentrate on middle-market companies, meaning companies we could eventually sell for between $200 million to $500 million. And in that middle market, we buy the market-share leaders in their small niche industries.

I want to interject here that what others call 'private equity' and we call 'corporate investment' is not just a matter of semantics: Ours is a different *process*. With private equity, as the term is understood in the industry, clients allocate resources to a fund, but they have no control over what companies that fund will buy; they simply have to rely on their knowledge of the fund manager's past track record. The Investcorp model is to bring our clients unique investments, something no one else can offer. When we buy a company, we go to our investors with the specifics of that company – its line of business, how it ranks in its field, what its management is like, how we see its future. 'Our investors,' says Steve Puccinelli, our head of CI for North America and Europe, 'want to know what the company does, and to feel good about it and *believe* in it. So, for example, when we took American Tire to them in 2005, we told them that this was the biggest distributor of tires to all the tire installation companies in the United States. And our investors said, "You know what, that makes sense to me. I got cars. They need tires. Tires wear out – there's always going to be a need for tires. I'm in."'

Post-acquisition management is one of our great strengths – we are known throughout the industry for adding value to the companies we buy. 'We've built the premier middle-market shop, both in North America and Europe, by really having rigor behind our processes,' says Steve. 'It consists of training our people in things like sales force management, lean manufacturing, IT, human resources – not that they would ever be experts in any of that, but so they'll know what to look for and to bring in the experts when needed. Post-acquisition starts with the fact that we don't run companies. We buy good companies with good management teams, and we bring to them tools that we have learned through doing this for thirty years. And they can either use those tools or not. But that is our game plan – how we make our deals, our companies, and our management teams the best they can possibly be.

'It starts with what we call our 150-day Plan. And we believe we were the first ones, back in 2001, to come up with that term. It means that in the first 150 days of owning a company, we spend an enormous amount of time with that company and its entire management team so we can understand them completely. Yes, we invested in them because we had strong views of what the company could do, but now we want to verify in the first 150 days that where we thought we could make money is in fact there. And what we try to come away with at the conclusion of that five-month period is: What are the three, four, or five best value-creation opportunities this company has – we want to identify them, agree with the company's senior management team about them, and then put together a timetable by which we're going to go after them, and measurements that we're going to use, incremental measurements, to know whether we're achieving our goals. We try to work with our management teams to help them get to the next level. With middle markets you can do that.

'The other thing about middle markets is that you have many different exits. You can take a company public, because you buy it small and you grow it; you can sell it to another private equity firm because you're middle market and they're bigger private equity firms; and you can sell it to a strategic buyer – someone who didn't buy it earlier because it was too small to make a difference. But now we've grown it to be a bigger, more influential company. So now this strategic buyer says, "This company can make a difference to my company, *now* I'll buy it." So you have multiple exit opportunities. Which is good to create value for your clients.

'Typically, the hold period is four to six years. When our model is working great, we buy four or five companies a year, we sell four or five companies a year. We sell the ones we bought five years ago, the five deals we bought five years ago we sell today, and the deals we bought four years ago we sell next year. And our model is working great when we can do that. And right now we're in a period of doing just that.'

We are also running smoothly in real estate. You may recall that Investcorp's very first deal, way back in 1983, was a real estate venture – a 50 percent interest in Manulife Plaza in Los Angeles. Through that initial decade of operation our real estate line experienced its ups and downs, and for a period of years in the early '90s we bought nothing, simply concentrating on cleaning out our portfolio. But even then I told our real estate team that we would someday be back in business, and in 1996 – more experienced, with the lumps to prove it, and wiser as a result – we started our real estate line anew. Jon Dracos joined the RE team in 1995, and now heads it. 'When we rebuilt the effort in '96,' he recalls, 'we first talked to our placement guys in the Gulf, trying to understand where they thought a good spot for us to position ourselves would be. So they went out and talked to our investors as well. And ultimately we decided to try and create a product that was a little bit different from corporate investment but also complementary. If an investor had a couple of million dollars, he could say, okay, I'm going to go for the higher return here – with CI – and the current return here – with real estate – and build a balanced portfolio.

'Today, we stress the same basic principles that we did when we re-launched in 1996: We tell our investors that we're going to be in the US only. To this day, we're Investcorp's only line of business that doesn't operate on both sides of the Atlantic – although I should say I think we'll go someday. We hear about it from our clients a lot: "We like what you've done in the States," they say. "Can you replicate that in Europe?" And there might be potential for us to do that in the next three or four years.

'For now, though, our strategy is to buy in the top thirty US markets. Our Gulf investors are very familiar with these markets – from going to school in California, say, or being treated at the Mayo Clinic in Minnesota, or attending a bachelor party in Miami, or doing oil business in Houston or Dallas, or traveling to Chicago or Atlanta, Denver or Phoenix, for whatever: "Oh, yeah, sure, been there a bunch of times." So we focus our energies on those markets, giving our investors commercial-quality real estate – office buildings, shopping centers, hotels, industrial buildings, even apartments. Which aren't commercial, they're residential – but they're for-rent residential. And in this way we both differentiate ourselves from CI as well as complement it: To our investors, we offer real estate, which gives them an annual or semi-annual dividend; and then we have corporate investment, which doesn't do that but which gives them a much higher return on a five-year basis.'

Today Investcorp has about seventy-five discrete properties in its real estate portfolio, and Jon sees every one of them at least once a year. 'It takes about four months of traveling once a week, for two or three days,' he says. 'But I like to get out and touch it, and then when I see our investors, I can tell them I make it a policy to see their investments once a year.

Since the financial crisis, we've tripled our effort on investor focus.'

Talking with the leaders of our businesses today, you will hear that refrain over and over – a renewed emphasis on investor focus. It is part of our return to our founding principles. 'Every day I remind myself that this is OPM, that we are managing other people's money,' says Savio Tung, head of all the lines of business. 'Whatever we do, it had better be for the benefit of the shareholders and our clients.'

In our hedge fund line, our most recent changes have made our Gulf investors happy while also positioning the firm for the future. 'Overall,' says Deepak Gurnani, who only recently retired from overseeing the hedge fund business, 'we've done extremely well, and have gone through three different phases: Phase One was from our launch in 1996 to about 2003; in this phase we were essentially a fund of hedge funds business, in which we were deploying our capital with external managers. And all of the capital that we raised was either from the Investcorp balance sheet or from our investors in the Gulf.

'Then around 2003, we spent some time internally asking what our hedge fund business should do next. Clearly the potential in the Gulf remains very strong, so one idea was to do nothing – just continue what we were doing. But we just felt that we could do more, so two other ideas emerged at that point – what I refer to as Phase Two of the business. The first was that in addition to raising capital in the Gulf, we should also raise capital from the US market, the US institutional market, which would be a first for Investcorp to do. Even though this was thought of as sort of a "risky" move, because the US is a very competitive market and so on, that was one initiative that was put on the table.

'The second initiative was to seed and set up new hedge funds. If somebody experienced leaves Goldman Sachs or JP Morgan, say, or leaves another hedge fund and wants to set up his or her own hedge fund, we provide them initial capital. We seed them to set up a new business, and we take a stake in that business.

'So in 2004 we started putting together a team to focus on those two activities, seeding new managers and raising capital from the US. We seeded our first manager in December 2004, and we've done several more since then. Until this phase, our whole hedge fund team was based in Bahrain. By the end of 2006, early 2007, most of the team had moved to New York. So that is what I call Phase Two of the business, and you could argue that it continues today, or you could argue that it went until 2008 – until the financial crisis.

'I personally call 2008 the start of Phase Three, because in fact there were a number of senior level changes at Investcorp in June 2009. It was around that time that the leadership within the hedge funds changed as well, and there was more focus on the US capital raising. So if I fast forward to today, about 70 percent of the capital within the hedge fund business is from the US – a big change from 2003/2004 when 100 percent of our capital was from the Gulf.

'This change has accomplished several things: First, Investcorp gains enormous strategic benefits from having so much capital coming from the US. And second, our board members and our Gulf clients really appreciate it. The fact that we do business with some of the best and the largest and the most sophisticated institutions here in the US gives us even more credibility with the Gulf institutions, enabling those institutions – sovereign wealth funds, pension funds in the Gulf – to do business with us, and that has a tremendous benefit on the high-net-worth and the ultra-high-net-worth individuals whom we do deals with. To them, this is sort of a confirmation that we are indeed a world-class firm with world-class products. So that has been a very important strategic benefit, and after 2008 what we also found is that the US institutions continue to add capital. We have, on average, raised $1 billion each year since – 2009, 2010, 2011, 2012. On average, we are close to raising $4 billion from the US, a billion every year.'

The last of our four lines of business is the Technology Fund. 'In the early 2000s, we made some mistakes by chasing the dotcom bubble,' says Savio Tung, 'and that caused us some time, money, and tension with investors. I was asked to "go fix this dotcom mess," to try to contain the damage and see what we can do out of it. We configured the business model, not to do early-stage venture capital but to do more what I call business technology, more stable companies.

'And today if you look at Investcorp, our private equity team includes professionals experienced in technology investing, but not, you know, semiconductors, not Facebook, none of that. We focus more on day-to-day business needs in technology, which I think is a lower risk – and more rewarding and more compatible to our culture.'

If the world *inside* Investcorp has again become smaller and more familial, our *outside* world has expanded dramatically.

Not only have we ramped up our efforts in Europe, we are also opening three new offices in the Gulf – one in Riyadh, Saudi Arabia; one in Doha, Qatar; and one in Abu Dhabi.

Many people look at Europe's current difficulties and cannot imagine setting foot into that situation. But we are not 'many people.'

'There are, I think, opportunities in Europe that did not exist before,' says Scott Freidheim, our executive in charge of European business development. 'And there are a range of specific themes that one can pursue to source opportunities. Going after companies that are based in the periphery countries – defined as Ireland, Spain, Portugal, Italy, Greece – but that have diminished reliance on those countries, that would be one theme to pursue to try to capitalize on the dynamics. Or if you had a company that did have reliance, that would clearly be an opportunity if it was getting punished from a valuation standpoint. There are several of these themes.

'I also think the dynamics of reduced demand and increased supply are going to shift the balance in favor of those in the ecosystem of private equity. Who can weather the storm? Right now there is a weathering of the storm that is required. Therefore, if you have permanent capital, you're clearly advantaged. We at Investcorp recently raised $250 million to strengthen our balance sheet. We don't have to go out to the marketplace and say, hey, you know, we have a $5 billion fund, we want to raise another one, please commit to the capital that you had promised pre-crisis. That would be a tough challenge.'

Our efforts in Europe reflect what I mean when I call

Investcorp a 'well-oiled machine.' We now have our European Advisory Board fully engaged and spread out across the Continent, ambassadors for the firm at the highest levels. Then we have Scott, who interacts with both the EAB and the executives of all of our businesses operating in Europe to help develop, enhance, and accelerate the economic productivity of the various lines; he focuses his time on creating relationships with people who could co-invest in deals, and also in sourcing deals. And, finally, we have our individual dealmakers, typified by Hazem ben Gacem and his 15-member CI Europe team. The Harvard-educated son of a Tunisian diplomat, Hazem grew up all over the world, eventually joining Investcorp in New York in 1994 – only to be sent nearly immediately to Europe to work on Ebel, the Swiss watchmaker we had just acquired. 'I had put on my CV that I was fluent in French,' Hazem laughs. 'They said, "You speak French? Okay, you go to London." And I've been working out of London ever since.'

Like all of us, Hazem is bullish on the opportunities in Europe for a firm like Investcorp. 'Our European team suffered from a fair bit of turnover at the leadership level over the years,' he says, 'and maybe we missed some attractive opportunities along the way. That being said, we are one of the oldest and the most established players in the European marketplace. Our team today is very young, but also very hungry and aggressive. Just to give an example, last summer we bought a building materials business in Spain. They do glazing for tiles, very high tech glazes, colors, and inks. If we tell anyone we bought a business in Spain in the summer of 2012, they probably think we're crazy. But I like to use this acquisition as an example because it has a lot of very interesting characteristics.'

The company that Hazem describes, called Esmalglass, is a textbook example of several of the 'themes' that Scott Freidheim identifies as opportunities in Europe these days. Based in Spain, it is from a periphery country, but it relies very little on its local market. 'Periphery countries since the beginning of the crisis have suffered the greatest headline risk,' says Scott, 'and have scared investors, thus competition for assets is weakest. Esmalglass has approximately five percent of its net sales coming from Spain plus over fifty percent from emerging markets. So while it is headquartered in Villareal, Spain, and suffered lack of buyer interest as a result, its economics are not driven by Spain, but rather by other countries. This company was also a legacy asset in an old private equity portfolio that had refinancing needs timed to previously established exit horizon limits. Thus, there was a lot of pressure on them to sell.'

'So if anything,' continues Hazem, 'the current market dislocation is for us an opportune time to go out and acquire business smartly. Another thing, and this is a very cultural aspect of Investcorp – we do not panic and run for the hills. We have been in Europe for the last thirty years; we will be in Europe for the next thirty. Europe will continue to be Europe, and there are only two markets in the world that have the transparency, the legal framework, the political stability, and the fluidity of both debt and exit markets which you as an investor can put money into – North America and Europe. That's it. So that's why when I think in terms of opportunities we feel we can be very shrewd in looking at Europe. We have pretty much all European nationals covered in our team, and we have the history and the scars to know what to do and what not to do – in France, in Germany, in Italy and in Scandinavia…

'Speaking of Scandinavia, we also just bought Georg Jensen, the hundred-year-old global luxury brand – they design, manufacture, and distribute jewelry, watches, fine silverware, and high-end homeware. The majority of this Danish company's sales today are in Asia, and our game plan is very much to develop the Asia angle. We hope it can be another Tiffany's!'

Meanwhile, in the Arabian Gulf, where Investcorp began and where everything we do eventually comes back to, Mohammed Al-Shroogi and his team are carefully cultivating our thirty-year-old roots. One way Mohammed did that was by the exemplary manner in which he left Citi after thirty-four years. 'I ensured a smooth transition,' he explains, 'and I offered myself to my former colleagues. I said, "Listen, guys, I am going to Investcorp, however, you can reach me anytime. Because after thirty-four years a lot of clients, public or private clients, know me very well. If I am needed I am at your disposal any time, even if I am with Investcorp." And my relationship, still, is impeccable with Citi – impeccable.

'When I joined Investcorp, many contacts assumed I would be calling them for business right away. However, I just kept in touch with my contacts through a difficult investment period during the financial crisis, providing them with guidance or advice when they asked, without really pushing any of Investcorp's investment directly. This, by the way, has helped me maintain my relationships and I can now leverage them as appropriate to ensure Investcorp really gets a fair shot at providing them a solution that really fits the client's need. For example, I was in Jeddah last week and I met with a client that I hadn't seen for three years, on purpose. So the sheikh said, "Where the hell were you?" And I told him I was staying away because I needed to understand the company I'm working with well. I needed to be sure that I know what I am selling you. You are a valuable client to me. It looks very bad for me to switch from Citi to Investcorp and come and ask you for money. Now I know the firm very well, and, comfortably, I'm telling you to come and invest with us, this is the history, this is what we are doing.'

By displaying personal integrity of such a high order, Mohammed has also confirmed Investcorp's reputation for integrity – in a region where integrity is valued above all else.

As I write, Mohammed has been with the firm for three-and-a-half years, in which time he, in concert with Mike Merritt and other partners, has effected remarkable improvements in our Gulf business – improvements that I believe position Investcorp to strong advantage for decades to come. The first achievement has been to dramatically upgrade our placement and relationship management (PRM) team in the Gulf – what we used to refer to simply as the placement team.

As you may recall, Mike was in charge of our placement people when he left in the mid-'90s, and he managed them, not by supervising their every move, but by giving them all the support they needed in order to do their job – 'the servant of the team,' he called himself. In 2010, when Mike returned to the firm, he first turned his attention to revising compensation policies; then he joined Mohammed to improve what he (Mike) calls 'the most important part of the business.'

When Mike retired in 1996, the placement team was very strong. By the time we got into the 2000s, however, those people had also retired, and it had been a challenge to develop the next generation. This was one of Mohammed's most pressing challenges when he took charge of our Gulf business. Then Mike came back and pitched in, streamlining the recruiting process, organizing it, controlling it, making it much more rigorous. 'I have a three- four-inch three-ring notebook of process, how we screen people,' Mike says. 'We had a process where we designated people for interviews. We assigned different kinds of questions and subject matter for interviewees so that we don't all ask the same question. We would test them on a business model kind of an exam: How would you handle this kind of problem? We would test them on their knowledge of the market. We would test them on their cultural fit, on their knowledge of the alternative investment industry, knowledge of Investcorp, and so forth.

'So we started out with this process and the focus was primarily on Saudi Arabia. Well, at the end of this last year, 2012, we had hired three outstanding young Saudis to join our team: one of them from Goldman Sachs, one from Morgan Stanley, one from one of the major French banks – though he was in fact the manager of a prince's investment office when we hired him. All of them are highly qualified, international degrees, great personalities. They are not coming for quick hits. They are here for a career.

'The result of all this is that we now have, unquestionably, the best capital-raising team in the Gulf, bar none. We're recruiting right now for a Relationship Manager for Abu Dhabi. So far we've screened three hundred and sixty people for that job and have not selected anyone. So we're very, very particular, the bar has gone way up. And of course when you have these kinds of standards, people get excited to be here. And Mohammed is in the field with them now fulltime. They're not by themselves. Mohammed gets on the plane and he goes to Jeddah. He goes to Kuwait. Wherever he's needed. He's a very good soldier. He's respected and he's not afraid to tackle any problem or issue. And so it's a great combination of Mohammed and me, in being a support mechanism for these guys.'

Part of that support will be in the form of three new Investcorp offices in the Gulf. 'Primarily,' says Mohammed, 'employees that are covering clients locally will now work from the respective local offices, in Riyadh, Doha, or Abu Dhabi. For example we have two people in Jeddah, they are Saudis, and we have three in Riyadh, they are Saudis, and one in Eastern Provence, she is Saudi. These people will now have an office in which to meet. Their boss can call a meeting in the office. They can discuss things in the office instead of meeting in the lobby of a hotel. Also, our staff will have good premises, and a good address, to meet clients and other stakeholders, which I believe will enhance the high-touch servicing aspect of Investcorp.

'But we will continue to meet clients primarily at *their* offices, hence there should be no change in the way we access and interact with the clients and our markets. Because

Investcorp has a norm and a standard, and that's the success of Investcorp.'

Self-confident. Self-motivated. Self-directed. Self-perpetuating – those are just some of the adjectives I would ascribe to this well-oiled machine that is the modern Investcorp. It is extremely gratifying to stand back and watch it percolate, listen to it hum. Thirty years ago my co-founders and I flipped a switch and turned it on, and now it runs under its own power, of its own volition. Like any machine, it has needed repairs over the years, and constant maintenance, and that will always be so. But I know for a fact that its operation today is smoother than ever. I also know that when I am no longer sitting in the Executive Chairman's chair, the machine will continue to run, under its own steam, in perpetuity. For it was built to last.

In that institutional spirit, I want to give the final word in this chapter to one of our young executives, a member of the generation presently at the peak of their power; I believe he speaks for the culture we have created over thirty years, a culture of openness and selflessness and vision: 'We've gotten through it, the financial crisis,' says Jon Dracos. 'We've re-engaged with our investors. We have a highly defensible recent track record and a good long-term track record. Our competitors have fallen away. Nemir has trained people, executives like us, and we understand how Investcorp operates, we understand the important relationship between products and investors and shareholders. We have a solid group of people now who are very much focused on Investcorp first and foremost. We truly have people who have Investcorp's interests at heart.

'Markets started to seize up in 2007, and we needed this seniority to get us through some pretty dark times. And we still need this seniority in the next three to five years to take advantage of this market-share opportunity, this liquidity in the Gulf region and in the United States, even though it's a slow-growth atmosphere – to cement our market-share gains and growth trajectory.

'But after that, I think the firm is really poised to start to elevate people to run businesses for the next ten to fifteen years. We should be grooming the next generation. We've added a lot of talent, especially in the Bahrain office. I've said to the real estate guys that are under me, the early-40s generation – I'm in my early 50s – "Look, three to five years, we're going to get this thing at the right place. And then you guys can take it from there."'

14
BETWEEN SUCCESS AND FAILURE

I am an inveterate collector of quotations. Through the words of great leaders or thinkers, I often find myself connecting to that which is best in me. The quote from Bobby Kennedy that began this book is a good example. In those two sentences he captured the essence of vision – the ability to see beyond what is in front of your eyes. The quote served as a great inspiration to me when I was trying to create the organization that became Investcorp. Time and again, after running up against blind opposition, I returned to Kennedy's hopeful words and took heart in their promise.

But I want to close out this book with some thoughts based on a different quotation. In 1984, after Investcorp was launched but before we had achieved our first notable successes, I came across the following passage:

> The line between success and failure is so fine that we scarcely know when we pass it, so fine that we are often on the line and do not know it. How many a man has thrown up his hands at a time when a little more effort, a little more patience, would have achieved success. As the tide goes clear out, so it comes clear in. In business sometimes, prospects may seem darkest when really they are on the turn. A little more persistence, a little more effort, and what seemed hopeless failure may turn to glorious success. There is no failure except in no lon-

> ger trying. There is no defeat except from within, no really insurmountable barrier save our own inherent weakness of purpose.

Looking back on my life's mission from the perspective of three decades, I can say that this quotation – from the American writer and philosopher Elbert Hubbard – could well be put on a plaque and bolted to the front of each of Investcorp's offices, as both a summary of, and a testament to, our achievement. Kennedy-like vision can spark the idea and help point the direction; but day by day and year by year, it is Hubbard-like strength of purpose that keeps the train on the tracks.

It is not enough for those qualities to reside solely in the organization's founder, however. An organization can become an institution only when the founder's vision and strength of purpose is somehow transferred to, or implanted in, the organization itself. Ultimately, the train must keep itself on the tracks.

This thought quite naturally takes on increased weight for me as we approach the day when I step down from the active running of Investcorp. Are we ready? Have I done what I needed to do as a leader to prepare for the passing of the torch? I have great faith in the new management team that emerged from the crucible of the world financial crisis. I have great faith in the employees of Investcorp worldwide, at every level. I have great faith in the direction we have set for ourselves for the future. And I have great faith that, building on the core values that have sustained us in the past – values that have come to reflect not just how we act, but *who we are* – we are prepared to meet every coming challenge.

There are many qualities of leadership required to guide a top-ranking firm. Leadership requires clarity of vision, as well as an ability to set direction and establish strategies for the realization of that vision. Good leaders challenge the status quo, create visions of the future, and inspire their followers to realize those visions. Leadership requires that when times are tough and the corporate future is at stake, the leader must take charge of the challenge and navigate through it with skill, determination, decisiveness, and coolness under fire. Leadership requires the ability to get people to move in the same direction by alignment, not by orders or organization. An effective leader identifies the right mission for his team to be pursuing at any given time. The members of his team need to understand the importance of accomplishing that mission and be committed to it. If the outcome is successful, the leader should give credit to his team. On the other hand, if the mission fails, the leader should accept total responsibility. In other words, effective leaders are those who credit success to others and take the blame for any failures.

A good leader is he who charts the right path for his organization with intelligence, instinct and authority. He must be able to create a spirit of confidence in those under him.

A good leader needs power not for what it could do for him but for what he could do with it.

But of all the necessary skills in a true leader's kit, the single most important is the ability to visualize, build, ensure, and maintain a distinctive corporate culture. That is the glue that binds everyone in the firm to the organization – and that is what I feel is my greatest accomplishment at

Investcorp. Over nearly three decades, involving hundreds of strong-willed and talented individuals from numerous nationalities, I have never shied away from depicting, projecting, invoking, narrating, characterizing, or defining the unifying essence we aspire to. We would not have succeeded in becoming an institution without it.

And I will say it yet again: As an institution, Investcorp is well aware of its character and its long-term mission – where no decision is taken without consideration of its future impact; where the driving forces are focus and concentration.

Investcorp believes in teamwork, honesty, and open dealings. It is open to criticism and is always ready to submit its intended actions to the scrutiny of expert opinion.

Investcorp is prepared to bide its time. When necessary, however, it can move with extraordinary swiftness, scrapping previous plans in a determined drive for the best alternative. It is, above all, a firm in which organizational procedures are never allowed to block the pursuit of opportunity. These are Investcorp's enduring values.

While much has been accomplished in the first thirty years, this is only the beginning for Investcorp. There is a great deal still to be done and the prospects are brighter than ever. The firm continues on its path, financially strong and high in profile and reputation, with a rising generation of talented young people determined to continue its progress into the future.

At the same time, the Gulf states continue to progress with phenomenal speed. To respond to the ever-changing needs and requirements of our target market, Investcorp must never stop evolving. We will of course maintain the focus and momentum in our core businesses while doing ever more to serve our Gulf clients.

Starting with white desert sand forty years ago, the governments of the Gulf states used the proceeds from oil exports to build massive infrastructure. Roads, ports, airports, hospitals, schools, and housing were among the first structures to be completed. Today these governments are still expanding and upgrading their infrastructure while also building large industrial projects. As a provider of goods and services, the private sector has benefited greatly from such an extraordinary transformation. Family businesses and conglomerates have mushroomed in every Gulf state.

In the years ahead, some of these conglomerates will be subject to break-ups and rationalizations. As a result, there is likely to be increasing demand for financial services in the area broadly defined as investment banking. This area includes mergers and acquisitions advice, underwriting capital market issues of bonds and shares, brokering in equity and debt instruments, market-making activities, research, institutional asset management, and private client wealth management. This is where I see Investcorp, with its distinguished brand, fulfilling a productive role.

Although we could expand into all of these new areas simultaneously, we as a firm have always been cautious about the risks that sudden and radical growth poses to our corporate culture. Our instinct is to grow carefully and organically. In keeping with our client-driven model, we want our growth in every case to be clearly directed toward satisfying client needs. As we develop and become successful in one area, we will naturally be led into additional areas as our clients grow and prosper.

As a first step, I believe that Investcorp has an opportunity to enter the investment banking business through a natural extension of its existing activities into advising clients on mergers and acquisitions and on capital structure and issues. There are a number of boutiques and branches of global firms in the Gulf that are engaged in the advisory business, but none has the unique combination of professionalism, Gulf reputation, and local understanding that Investcorp can offer. Success in this business is about developing the best skills and talent, and having the ability to access clients at senior decision-maker levels. The capital required is intellectual rather than purely financial. These criteria play to our strengths.

As our client needs evolve, it is my hope and expectation that Investcorp too will evolve – and that may include structurally – in order to add the capabilities needed to meet those enhanced client needs with our expected professionalism and success. In the years ahead I see the potential for revising – and by this I mean improving – Investcorp's ownership structure. In its first three decades, the firm was predominantly owned by the private sector in the Gulf, with around twenty percent held by its management. While management should retain its ownership, another block should be attracted in the years ahead – sovereign wealth funds or pension funds, for example. The share in the hands of the private sector would be reduced to accommodate this new block.

If such proposed potential ownership is successfully

engineered, Investcorp may choose to stay publicly owned or go private. Each of these two alternatives will have pros and cons that should be evaluated when the time for action is ripe. But whatever specific changes develop, Investcorp should be well positioned to broaden its activities as the firm's capital structure continues to strengthen and develop. With its strong culture, deep local ties and understanding, diverse pool of world-class talent, and connections to the global capital markets, Investcorp should be poised to become the preeminent Gulf investment bank.

A potential anchor investor will of course be free to revise the composition of the firm's Board of Directors, whose role is, after all, to represent shareholders. It will be the board that selects the future Executive Chairman to replace me. And here I want to emphasize that I was successful in my job because I enjoyed the full support and confidence of the existing owners and the current Board of Directors. My successor, to be effective, will need the same access and empowerment from the future owners and directors. If he is appointed by them based on long-established trust and confidence, he will be well positioned to use this sophisticated machine extremely productively.

Every machine should come with an 'operating manual,' however, and I hope this book will help to serve future Investcorp leaders in that capacity; that is one of the reasons I wrote it.

And as this is the final chapter, I want to take one last opportunity to reinforce certain philosophical principles that I believe greatly influenced my success at Investcorp.

Whenever I was confronted with a choice, or had a decision to make, I never accepted a recommended course of action that was merely legal; in addition, it had to be both ethical and defensible. Suggestions therefore had to pass three tests in order to be considered.

I never believed in managing by decree or intimidation. Nor did I believe in a hierarchical divide. I encouraged an environment in which people were expected both to ask what they should do *and* why they should do it.

I surrounded myself with subordinates who were free to contradict my view if they disagreed with me. I did not consider that to be insubordination during the deliberations, but rather a way of protecting myself from a wrong move. Once a decision was made, however, I expected full and unwavering dedication to it and to its implementation.

After I had decided on a particular course of action, I never felt a shortage of courage to make it happen, irrespective of the obstacles.

To do my job effectively, I had to draw my power and support from different constituents among Investcorp's stakeholders. The most important of these constituents were, first, the Board of Directors and, second, the employees of the firm I was expected to lead. Before I could win the total confidence and loyalty of the staff, they had to be convinced that I was honest, steady, reliable, and fair.

In order to gain an influential position with my fellow board members, I first had to establish credibility, which grows out of expertise and relationships. To earn their respect for my expertise, I had to demonstrate sound judgment and achieve a good track record over several years.

Winning battles helped. Some of the battles – for example the Tiffany transaction, which was opposed by two board members including the then Vice Chairman, or the dispute with the Central Bank of Bahrain – emboldened my supporters on the board while defusing my opponents. The result was that, going forward, I had the board's trust.

Some people may have felt – or may yet feel – that the influence I gained was due to my being the founder of the firm. While that is partially true, it is not the full answer. When I stepped in at critical times to save the Tiffany, Gucci, or Circle K transactions, for example, the impact on the Investcorp staff was tremendous. My taking charge in 2009 to turn the firm around during the world financial crisis made an equally strong impression.

A leader gains stature by leading. That is what is required to meet the innumerable daily challenges described by Elbert Hubbard in the quotation at the start of this chapter. When do you keep going and when do you change course? How do you inspire the troops when spirits are down? When do you take action and when do you sit still? How do you tell when darkness is just a promise of dawn? These are all questions that every leader must answer for himself nearly every day.

For me, the pivotal line of the Hubbard passage is this: 'There is no defeat except from within, no really insurmountable barrier save our own inherent weakness of purpose.' I interpret that to mean that a leader – and, by extension, the organization he presides over – must possess (a) an ironclad sense of self; and (b) an unwavering devotion to the realization of stated goals.

As leader of Investcorp, I was tested constantly. My

opportunities to stand up for my – and my institution's – professed values were as limitless as the number of people prepared to contest our honor and resolve in ways both serious and absurd. Let me tell you three stories.

The first concerns Savio Tung and the Governor of the Bahrain Monetary Agency. The time was the 1980s, soon after Investcorp was launched. Hovering in the background to this tale is the feeling, among some in Bahrain, that I was headstrong and perhaps too ambitious, qualities that were not appreciated by some in authority. My direct access to the top people in government might have created part of that discontent.

One day I received a call to see the Governor of the Bahrain Monetary Agency, which had supervisory and regulatory authority over the banks. When I went to the Governor's office, he told me there was a sensitive issue that needed quiet resolution. He said it involved Savio Tung, who had just joined Investcorp. The Governor asked me to terminate Savio's employment. I was shocked – dumbfounded – and asked why. He said there were reasons that could not be explained to me, but action on my part to execute his order was demanded.

My reply was clear. 'I will not take action unless I know the reason and become convinced of its validity.' The Governor was outraged and protested that I was defying his instructions. As a higher government official, he felt my insubordination was unacceptable. He insisted that he had the facts, that he would not share them with me, and that I had to trust his judgment and conclusion. The meeting ended in high temper.

The following week I was summoned for a second meeting with the Governor, who asked very calmly if I had reconsidered my position. When I said no, he threatened to address the Investcorp board. I left his office again in anger. I contacted the Chairman and Vice Chairman of Investcorp and informed them that I would not change my position, at whatever cost. It was a matter of principle to me. I would not bend.

Next, I was invited to meet with the Minister of Finance, who was very cordial and asked me to soften my stand. I thanked him for his courtesy but insisted that my position would remain unchanged.

In the meantime, I called Savio in New York and asked him to come to Bahrain and respond in person to my question: 'Is there any reason that you are aware of for this strange development?' When Savio arrived, he emphatically assured me that there had been no wrongdoing on his part. But he suspected that his association with Arab Asia Bank, which he had joined after leaving Chase and before coming to Investcorp, might be the cause. Arab Asia Bank was then under investigation, and was later found guilty and closed down.

I asked Savio to go to the Bahrain Monetary Agency and clear his name with them. That he did, and then he left Bahrain and went back to his work in New York where, as you know from reading this book, he has enjoyed a long and impressive career with Investcorp. But Savio's explanation did not discontinue the Governor's anger toward me.

The second story concerns Saks Fifth Avenue. In spite of all the fame and attention that the acquisition of Saks had attracted to Investcorp, there were some facets of the transaction that were not nearly as pleasant.

For example, Saks had issued VIP cards to its valuable customers; anyone presenting one of these cards would receive extra attention. All Investcorp board members were given the cards, of course, and one of our directors also wanted to extend a VIP card to a prominent member of his country's royal family.

So on his next visit to New York, this man, whom I will call The Official, went to Saks and presented his card very proudly. He expected a meaningful discount, but was courteously informed that the card entitled him to receive attention but no discount. The Official insisted and the store employee persisted. Finally The Official left the store very unhappy.

Next thing I knew, my office in New York had received a harsh letter and the return of the Saks card that had been issued to this man. I immediately sent The Official a very apologetic response for any misunderstanding, and I also asked the Chairman of Saks to visit him and re-invite him to the store. I asked the Chairman to send me the bill for settlement.

Of course Investcorp, as a matter of policy, cannot offer anyone a discount on any of its investments. Our mission is to represent our investors and encourage the target company to maximize its margins for achieving increased profitability – not discount the margins for reduced returns. The members of the investors group are the ones who own the company, and we are entrusted as custodians to look after their best interests.

This episode was shockingly expensive and very unpleasant. The relationship with The Official was never repaired. In that important country in the Gulf we lost a key contact over something as silly as this.

The final story concerns another Gulf royal. On one of my visits to Riyadh, Saudi Arabia, I was invited to a dinner by an influential young prince at his palace. The dinner included my colleagues from Investcorp who were accompanying me. The prince was a most gracious host, and when the evening had ended and I was leaving the front porch to get into my car – having already expressed my thanks and said goodbye to the prince – he and his assistant stopped me to make a request.

The prince told me that both he and his assistant wished to fill two positions on Investcorp's Board of Directors. Again, I was dumbfounded. First, the subject had never come up in the two and half hours I had just spent with them inside the palace. Second, I did not understand why he had chosen, literally, the last moment of the evening to make such a request. Finally, Investcorp had no vacancies on the board, nor were we close to election time.

Unable to hide my total amazement, I responded that there was no board vacancy to be filled. The prince insisted that what he needed were *two* positions, not one, and said he believed that if I wanted to make it happen I could find a way. As he became more persistent, insisting that I should accede to his demands, I decided to be firmer – while remaining very polite, of course. I gave him two reasons for my refusal. One, I said, it was true that there were no open positions. Two, I explained that I wanted him, as a prince, to be our *client,* and a client is always a boss and not a member of the board.

He ignored my second reason and addressed the first. If he were to ask two existing Investcorp board members to step down, he said, would I make his wish happen? At this point I was upset and said that I hoped no one on our board would resign for that reason. But if anyone did – and here I was adamant – Investcorp would have to elect the most appropriate successor based on our established criteria. Thus, I stressed, the route that the prince outlined could not possibly be advantageous to him.

When I returned to Bahrain, at the next board meeting one of our Saudi board members approached me to say that we had a problem. When he indicated what it was, I responded that the answer was 'absolutely not' and that he should not feel obliged in any way to accede to the prince's pressure to step down.

That was the end of that. The prince unfortunately died a few years later at a young age. I never saw him again following the sumptuous dinner at his splendid palace.

What is the moral of these stories? What lessons should we take from them? On the surface they appear to be unconnected anecdotes, three more stories in a book chock-full of them. And yet I think the sheer 'randomness' of these three accounts is important to consider. You never know when you are going to be tested. The next door that opens, the next phone that rings, the next letter that arrives, may bring with it challenges to your value system. Some will be more serious than others, but even a small challenge successfully waged can chip away at the integrity of the whole.

We are speaking of leadership here. A true leader will always know the reading on his internal compass. That does not mean that all his decisions will be easy, but it does mean that he has an instinctive and ready sense of what feels right and what feels wrong – no matter how forcefully others, with other agendas, may argue. Such a leader will do everything in his power to imprint that internal sense of self onto the organization over which he presides. That is why I have striven so to inject my father's three-pronged philosophy of success – the importance of being needed, being respected, and being trusted – into the DNA of a living business institution. Such core values are important in any organization, but most especially in one whose business is the managing of other people's money.

Like all things worth accomplishing, however, this three-decade effort of creating and maintaining an appropriate corporate culture, while steering that inspired and unified body toward the realization of our goals, has required great reserves of stamina and persistence. This is the 'strength of purpose' of which Hubbard wrote. And that reminds me – naturally enough for an inveterate quotation collector like myself – of one last quotation that I want to share with you.

In January 2006, I was honored to be able to welcome former US president Bill Clinton to Bahrain, to a gathering held under the patronage of His Highness, the Crown Prince of the Kingdom of Bahrain. In preparing my introductory remarks, I turned to President Clinton's fascinating autobiography, *My Life,* and found in it many worthy candidates for my archive of inspirational quotations.

But one passage stood out. One spoke to me in a way that

echoed through all the struggles and strivings of my life:

> There's a lot to be said for showing up every day and trying to push the rock uphill. If you're willing to win in inches, as well as in feet, a phenomenal amount of positive things can happen. If ... you have something you want to do, and you put together a good team, and you're willing to be relentless and exhaust yourself in the effort, the results will come.

They will come if you are fearless, undaunted by the most awesome difficulties. If you refuse to accept defeat until every possible line of attack has been tried. If, when obstacles cannot be crushed or removed, you look for ways to go around them. And if, when necessary, you are ruthless in your resolve, tolerating no resistance from anyone who stands in your path.

I have often said that if I had allowed myself to become preoccupied by the magnitude of the challenge, I would never have started Investcorp. Fortunately, I did not dwell on the difficulties, only the goal. What was essential was a fierce determination to stay on plan – to summon all the energies we could muster, and to focus them solely on what we were determined to achieve.

Only the goal. *Only the goal.*

EPILOGUE

And now the time has come – the time to speak candidly of my thoughts about a successor. What else is left for me to do? I look at the firm and see that my ideal management structure is now in place. Our world-class lines of business are all headed by skillful, competent people – a cabinet of experts. Finishing the assembly of this well-oiled machine was a major mission in my life, and I had to stay to get it done. Now, looking to the next phase of my own journey, I feel that it is my duty to end this book by offering what I think are appropriate criteria for the person who should take my place.

I have given it considerable thought. If tomorrow my chair is empty and needs to be filled, my recommendation is that the appropriate person to succeed me must, among other attributes, be a statesman. Such a person must be able to meet, on Investcorp's behalf, with the rulers of the Gulf countries. To do that, he must be accepted in the Gulf community as a very senior man. At the same time, because Investcorp's culture spans the Middle East and the West, he must also be well received in New York and London.

His view is international. His talent is an ability to navigate the globe's cultural, economic, and political waters.

His strengths are judgment, imagination, and foresight – in other words, *vision*.

As you know from reading this book, I have given my all to building this institution known as Investcorp. When the time for me to leave it is near, I intend to do it with the same care that I have invested in every single day of this thirty-year mission: I intend to pass the torch.

Then, and only then, will I be able to say, 'Mission accomplished.'

ACKNOWLEDGEMENTS

The substance of these memoirs is drawn from my personal notes, handwritten over the years on yellow pad pages which I kept in a special file. The information they contain was transformed into this book by James Morgan, who also had access to media reports, company files and other relevant material. While the stories are mine, the crafting of this book and the way the content is presented are his. He has done incomparably well and all I can say from the bottom of my heart is, 'Thank you, Jim.'

Jim's work, in turn, draws on the contribution of Andrew Osmond, a professional writer whom we commissioned to record Investcorp's management meetings for many years. Andrew interviewed every board member to record their recollections of Investcorp's early decades. He also gathered the memories of the firm's founders and senior management, most of its key investors, a number of its professional allies and advisors and the chief executives of some of the companies that Investcorp owned over the years.

Andrew sadly died in 1999, but his manuscript was completed and printed after his death with the help of Robert Fearnley-Whittingstall and later made available to Jim Morgan.

At Investcorp, enormous thanks must go to Elizabeth Pires, who has tirelessly overseen the entire project. Betty brought extraordinary focus and dedication to the task and earned the respect and admiration of all those involved. Without her drive, initiative and unfailing cooperation and effort, this publication would never have seen the light of day. I owe her a debt of gratitude that no words can adequately express.

I must also express my gratitude to Lord Weidenfeld of Weidenfeld & Nicolson and Alan Samson of Orion Books for their encouragement and support in bringing the book to publication. Finally, I thank my editor, Lucinda McNeile, for her professional advice and assistance in polishing the manuscript. It has been a privilege to work with them all.

APPENDIX I

Investcorp's Founding Shareholders

Saudi Arabia

HRH Prince Sattam bin Abdulaziz
HRH Prince Mohamed bin Fahad bin Abdulaziz
HRH Prince Faisal bin Abdulla bin Abdulaziz
HRH Prince Faisal bin Sultan bin Abdulaziz
HRH Prince Saud bin Naif bin Abdulaziz
HRH Prince Faisal bin Salman bin Abdulaziz
HRH Prince Fahad bin Salman bin Abdulaziz
Sheikh Abdalraouf M.S. Abuzinadah
Aggad Investment Company
Dr Farouq Mohamed Akhdthar
Sheikh Teymour Alireza
Mr Rami Shafiq Al Akhras
Sheikh Abdul Wahab Saud Al Babtain
Sheikh Abdulla Al Blehed
Sheikh Fahad Saud Al Dugaither
Sheikh Abdul Kader Mohamed Al Fadl
Sheikh Faysal Mohammed Al Gosaibi
Sheikh Abdul Ghani Al Ishi
Sheikh Diab Al-Jobar
Sheikh Saad Al Mojil
Sheikh Mohamed Al Otaiby
Sheikh Sulaiman A. Al Saleh
Sheikh Abdullah Abdulaziz Al-Sudairy
Sheikh Khalid bin Turki Al-Sudairy
Sheikh Abdulaziz Al-Abdullah Al-Sulaiman
Sheikh Omar Mahmoud Al Tabari
Sheikh Ibrahim A. Al-Touq
Sheikh Abdul Rahman Ali Al-Turki
Mr Hamad Abdulla Al Zamil
Mr Abdullah Taha Bakhsh
Sheikh Ali Abdullah Bugshan
Sheikh Salem Ahmed Bugshan
Sheikh Mohammed Said Hassan Farsi
Sheikh Abdulla Fouad
Sheikh Jamal Hassan Jawa
Mr Abdul Aziz J. Kanoo
Sheikh Mohamed Eyad Kayali
Sheikh Mansour bin Juma bin Mani
Mawarid Investment Limited
Sheikh Ali bin Hussain bin Musallam
Rolaco Trading & Contracting
Abdulaziz Al-Abdullah Al-Suleiman & Company
Sheikh Amin Sejiny
Sheikh Abdulrahman Sharbatly
Sheikh Ali Shobokshy
Sheikh Fahad Shobokshy
Sheikh Ali Zaid Al Quraishi
Dr Nasser Al Rashid

Mr Abdulaziz Saud Al Saleh
Sheikh Nasser Mohammed Al Saleh
Taher Investment & Trading Company Limited
Sheikh Ali A. Tamimi
H.E. Sheikh Ahmed Zaki Yamani

Bahrain

National Bank of Bahrain B.S.C.
Al Ahli Commercial Bank B.S.C.
Bank of Bahrain & Kuwait
Al Ahlia Insurance Company B.S.C
Bahrain Investment Company B.S.C
General Organization for Social Insurance
Sheikh Rashid bin Isa bin Salman Al Khalifa
Sheikh Ibrahim Abdulla bin Khalid Al Khalifa
Sheikh Khalid bin Abdulla bin Khalid Al Khalifa
H.E. Sheikh Khalifa bin Salman bin Mohammed Al Khalifa
Sheikh Abdul Rehman Faris Al Khalifa
Sheikh Daij bin Khalifa bin Mohamed Al Khalifa
Sheikh Hamad bin Abdulla bin Hamad Al Khalifa
Sheikh Khalifa bin Ahmed Al Khalifa
Sheikh Mohammed Abdulrahman Mohamed Rashid Al Khalifa
Sheikh Abdulla bin Salman Al Khalifa
Sheikh Isa bin Mubarak Al Khalifa
Sheikh Khalid bin Ahmed Al Khalifa
Sheikh Khalid bin Mohammed bin Ebrahim Al Khalifa
Sheikh Khalid bin Salman Al Khalifa
Sheikh Mohammed Khalifa Al Khalifa
Sheikh Salman Khalifa Al Khalifa
Sheikh Sabah bin Daij Al Khalifa
Sheikh Khalifa bin Abdulla bin Hamad Al-Khalifa
Sheikh Salman bin Hamad bin Isa Al Khalifa
Sheikh Ali bin Khalifa bin Salman Al Khalifa
Sheikh Talal bin Mohamed Al Khalifa
Sheikh Tariq Mohamed Al Khalifa
Sheikh Isa bin Abdulla bin Hamad Al Khalifa
Sheikh Isa bin Ali Al Khalifa
Mr Farouq Al Moayyed
Mr Khalid Al Moayyed
Dr Towfiq Abdulrahman Al Moayyed
Mr Ghazi Radi Al Musawi
Mr Mohamed Al Mutawa
Mr Abedali Essa Al Nooh
Mr Khalifa Al Saad
Mr Jassim Mohamed Al Safar
Sheikh Abdulrahman Saggar Al Khalifa
Mr Yusuf Ahmed Al Saie
Mr Ali Saleh Al Saleh
Mr Ali Al Sayrefi
Mr Nabil Al Zain
Mr Mohammed Abdulla Al-Zamil
Al Zayani Investments
Messrs Fayeq and Fawaz Al Zayani
Mr Jassim Abdulrahman Al Zayani
Mr Khalil Al Zayani
Mr Mohamed Jassim Abdulrahman Al Zayani
Mr Rashid Abdulrahman Al Zayani
Mr Essa Al Zeerah
Mr Khalid Ashoor
Dr Hussain Mohamed Al Baharna
H. E. Mr Majid Jawad Al Jishi
H.E. Mr. Yousif Ahmed Al Shirawi
H.E. Dr Ali Mohammed Fakhro
H.E. Mr Ibrahim Humaidan
Mr Ali bin Ebrahim Abdul A'Al

Bahrain: continued

Mr Ebrahim Eshaq Abdulrahman
Mr Mohammed Ahmadi
Mr Yusuf Amin
Mr Haj Hassan Al A'Ali
Mr Faisal Jaffar Al Alawi
Mr Hamad Al Amer
Mr Ahmed Mohammed Al Aseeri
Mr Abdul Wahab Al Asoomi
Mr Ali Al Awadi
Messrs Sadiq and 'Taqi Al Baharna
Mr Khalifa Ahmed Al Bin Ali
Mr Najeeb Al Hamar
Mr Ali Al Jalahma
Mr Ahmed Al Jawahery
Mr Yusuf Ahmed Abdulrahman Al-Khoozi
Mr Farouq S. Al. Maawdeh
Mr Mohamed Sakhar Al Maawda
Mr Abdulla Rashid Al Madani
Mr Ali Al Mahrouss
Mr Khalifa Abdulla Al Mannai
Mr Mohamed Abdulla Ahmed Al Mannai
Mr Mohammed Abdulla Al Mannai
Mr Rashid Ismael Al-Meer
Mr Ibrahim Hassan Kamal
Dr Abdulatif Kanoo
Mr Abdulla Khalil Kanoo
Messrs. Mohamed & Fouad Ebrahim Khalil Kanoo
Mr Ali Abdulla Karime
Mr Isa Khalaf
Mr Khalifa Khalfan
Mohammed Jalal & Sons Co.
Bahrain Trading Agencies
Mr Ismail Baluch
Mr Mohammed Hussain Haji Baqer
Mr Khalifa Salah Buachalah
Mr Ahmed Abdulrahman Bu Ali
Mr Abdulla Buhindi
Mr Mohamed Hassan Dawani
Mr Abdulnabi Daylami
Dilmon Trading and Services Establishment
Mr Abdulrahman Abdulla Fakhro
Mr Abdulrahman Yusuf Fakhro
Mr Ali Yousuf Fakhro
Mr Hassan Abdullah Fakhro
Mr Jassim bin Mohammed Fakhroo
Mr Qasim Ahmad Fakhro
Mr Abdulreza Faraj
Gulf Shipping & Commercial Agencies
Gulf Trading & Export Agency
Mr Isa Hilal
Mr Mahmood Mahmood Hussain
Mr Mahmood Mohamed Hussain
Mr Hamad Abdulla Abul
Mr Sami Mohammed Jalal
Mr Hussan Jenahi
Mr Abdulrahman Juma
Mr Hassan Ali Juma
Mr Najeeb Juma
Mr Sami Kaiksow
Mr Abdulla Ahmed Nass
Mr Ali Obaidli
Mr Abdulrahman Rafeea
Mr Ahmed Sallahuddin
Mr Ebrahim Sallahuddin
Mr Mohamed Sallahuddin
Mr Yousif Sallahuddin
Mr Abdulrahman Taqi
Mr Hussain Ali Yateem
Mr Aref Saleh Mohamed
Mr Abdul Karim Mohsin
Mr Ali Mohamed Murad
Mr Jassim Mohammed Murad
Mr Murad Ali Murad
Yusuf bin Ahmed Kanoo W.L.L.
Mr Hassan Mohamed Zainalabedin
Mr Mohammed Jaber Zubari
Gulf Investors Group E.C.
Arabian Investment Resources E.C.

Kuwait

Sheikh Khalifa Abdulla Khalifa Al Sabah
Sheikh Ali Jarrah Al Sabah
Sheikh Mohamed Khalifa Al Sabah
Abdulaziz & Ali Al-Yousif Al Muzaini Company
H E Abdul-Rahman Salim Al-Ateeqi
Mr Khalid Saleh Al-Ateeqi
Mr Mohammed Hadi A. Alawadi
Mr Abdulaziz Ahmed Al Ayoub
Mr Abdulla Ahmed Al-Ayoub
Mr Adnan Ahmed Al-Ayoub
Mr Salah Ahmed Al-Ayoub
Mr Tariq Ahmed Al-Ayoub
Mr Barrak A. Al Babtain
Mr Khalid Abdul Mohsin Al-Babtain
Mr Fayez Saud Al-Dabous
Mr Faysal Saud Al-Dabous
Mr Saad Abdul Latif Al-Dousary
Mr Abdul Malik Al Duaij
Mr Mohammed Said Al-Dwaisan
Mr Ebrahim Al Ebrahim
Mr Abdullatif A. Al Fulaij
Mr Adnan A. Al Fulaij
Mr Sulaiman Ahmad Al Gadheebi
Mr Bassam Yusuf A. Alghanim
Mohammed Dakhil al Ghuneiman
Mr Fahad Al Hasawi
Mr Fadil Ibrahim Al-Hathran
Mr Ahmed Abdulaziz Al Jarallah
Mr Saleh A. Al-Muzaini
Mr Yousef Abdul Aziz Al Muzaini
Mr Mahmood Abdulkhaliq Al-Nouri
Mr Ebrahim Yousuf Al Ragum
Mr Jarrah Yousuf Al Roomi
Mr Mohammed Yousef Abdulla Al Roomi
Mr Abdulaziz Al Rumaih
Mr Saad Mohammed Al Saad
Mr Abdulla Mubarak Alsabij
Mr Wael Jasim Al Sager
Mr Mohammed Yousef Ahmed Al Saif
Mr Dawood Musaad Al Saleh
Mr Khalid Nasser Al Saleh
Mr Najib Hamad Musaad Al Saleh
Mr Yousef Hamad Al Sane
Mr Hamoud Ibrahim Al Saqabi
Mr Abdulla A. Al Sharhan
Mr Abdulwahab A. Al Tammar
Mr Marwan Marzook Boodai
Mr Mustafa J. Boodai
Mr Jawad Ahmed Bu Khamseen
Mr Jawad Ahmed Bu Khamseen
Mr Samer Subhi Khanshah
Mr Yousef Mohamed Abdulaziz El Shemali
Mr Abdulridha A. Khursheed Ahmad
Mr Waleed Abdulridha A. Khursheed Ahmad
Mr Faisal K. Jaffar
Modern Trading & Contracting Company
Musaad Al Saleh & Sons Investment Group Limited
Mr Fahad Abdulrahman Al-Mojil
Mr Barrak Abdul Muhsin Al Mutair
Mr Ghazi Abdul Kader Al Mutawa
Mr Jasem Mohammed Khaled Al Mutawa
Mr Najeeb Mohammed Khaled Al Mutawa
Mr Abdullah Abdulaziz Al Muzaini
Mr Hussain Jawad Abdul Rasool
Mr Hassan Ali Subei
Mr Khaled Abu Su'ud
Mr Ali Mahmoud Tifouni

United Arab Emirates

National Bank of Sharjah
Dubai Bank Limited
Gulf Financial Center
H. E. Saeed Ahmad Ghobash
H. E. Sheikh Suroor bin Mohammed Al Nahyan
Mr Khalaf Al Habtoor
Mr Abdul Malik Al Hamer
Mr Juma Al Majid
Al-Mazroo Trading & Industries Company
Mr Ghanim Faris Al Mazroui
Mr Mubarak bin Abdulla Al Muhairy
Dr Mana Saeed Al-Otaiba
Mr Saeed Ahmed Al Otaiba
Mr Hamad Al Sabah
Mr Abdulla Juma Al Sari
Mr Obaid Rashid Al Shamsi
Mr Abdul Rahman Arif
Mr Abdulrahman Mohamed Bukhatir
Mr Fardan Ali Fardan
Mr Abdul Latif Galadari
Mr Abdul Rahim Galadari
Mr Abdulla Ismail
Mr Hameed Jaffar
Mr Mohamed Mir Hashem Khoory
Mr Mohamed Hussain Shamali
Mr Sultan bin Khalifa bin Sultan
Mr Abdulla Imran Taryam

Qatar

Qatar National Bank, S.A.Q.
Commercial Bank of Qatar, Q.S.C.
Sheikh Ahmed bin Khalifa Al Thani
Sheikh Ali bin Ahmed bin Khalifa Al Thani
Sheikh Ali bin Jaber Al Thani
Sheikh Ali bin Khalifa Al Thani
Mr Khalid Al Attiya
H.E. Ali Abdul Rehman Al Muftah
H.E. Ebrahim Ahmed Hussain Namah
Mr Mohammed Yousef Al Ali
Mr Abdullah Khalifa Al Attiya
Dr Abdulla Abdul Rehman Al Bakar
Mr Akbar Yousef Al Bakar
M. Hussain I. Al Fardan
M. Abdulla Mohamed Al Ghorairi
M. Ali Mohamed Rashid Al Khater
M. Mohamed Saif Al Maadadi
M. Yaocoub Yousef Al Maadadi
Mr Ali Ebrahim Al Malki
Mr Mohamed Hamad Al Mana
Mr Ahmed Ali Maarafi
Mr Fahad Mohamed Al Musallam
Mr Jassim Mohammed Al-Mussalam
Mr Yasser Mohamed Al Musallam
Mr Mohamed Sheikh Hussain Ali
Mr Ahmed Hassan Belal
Mr Abdul Ghani Abdul Ghani
Mr Abdul Jalil Abdul Ghani
Messrs Nasir and Abdul Razzak Abdul Ghani
Mr Ali Mohamed Jaidah
Mr Jassim Mohammed Jaidah
Mr Yakoob Yousef Jaidah
Mr Jasim Yousef Jamal
Kontra Technical Company Limited
Mr Abdullah Mohammed Ebrahim Mannai
Mr Ahmed Abdullah Al Mannai
Midmac
Nasser bin Khalid Al Thani & Sons

Oman

Bank of Oman, Bahrain and Kuwait
Union Bank of Oman, O.S.C.
H.E. Sayied Hamed bin Hamoud
H.H. Sayied Shabib bin Taimur
H.E. Mohamed Musa A. Al Yousef
H.E. Mr. Ahmed Macki
H.E. Qais Zawawi
Mr Hamoud bin Abdulla Al-Harthy
Mr Murtaza Hassan Ali
Mr Mohsin Haider Darwish
Mr Mohamed Jamali
Mr Abdulla Moosa
Dr Ali Moosa
Mr Mansoor Ali Suleimi
Mr Mustafa Abdul Reda Sultan
Dr Omar Zawawi
Zubair Enterprises

APPENDIX II

Trust Board of Directors

Over the years, Investcorp's shareholders have elected prominent individuals from across the Gulf and Saudi Arabia to represent them on the Board of Directors. Listed below by country are current members of the Board along with all those who have served in the past.

Kingdom of Bahrain

Current members

Mohammed bin Isa Al Khalifa
Nemir Amin Kirdar
Farouk Yousuf Almoayyed
Khalid Rashid Al Zayani

Former members

Mohammed Yousef Jalal
Ahmed Ali Kanoo
Mohammed Abdullah Al Zamil

State of Kuwait

Current members

Abdul-Rahman Salim Al-Ateeqi
Mustafa Jassim Boodai

Former members

Khalid Abdul Mohsin Al Babtain
Fahad Abdulrahman Al Mojil
Dawood Musaad Al Saleh

Sultanate of Oman

Current members

Mohammed bin Mafoodh Al Ardhi

Former members

Mohamed Musa Abdullah Al Yousef

State of Qatar

Current members

Hussain Ibrahim Al-Fardan
Jassim bin Abdulaziz Al Thani

Former members

Ahmed Abdulla Al Mannai

Kingdom of Saudi Arabia

Current members

Abdullah Mohamed Alireza
Abdul Aziz Jassim Kanoo
Abdul Rahman Ali Al Turki

Former members

Mohammed Abalkhail
Omar Abdul Fattah Al Aggad
Abdullah Taha Bakhsh
Bakr Mohammed Binladin
Nasser Al Rashid

Abdulaziz Al Sulaiman
Ali Abdullah Al Tamimi

United Arab Emirates

Current members

Majid bin Saif Al Ghurair
Abdullah Mohammed Mazrui

Former members

Abdulrahim bin Ebrahim Galadari
Easa Saleh Al Gurg
Faraj Ali bin Hamoodah
Jawad M. Hashem
Juma Al Majid
Ghanim Faris Al Mazroui
Khalaf bin Ahmed Al Otaiba

APPENDIX III

Trust European Board Members

The individuals chosen to serve as members of Investcorp's European Advisory Board (for a discussion of the purpose and formation of this body, see page 282) are:

H.E. Kofi Annan
Chairman, Kofi Annan Foundation
Two-term Secretary General at the United Nations

Prof. Giuliano Amato
Twice Prime Minister of Italy. Also served as Minister of the Treasury and Minister of Interior
Emeritus Professor at the European University Institute in Florence and Visiting Professor at Columbia University's School of Law

H.E. Ambassador Wolfgang Friedrich Ischinger
Global Head of Government Relations for Allianz SE
Long-serving member of the German foreign service; previous roles include former Ambassador of Germany to the United States of America and to the United Kingdom as well as deputy foreign minister (State Secretary)

Mr Alain Juppé
Served as Prime Minister and Minister of Foreign Affairs, France
Mayor of Bordeaux

Dr Pierre Keller
Former Senior Partner of Lombard Odier & Cie Private Bankers in Geneva, former Vice-President of the International Committee of the Red Cross. Currently Chair of the Europaeum Board of Trustees. Member of the Board of Trustees of the Institute for Strategic Dialogue, and member of the Advisory Board of the Weatherhead Center for International Affairs at Harvard University

Ms Ana Palacio
Foreign Minister of Spain in the government of Jose Maria Aznar
Member of the Spanish Council of State
Senior Vice President and General Counsel of the World Bank

Dr. h.c. Otto Schily
Minister of the Interior in the cabinet of Chancellor Gerhard Schroder
Long-serving member of the German Parliament (until 2009)

Dr Wolfgang Schüssel
Served as Chancellor of Austria and President of the European Council
Member of the Supervisory Board of RWE AG and Board of Trustees of the Bertelsmann Foundation

Professor Klaus Schwab
Founder, President and Executive Chairman
World Economic Forum

Baron Weidenfeld of Chelsea, GBE
Founder and Chairman of Weidenfeld & Nicolson
President of the Institute for Strategic Dialogue

INDEX